HUNGRY for PARIS

The
Ultimate Guide to the City's
102 Best Restaurants

ALEXANDER LOBRANO

Photography by Bob Peterson

HUNGRY FOR PARIS

RANDOM HOUSE TRADE PAPERBACKS

New York

TO BRUNO MIDAVAINE
FOR HIS REMARKABLE PALATE,
EXTRAORDINARY COOKING,
AND INVALUABLE PATIENCE

CONTENTS

...

1ST *and* 2ND
ARRONDISSEMENTS

TUILERIES, LES HALLES, BOURSE

3RD and 4TH
ARRONDISSEMENTS

LE MARAIS, THE ISLANDS

5TH, 6TH, and 7TH
ARRONDISSEMENTS

LATIN QUARTER, SAINT-GERMAIN-DES-PRÉS, FAUBOURG-SAINT-GERMAIN

9TH *and* 10TH
ARRONDISSEMENTS

LA NOUVELLE ATHÈNES, GARE DU NORD, GARE DE L'EST, CANAL SAINT-MARTIN

11TH *and* 12TH
ARRONDISSEMENTS

RÉPUBLIQUE, OBERKAMPF, BASTILLE, BERCY

The Rise and Fall of the Parisian Brasserie 326

13TH, 14TH, and 15TH
ARRONDISSEMENTS

PLACE D'ITALIE, GOBELINS, MONTPARNASSE, GRENELLE, CONVENTION

Fashion Plates: A Brief History of Stylish Dining in Paris 366

16TH *and* 17TH
ARRONDISSEMENTS

TROCADÉRO, VICTOR-HUGO, BOIS DE BOULOGNE, L'ÉTOILE, TERNES, WAGRAM, CLICHY

18TH, 19TH, *and* 20TH
ARRONDISSEMENTS

MONTMARTRE, BUTTES-CHAUMONT, NATION

..

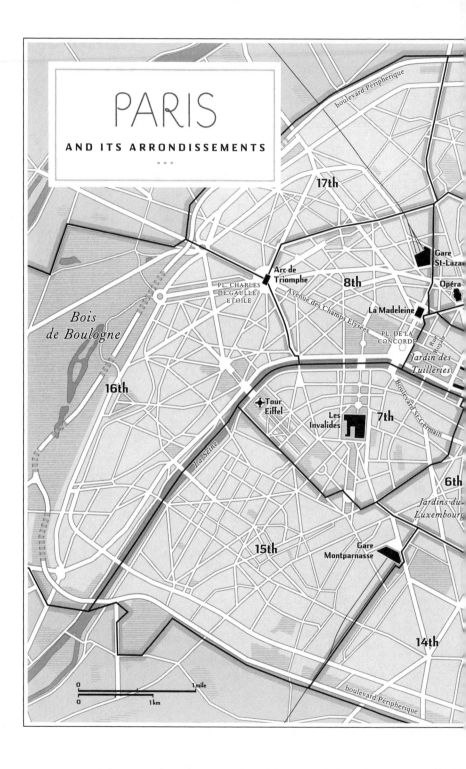

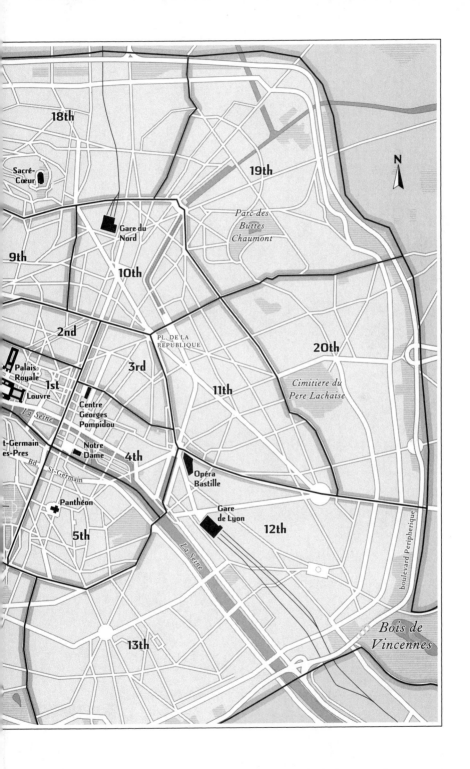

PREFACE

MY PASSION FOR PARIS

. . . .

PARIS, AUGUST 1972. THE CITY WAS STINKING HOT, THE mysteriously empty Champs-Élysées (my family knew nothing about the month-long August holiday of the French) was paved with bumpy cobblestones, and most French cars looked like funny metal beetles.

After six weeks of maternally led but basically autonomous splendor in Italy, Austria, Switzerland, and Germany, my mother, two brothers, and I were meeting my father and sister in Paris. Our first meal was spent at the Androuët, a restaurant that specialized in cheese. We all loved cheese. So off we went in two small taxis; the one I was in included a smelly, drooling German shepherd looking over the front seat and a driver who managed two deliciously ripe-smelling Gitanes before we got to the restaurant, maybe a fifteen-minute drive. The blue cigarette packet on the dashboard was decorated with a fan-wielding gypsy encircled by a blue curl of smoke, possibly the stuff of erotic musings, but the best was yet to come.

The strange little restaurant with rough white stucco walls and wrought-iron fixtures shocked with a hairy dairy stink: cheese. We ate salad with hot *goat* cheese (with all due respect to Miss Healey, my third-grade teacher and the one charged with the awkward business of teaching us about mammals, it had never occurred to me that goats had milk, much less that you could make cheese from it) fondue, which made us kids nearly drunk with its kirsch fumes; Roquefort soufflé—served with walnut bread; a small salad dressed with sharp vinaigrette, and sublime cheese; cheese; and more cheese. We went back the next night, and maybe the following one, but on our last night in Paris we ended up in a stifling cellar in the Latin Quarter, where we all ordered onion soup and boeuf bourguignon.

The beef was chewier than what I knew at home, but I'd never eaten a sauce like that in my life. What did it taste like? Smoke, beef, blood, salt, onions, mushrooms, and wine. I spooned, dunked, and licked until not a drop of the velvety garnet-colored sauce was left and later spent a restless night knowing that I'd never be free of a powerful, permanent craving for more. Little did I know then that this addiction would become the compass by which I would live my life.

Four years later I was in Paris again, dumb from the misery of British food on a student pauper's pocket in late-seventies London and desperate for goat cheese and more of that sauce. But, on a night so cold it made your eyeballs ache, I discovered choucroute garnie, a vast smoking platter of tart sauerkraut mounted with several kinds of sausage, fatback, and brined pork loin. Eaten with waxy white potatoes and nostril-stinging mustard, it's one of the world's great winter dishes and immediately became a firm favorite. I amazed the waiter but not myself by polishing off every blond shred of cabbage, every nubbin of pork, along with a second serving of potatoes, yet secretly, I was still yearning for boeuf bourguignon.

The punitive wages of New York publishing subsequently kept me away from Paris again for a long time. Then, the next time I finally visited the city, and after a night of revelry, I found myself flat broke and walking back to my hotel without a map as the city was waking. Shop owners opened wheezing metal gates, a florist was secateuring lily stems into the gutter, and waiters in snug waistcoats set up regimented burgundy-and-ivory wicker chairs on café terraces. The air smelled of melted butter, coal smoke, cigarettes, stale wine. Too tired to be completely panicked, I just walked, dazed but intrigued by the quickening pulse of the city. Somewhere I came across a small market, just setting up so early in the day. "J'espère qu'elle l'a valu!" shouted one of the stallholders, to the laughter of colleagues, and though it was five years before I understood the remark ("I hope she was worth it," a reference to my disheveled appearance, assumed to be the aftermath of an amorous evening), I knew that being teased was also being included in a Parisian morning. I stopped and stared into an open wooden crate at fat bronze pears that not only had little gold labels with black Gothic lettering but had had their stems dipped into crimson wax (why?). Before I could even wonder if I had enough to buy one, a barrel-shaped woman in a knit cap handed me one that had been bruised. I didn't realize that it was a gift and tried to pay her, but she waved me away. I carried the surprisingly heavy pear in my pocket until I was in the middle of the Pont des Arts, and then, leaning on the railing, I bit into the fruit and rich, sweet juice sluiced through my fingers and ran into my sleeves. Happier than I'd ever been, I crossed the river and found the Hotel La Louisiane, knowing, when I slid back into my lumpy bed, that I was meant to live in Paris. After all, I'd just walked home like someone who'd been born there, and my forearms were sticky with pear juice.

But it was some years later back in New York at a dreary

Third Avenue coffee shop where my fate was sealed. "Alec?" Where else would I find a friend whom I not only hadn't seen in five years but who knew about a job opening in Paris, the idea being that I could live in France? I applied for the job that afternoon and was hired.

MY PASSION FOR FRENCH FOOD

SEPTEMBER 1986. I MOVED TO PARIS WITH TWO SUITCASES, left them unopened at the hotel, and went out to discover that the Latin Quarter place with boeuf bourguignon had become a Greek restaurant. I was disappointed but undaunted. My first weekend in Paris was spent in a heightened haze of elation and loneliness, but I did buy five restaurant guidebooks. I may not have known a soul in Paris, but rather than moping around the Luxembourg Gardens all afternoon, or hurriedly scarfing down an omelette in a café, I decided to make the best of things, like the fact of being in Paris, along with a company expense account for all meals, and find the best boeuf bourguignon in town. Being on a quest is the best way to learn any city, and in search of my stew that fall, I mastered the Métro system, and even more valuably, how to eat alone and be happy.

I found my calling as a food writer in a rather unlikely setting, as a writer for Fairchild Publications, the New York-based fashion publishing group, when I started work in their Paris offices. Most of the work I did for them revolved around fashion, and I found my occasional assignments to report on restaurants in Paris, Milan, or Florence vastly more interesting than any-

thing having to do with fabrics or silhouettes. The job came with a very generous expense account, however, which enabled me to begin my assiduous discovery of French food and Paris restaurants.

Three years later I left Fairchild to become a freelance writer and immediately sought out as many food-oriented assignments as I could. I was fortunate to write for the now sadly defunct *European Travel and Life* as well as for *Travel and Leisure*, *Time Out Paris*, and many guidebooks, including *Frommer's* and *Fodor's*. Along the way, I became European editor for *Departures* magazine and also wrote regularly on French food and restaurants for *Food & Wine*, *Bon Appétit*, and *Gourmet*, for whom I worked as European correspondent from 2000 until its most regrettable closing in 2009.

During the course of this work, I've been privileged to

spend hours talking to the best chefs in Paris, often behind their kitchen doors, and also to take dozens of cooking classes. I love to cook and consider that a personal working knowledge of the ingredients and techniques used in French cooking has been essential to my ability to understand and appreciate the meals I am lucky to enjoy in the city's restaurants.

In any given week in Paris, I usually try a half-dozen new restaurants and return to a few old favorites. All of the restaurants profiled in this book are places I've been to many times, and though that doesn't guarantee that you won't try one of them on an off night, I can vouch for the seriousness, reliability, and quality of their cooking.

Needless to say, I never moved back to New York. Instead I fell hard for Paris, and began two decades of singularly spectacular eating as well as earning a living writing about it. And there's no city in the world where you eat better. Period. As is true of all big cities, what you really need, however, is a local friend to tell you where to go, and that's the whole idea of this book. Consider me to be your friend in Paris, the amiable obsessive who's spent years tracking down everything from the best boeuf bourguignon in town to those haute-cuisine tables that are actually worth a major wound to your wallet, from the world's best oysters, to onion soup so good you'll get teary-eyed. I know that I've been lucky, and I want to share. Bon appétit!

—ALEXANDER LOBRANO

Paris, AUGUST 2010

HUNGRY FOR PARIS

A READER'S GUIDE
HOW TO USE THIS BOOK

. . . .

THIS BOOK CONTAINS MORE THAN A HUNDRED PROFILES of Paris restaurants. Each portrait is intended to convey the personality of the table and its cooking, and together they offer a portrait of Paris seen through the prism of the city's best food.

As someone who travels constantly, I spend a lot of time with travel and guidebooks, and what I need from them most often is good recommendations of where to eat. While there are many sources for information on a given city's museums, for example, it's much more of a challenge to find restaurant advice that I can trust.

Some books are excellent, some less so. With their shortcomings in mind, I decided to write the Paris restaurant book that I'd hope to find if I were a food lover traveling to Paris, a book that would, I hoped, be companionable, reliable, and usefully opinionated, and also a book I'd enjoy reading as much for pleasure as I would using it for valuable reference. In the age of the Internet, hundreds of Web sites offer suggestions and restaurant reviews, but I also wanted to offer something I often find missing in cyberspace, which is a friendly, knowledgeable, and authoritative voice one can rely on.

With this ambition, I faced the delicious but challenging task of selecting which restaurants merited inclusion. My original list ran to more than two hundred tables, which I winnowed down to some hundred-plus restaurants where I know you'll have not only a great meal but also a great experience of Paris.

This book covers the entire spectrum of Paris restaurants, from globally renowned haute cuisine restaurants to the city's best falafel sandwich. The largest number are, of course, the bistros that are emblematic of eating in Paris and that also serve up some of the city's best food at relatively reasonable prices.

Every restaurant included in this book has a full-length profile, followed by "In a Word," a quick summary of that table for anyone in a hurry, plus a list of recommended dishes and a tagline that includes its number on the map, address and phone number, the Métro station nearest to the restaurant, its opening hours, and the average price of a meal for one without wine. French dishes that may be unfamiliar are explained in the longer profile but not in the list of recommended dishes, so if you want further information on a given dish, refer back to the main text.

Prices are indicated according to the following scale:

. . . .

INEXPENSIVE:	$	*Less than €30*
MODERATE:	$$	*€30–50*
EXPENSIVE:	$$$	*€50–75*
VERY EXPENSIVE:	$$$$	*over €75*

. . . .

Indexes at the end of the book group the restaurants according to type, price range, and places that are open all or part of the weekend.

THE HAPPY EATER'S ALMANAC:
HOW TO HAVE A PERFECT MEAL IN PARIS

T

O HAVE A WONDERFUL MEAL IN PARIS, IT HELPS TO HAVE an informed and sympathetic understanding of the different expectations that the French and most North Americans bring to the table. For starters, consider the balance of power. Americans believe the customer is entitled to have a meal his or her way. The French, deeply admiring of the culinary profession, are more willing to submit to the chef—you never hear Parisians asking if they can have it without the garlic, with no salt, or made with lemon juice instead of vinegar—and are brought up to believe that any restaurant meal follows the same script. You study the menu over an apéritif and begin with a first course, followed by a main course, then maybe cheese, and finally dessert and coffee. You don't ask if you can have cheese as a starter or two desserts instead of a main course, since it disturbs the essential, ancient logic of a well-constructed meal.

Parisians also have a much more relaxed attitude toward what they eat than do North Americans, who are often surprised by what appears to be their relative indifference to health considerations at the table. The reality isn't that the French are oblivious to the benefits of eating less fat, salt, or sugar. Instead, they believe in moderation and eating a well-balanced diet—

the French rarely snack between meals—and also that gastronomic pleasure is more important to one's physical well-being than obsessive calorie counting. In contrast, North Americans tend to have a more anxious relationship with food. No country in the world other than the United States could have invented the concept of the chocoholic, a term that is freighted with puritanical connotations, since it implies an unhealthy dependency on chocolate. Considering all of the other possibilities for destructive vice, I think an outsized love of chocolate is relatively harmless. Similarly, Americans want their food engineered to create and sustain health. Compared to the French, they think they've seen the "Lite," and they want meals that are low cal, low fat, low salt, and high fiber. The French will tell you that all of these worries are addressed by eating three balanced meals a day.

To be happy in a Parisian restaurant, it also helps to take a few pointers from the locals. For example, even though Parisians are deferential to chefs, they're otherwise assertive and engaged diners. This begins with insisting on being well seated when they arrive in a restaurant and then establishing a cordial complicity with the waiter or waitress. What's understood is that you'll be working together to create a successful meal. This is why servers in Paris restaurants proudly explain their menus in painstaking detail and are usually pleased when their clients are inquisitive or curious. Ordering is a process of friendly but serious discussion and consultation that's undertaken with the goal of composing a suite of dishes that flatter one another. If you order smoked salmon as a starter and grilled salmon as a main course, the waiter may try to guide you toward a more varied set of choices. Similarly, if you order a strong-tasting first course and a delicate main one, the waiter may suggest an alternative appetizer that won't overwhelm your second course. You're never obliged to follow his suggestions, but it helps to understand his well-intended motivation.

Parisians also know that good cooking takes time and so happily allot at least two hours for a typical restaurant meal. They'd never dream of trying to rush the kitchen either, since they understand that dining in a restaurant is a glorious public ceremony that has been refined over the course of centuries to enhance two of the most essential and wonderfully recurring pleasures of civilized daily life: great food and good conversation. The following section addresses various subjects and issues that you may encounter when dining in Paris.

APÉRITIFS (before-dinner drinks): Parisians rarely drink cocktails or hard liquor before a meal—they consider that these drinks dull the taste buds. Instead, they prefer a glass of Champagne or white wine or maybe a kir, white wine dosed with crème de cassis (black currant liqueur), crème de mûre (blackberry liqueur), or crème de pêche (peach liqueur). Popular non-alcoholic quaffs include tomato juice and Perrier, which the French never drink with meals because they think its large bubbles make it too gaseous to go well with food.

BREAD. I learned the importance of bread to the French through poignant firsthand experience. In the 1970s, my family hosted a French foreign exchange student, the son of an oyster fisherman from the southwestern town of Arcachon, at our home in suburban Connecticut. The first night that the genial Francis sat down with us for dinner, he scanned the table with a slightly panicked expression and then asked my mother if we had some bread. She excused herself and returned to the table with several slices of Pepperidge Farm white bread in a basket. He thanked her but still looked crestfallen when he peered into the bread basket.

Several days later, in my brother's French class, Francis talked about what he liked most and least about the United States. It turned out that he'd fallen hard for New York City, pizza, Chinese food, and pancakes with maple syrup but he found American houses overheated—even though it was a bitterly cold winter, my mother had to close the windows in his room every morning—and that he was suffering from severe bread deprivation. "Eating American bread is like eating a towel," he told the class to great hilarity. The following Friday, my father thoughtfully brought a baguette home from a bakery in New York, and Francis almost yelped with joy when he saw it.

Suffice it to say that bread is a vital and much-loved part of any meal in Paris. The most commonly served bread is a sliced baguette, or long crispy golden wand of wheat-flour bread. If you order oysters, you'll be served pain de seigle (rye bread) with butter, but otherwise butter is almost never served with bread in French restaurants. Some restaurants also serve pain de campagne, which comes to the table as slices of a crusty loaf baked with unbleached flour.

CHEESE. Though the cheese course is a waning institution at most Paris restaurants—even Parisians have become more calorie-conscious, and it is expensive to maintain a good selection of properly aged cheese—many better restaurants still serve a cheese tray between the main course and dessert. On a well-stocked tray, the cheeses are arranged clockwise, with the mildest one, usually a chèvre (goat cheese) or a gentle cow's milk cheese at "noon," to the strongest one, generally a blue cheese, at "eleven." A well-composed French cheese course stops several times on this clock according to individual taste. Cheese in France still remains a highly seasonal product. The best time of the year to eat most chèvres, for example, is in the spring, when the goats are eating fresh grass again after the winter months, while Mont d'Or, a creamy Alpine cheese, is at its best during the winter. Don't hesitate to ask the waiter for suggestions, and if you're wondering why cheese tastes so much better in France than it does at home, it is because French cheeses are still generally made with raw, as opposed to pasteurized, milk. Pasteurization kills off the friendly bacteria that give cheese its unique taste. Despite USDA regulations, eating cheeses made from raw milk is not only perfectly safe but essential if you're to appreciate them fully.

CHILDREN. Parisians very rarely take their children when they go to restaurants, but this is no reason why your well-behaved young ones won't be welcome. Be forewarned, however, that few Paris restaurants have children's menus and that the leisurely pace of Parisian dining can try smaller nervous systems. As a general rule of thumb, brasseries are good bets for kids, since their service is brisker, their menus generally offer things that kids like to eat, and the animation in the dining room provides helpful distraction.

COFFEE. The French never drink coffee with their meals and order coffee with milk (café au lait) only at breakfast. The standard French coffee is a small, dark espresso-style coffee known as a café or express. If you want coffee with milk during the day, order a café crème (coffee with steamed milk) or a noisette, which is an espresso-style coffee with a shot of milk. American-style coffee (café américain) is generally available in hotel restaurants or places with large tourist clienteles, but few Paris restaurants are likely to have it on hand, since the French find it too thin. Decaffeinated coffee, or un décaféiné, is commonly available, but very few Parisian restaurants serve cappuccino, to say nothing of low-fat mocha lattes. Artificial sweeteners are generally available.

COMPLAINTS. Many Anglophones are uncomfortable making complaints in restaurants. Parisians don't suffer from the same inhibition—if their meat is over- or undercooked, they won't hesitate to send it back and neither should you. Similarly, if you're unhappy for any other valid reason—you don't like your wine, or you're disappointed by something you've ordered—signal the waiter and politely but firmly explain your problem.

CREDIT CARDS. Most Paris restaurants accept at least one credit card, but to avoid an awkward surprise, it's a good idea to check when you're booking a table. The most commonly accepted card is VISA, and most restaurants also take Master-Card. American Express and Diners Club cards are less common.

DIGESTIFS (after-dinner drinks). According to the consensus of good manners, Parisians stop drinking wine when their coffee is served at the end of a meal, and though the tradition of concluding with a Cognac or an Armagnac is waning, they remain a glorious way of winding up a memorable meal. Single-malt scotches are also popular, as are Alsatian eaux-de-vie, clear spirits distilled from plums, pears, raspberries and other fruits—the latter being a real treat when served chilled on a warm summer night. A glass of Champagne also makes for a lovely nightcap, but the French never order cocktails following a good feast.

DINING HOURS. With few exceptions, lunch is served from noon to 2 P.M., dinner from 8 P.M. to 10 P.M. If you're hungry outside regular dining hours, try a café—most of them serve sandwiches, salads, and omelettes all day long—and if you want to eat late, your best bet is a brasserie or hotel restaurant.

DOGS. Don't be surprised to find yourself sitting next to a poodle in a Paris restaurant. Parisians love their pooches and often bring them along when they go out. Birds and reptiles are less well received, and cats stay home.

DRESS CODE. The Parisian idea of informal dressing is still very different from what passes for relaxed in most English-speaking countries. Deeply groomed in the art of public life, Parisians take pride in their appearance, and you'll rarely see them wearing T-shirts, shorts, or running shoes anywhere but at the gym. If you'd like to look local, women will never go wrong with the proverbial little black dress or a nicely cut pair of trousers and a blouse, while dress-down for men means a long-sleeved shirt with dark trousers and maybe a sweater or the quintessentially French white shirt with jeans and a blazer. Very few top-flight restaurants still insist that men wear ties, but you can avoid the ignominious fate of having to wear the ill-fitting house jacket by packing a lightweight blazer. And throw a tie into your luggage just in case.

FISH. Fish is often served whole in Paris restaurants. Parisians rightly believe that this offers a visible guarantee of freshness and also that fish cooked on the bone is more flavorful. If you don't want to bone your poisson yourself, ask the waiter to enlever les arêtes (remove the bones) for you. Certain fish, including tuna and salmon, are regularly cooked rare. If you want your fish cooked through, ask for it bien cuit (well done). The quality of fish and shellfish in Paris is excellent, but since the wholesale market is closed on Monday, meaning the last delivery was probably on Saturday, you might want to wait for Tuesday to get the freshest catch of the day.

LANGUAGE. Almost all restaurants in Paris now have a staff member or two who speaks English, but if you're not French-speaking, it is still not a bad idea to tuck a dictionary in your pocket on the off chance that you end up on a linguistic sandbar. Aside from a few brasseries and hotel restaurants, English-language menus are still uncommon in Paris. Don't assume that anyone speaks English, however. Instead, ask, "Parlez-vous anglais?" ("Do you speak English?") and hope that the answer will be "Yes." A few common French words and phrases will always make you more welcome, including "S'il vous plaît," the French equivalent of "please" and the politest way to attract a waiter's attention; and "Merci" (thank you).

LEFTOVERS. Since the portions served in Paris restaurants are more moderate than those found in North America, it's unlikely you'll end up with many leftovers at the end of a meal. Parisians almost never ask for a doggy bag, and few restaurants are equipped to serviceably pack up anything you haven't eaten. But if you end up with a tasty morsel on your plate that would be good as part of a picnic, you can always ask if you can take it home—"Est-ce-que je pourrais garder ça pour mon chien?" ("May I please keep this for my dog?"). In my opinion, avoiding waste and exercising a little thrift trump cultural differences.

MANNERS. Parisians are very polite and always greet the maître d'hôtel or hostess with a pleasant "Bonjour" or "Bonsoir" when they arrive in a restaurant, and an "Au revoir" when they leave. Conversational levels are also lower in Paris than they are in many other cities, so keep your voice down to assuage the locals.

Should you have the occasion to dine with French people, be advised that their casual conversational style is very different from that of North Americans. The French never ask personal questions—Are you married? What do you do?—until they've become reasonably well acquainted, and they are often flummoxed by what they see as our disorganized chatter. When it comes to any serious discussion, the French approach is leisurely and empirical, beginning at the broadest base of an issue or idea and winnowing it down to a careful conclusion. This may strike you as long-winded or dull, but bite your tongue and don't interrupt. Religion and politics are rarely discussed among people who don't know one another well, and to their credit, the French are brought up to believe that listening attentively is as important as expressing every thought that comes into your head, so when in doubt pinch your pie hole (be quiet).

MEAT. The French generally eat their meat rare, correctly believing that well-done meat has lost its flavorful juices. If you want your meat well done, order it bien cuit (well done). Rare is saignant, medium, à point.

MENU VOCABULARY. Somewhat confusingly, first courses in Paris restaurants are known as entrées—how the term came to mean a main course in English remains a mystery. Main courses are called plats, and plats du jour are the daily specials, often special seasonal dishes or recent inspirations of the chef. Fromage, or cheese, follows the main course. *Dessert* is a word that the English language borrowed from French.

NOISE. With some exceptions, notably the city's large brasseries, Parisian restaurants are quieter than those in large cities such as Los Angeles, Chicago, New York, and London. The French generally dislike noise while they're eating and attempt to keep the conversational volume at a discreetly low level.

OYSTERS. The French are mad for huîtres (oysters), and, contrary to the old dictum that they should be eaten only during a month with an *R* (September to April), they scarf them down all year long. (The reason for the *R* rule, by the way, is that oysters become laiteuses, or milky, during their reproductive season, and many people find that this masks their true taste.)

France produces some 130,000 tons of oysters annually, which makes it Europe's largest and the world's fourth largest producer. The main oyster-producing regions are Normandy, Brittany, Charente-Maritime, the Arcachon Basin, and the Mediterranean. Connoisseurs insist that you can immediately tell in which of these waters an oyster originated in the same way that you attribute a wine to a specific region of France, since the varying salinity and plankton levels affect the taste and size of these tasty morsels.

As befits a great Gallic delicacy, French oyster terminology is as detailed and complex as that used to identify and classify the country's wines. France produces two types of oysters—plates, which are flat, and creuses, which have convex shells. Plates are usually more expensive, since they're harder to grow. The two main varieties of plates you'll find on a shellfish menu are belons, from Brittany, and marennes, from the Loire-Atlantique. Oysters are then calibrated according to size. Creuses, the most common oysters, range in size from No. 5, the smallest, to No. 0, the largest. Plates oysters run from No. 4, the smallest, to No. 000, the largest, and spéciales, which are larger and meatier than creuses, start at No. 4 and run to No. 1. Big or small, they're all delicious, although recent fashion has favored smaller oysters, including boudeuses, which weigh in at just over an ounce, and the slightly larger papillons. Other terms you'll run into include fines, which indicates small to medium-sized oysters; spéciales, larger and meatier than fines; fines de claires, which are fattened at lower density in saltwater claires, or marshes, than spéciales; spéciales de claires, which usually have a more pronounced taste of the sea since they're finished in lower-density claires than are fines; and the connoisseur's choice, pousses en claires, which are fattened longer and at lower density than any of the others. Gillardeaux are especially plump, delicious oysters from Brittany. Confused? Throw caution to the winds and just enjoy them—French oysters are the world's best.

PRICES. Contrary to popular wisdom, you can eat extremely well in Paris without spending a small fortune. Many bistros offer a good-value prix fixe menu that includes a starter, main course, and dessert for a single set price, and plats du jour, or daily specials, are also often a good buy. Keep your bill down by skipping a drink before dinner and bottled water, and also by ordering the house wine. Sharing first courses and desserts is perfectly acceptable, too.

Restaurants in this book are rated according to the following price scale, which represents the cost of an average meal per person without wine.

· ·

INEXPENSIVE:	$	*Less than €30*
MODERATE:	$ $	*€30–50*
EXPENSIVE:	$ $ $	*€50–75*
VERY EXPENSIVE:	$ $ $ $	*over €75*

· ·

RESERVATIONS. Reservations are absolutely essential in Paris, especially if you want to eat at one of the city's more popular tables, in which case you should book as far ahead of time as possible. For Parisians, making a reservation not only ensures a table but is a sign of commitment and respect toward a restaurant and its staff. Parisians take reservations seriously, too. If you no longer need or want the table you've reserved, you should *always* cancel your reservation. An empty table punches a hole in the fragile finances of a restaurant, especially in a city like Paris, where one seldom runs into the double or triple seatings for the same table that are common in North American cities. Though some restaurants have double sittings during a given service, most Parisians will not put up with being rushed at the table—as far as they're concerned, once you've been seated, you shouldn't have to keep an eye on your watch.

RESTAURANT TYPES. Anyone accustomed to the generic hybrids that pass for "French" restaurants back home—in many places, "French" is still synonymous with "fancy"—may be confused by the different styles of restaurants in Paris, so a word of explanation is in order.

The bistro is the bedrock of Paris dining. Bistros are generally small, casual restaurants that are best known for their traditional plats mijotées, or simmered dishes, such as boeuf bourguignon (beef braised in red wine with onions, mushrooms, and cubed bacon) or blanquette de veau (veal in a lemony cream sauce). They also serve roasts and grills, are often crowded and convivial, and reflect the personality of the owner, who is often in the kitchen while his wife or her husband runs the dining room.

Within recent years, a new generation of chefs has reworked the bistro idiom by serving contemporary French cooking that's often lighter and more creative than what's on offer at traditional bistros. Many famous chefs have also branched out by opening bistros where you'll find their signature touch applied to bistro cooking, with delicious results.

The brasserie is perhaps the other best-known Paris restaurant category. These large, swift-paced establishments came into their own in the second half of the nineteenth century, when France's expanding rail network brought an influx of travelers to the capital and the city's growing population and booming tourist trade caused a restaurant boom. Many famous Parisian brasseries have Alsatian roots—the word means "brewery" in French—and Alsatians fleeing the eastern region of Alsace after it was occupied by Germany following France's defeat in the Franco-Prussian War (1870–1871) brought the brasserie tradition (breweries in Alsace often served food in taverns adjacent to their brew halls) to Paris. Traditionally, brasseries serve oysters, grills, and choucroute garnie, an Alsatian specialty of sauerkraut garnished with sausages and various cuts of pork. Many of them have a grand decor, are open daily, and serve late. Animated and convivial, brasseries are a good choice for weekend and holiday dining and perfect for large groups.

Regular restaurants tend to be more expensive, formal places that often cater to a business clientele at noon and serve traditional French bourgeois cooking—that is, richer, more elaborate dishes than you generally find in bistros and brasseries. Haute cuisine restaurants are the pinnacle of the French food chain. Often found in hotels, they have elegant decors, soigné service, and lavish menus. These places tend to be very expensive and require reservations to be made several weeks in advance.

SALADS. Once or twice a year during the summer, I see the same handwritten sign. "Pas de salade comme plat/No salad as a meal!" a warning to salad-mad North Americans that they cannot order salad as a main course in the restaurant where the sign is posted. This is because salads are usually eaten either as appetizers or after the main course in France, not as main courses, and restaurant owners don't like serving a bowl of modestly priced greens when they could sell a sturdier and more expensive main course.

If you want a salad as a main course, your best bet is a café. Most of them offer a variety of salades composées, salads garnished with cheese, hard-boiled eggs, tomatoes, potatoes, ham, chicken, fish, or shellfish. The standard French salad dressing is oil and vinegar, but you'll occasionally come across blue cheese dressings. If you'd like a simple green salad with your meal, ask for a salade verte. A salade mixte is a green salad with tomatoes.

Popular first-course salads on Paris menus include salade

folle (crazy salad), with greens, green beans, and thin slices of foie gras; frisée aux lardons, curly endive with croutons and sautéed chunks of bacon; salade de tomates, tomato salad; salade de mâche et betteraves, lamb's lettuce with chopped beets in a creamy vinaigrette; salade aux noix, mixed greens with walnuts; salade lyonnaise, mixed greens with bacon, soft-cooked eggs, and occasionally anchovies, herring, chicken livers, or sheep's feet. A salade niçoise is a meal-sized bowl of mixed greens garnished with anchovies, tomatoes, tuna, black olives, potatoes, and green beans.

SALT AND PEPPER. Some restaurants don't put salt (sel) and pepper (poivre) on the table, the implication being that the chef's food is already perfectly seasoned. If you want salt and pepper, don't hesitate to ask. In addition to regular white table salt, you may also come across coarse sel gris, which is made by evaporating seawater and is considered to have better flavor and also be rich in trace minerals, or fleur de sel, the fine white salt crystals that form as seawater evaporates in open salt pans and are laboriously gathered by hand. You'll find regular black pepper in most pepper mills, but some southwestern restaurants and contemporary bistros may serve small open dishes of bright orange piment d'Espelette, which is made by grinding long red peppers from the Basque country village of Espelette.

SMOKING. One of the great banes of Paris restaurant dining has been stubbed out. As of January 1, 2008, all restaurants in Paris officially became nonsmoking.

SOFT DRINKS. If you want to drink Coca-Cola with your foie gras, that's your prerogative, but expect visible consternation, even indignation, from your waiter. The French almost never drink soft drinks or iced coffee or tea with a meal, and diet soda is still not common in most French restaurants. Parisians who don't wish to drink wine with their meals order water, which is the best diet drink of them all.

SPECIAL REQUESTS. Though most Paris restaurants will try to accommodate common dietary considerations, many kitchens bridle when customers become too specific with special requests. It's fine to ask for the sauce on the side, but don't expect a friendly reception to a request that the chef omit an ingredient such as garlic or onions.

TIPS. Service is *always* included on any bill in a Paris restaurant, and you are not obliged to leave an additional tip. Customarily, however, a little extra change is welcome. On a €100 bistro meal, I might leave €5 extra, while excellent service at a haute cuisine restaurant may warrant a €20–40 tip. Tips are always in cash, since French credit card terminals do not allow the addition of a tip. Coat check attendants are usually happy with €2 per chit.

VEGETARIANS. Though Paris is still not as vegetarian-friendly as cities such as New York, San Francisco, and London, vegetarians are much better catered for today than they were in the recent past, when the only dedicated vegetarian restaurants in Paris were sad-sack sixties-vintage Latin Quarter holes-in-the-wall. Restaurants in this book that are particularly vegetarian-friendly include Au Coin des Gourmets (Vietnamese), Arpège, L'Astrance, L'Atelier de Joël Robuchon, Le Bambou (Vietnamese), Breizh Café, Le Dôme (fish), Les Fables de La Fontaine (fish), Liza, Pierre Gagnaire, Le Pré Verre, and Ze Kitchen Galerie. Many other restaurants are happy to offer salads, soups, omelettes, and vegetable plates, however—just alert the waiter as soon as you arrive that you're a végétarien (male)/végétarienne (female).

WAITERS AND WAITRESSES. Waiting tables is a respected profession in France, which explains the seriousness with which many waiters and waitresses do their jobs. Don't mistake this professionalism for unfriendliness. The French prefer a polite distance when being waited on and are unlikely to discuss anything other than what they're eating and drinking with the staff. Servers never introduce themselves, and though you may occasionally see staff wearing name tags in hotel dining rooms, it's considered impolite to address anyone by his or her first name.

WATER. Parisian tap water is perfectly potable, so unless you prefer mineral water, request a carafe d'eau, a carafe of water, which restaurants are required by law to serve you. The most popular still mineral waters are Evian and Volvic, with Alsatian Watwiller, a nitrate-free still water said to aid digestion, turning up at some haute cuisine tables. Badoit is the most popular brand of French sparkling water, though the Italian San Pellegrino is also common. Chateldon, marketed as a premium water and the favorite sip of King Louis XIV, comes from the Auvergne region and is served at many upmarket restaurants.

WINE. The arrival of the wine list in a Paris restaurant is often a source of quiet panic for the simple reason that many people assume that they don't know enough to make an informed choice. If you're one of them, rest assured that you're in good company. Most people, even Frenchmen, know a lot less about wine than they let on. So relax and remember that the whole point of wine is pleasure and that learning to pair wine with food is a joyous lifelong process of trial and error.

Armed with this outlook, consider the waiter or the sommelier (wine steward) to be your helpful, if not unfailingly disinterested, teacher. Ask for suggestions, and don't be cowed into thinking that price is the unfailing guarantee of a good wine. When presented with the bottle you've chosen, read the label carefully to make sure it's the wine you've ordered, and remember that the main reason you taste it after it's been uncorked is to make sure it isn't bouchonné, or corked. Corked wine has a moldy taste and musty smell that occurs when the cork used to close the bottle was contaminated with TCA (2,4,6-trichloroanisole), a chemical compound that occurs when natural airborne fungi come into contact with the chlorophenol contained in cork. If you're not sure if your wine is corked, ask the sommelier or waiter to taste it, too.

Happily, a new generation of Parisian sommeliers is not only demystifying the whole business of choosing wines but takes pride in helping you find something that will suit both your tastes and pocketbook. Many of them are also likely to propose wines from some of France's lesser-known wine regions, especially Provence and the southwestern Languedoc-Roussillon, the latter being France's largest wine-producing region. Their thinking is that these wines are somewhat bigger and stronger-tasting than most French wines and so will please anyone used to drinking New World wines as those from Chile, California, New Zealand, and Australia are known. If you prefer quieter, subtler Old World–style wines, make this known.

Parisian wine lists are most often organized according to the major French wine regions, specifically Alsace, Beaujolais, Burgundy, Bordeaux, Côtes du Rhône, Languedoc-Roussillon, Loire Valley, and Provence. Other important wine regions include Corsica, the Jura, and the southwest. Wines are grouped under these regional subheads by color—blancs (whites), rosés, and rouges (reds). Unlike many Americans, Parisians never order wine by the cépage, or grape variety. If being deprived of such familiar classifications as Pinot Noir, Merlot, Chardonnay, or Sauvignon Blanc leaves you without bearings, don't hesitate to explain to the waiter or sommelier (wine steward) what style of wine you like and also your budget. Don't feel pressured into accepting his or her suggestions, either. Good fail-safe wine choices include Sancerre, Chablis, and Graves if you want to drink white and Côtes du Rhône if you're after an affordable medium-bodied red.

Many Paris restaurants have a house wine that's often a decent buy for the money, and more and more of them also serve

wine by the glass. Brasseries and bistros often offer perfectly drinkable wine by the carafe, too.

WHAT IS FRENCH FOOD?

For many years, French food was a mystery to me, and from the regular visits of friends and family I know that for many people it remains an alluring enigma. Though the idea of sitting down to a Gallic meal provokes heightened expectations—France's gastronomic reputation precedes any actual experience of its food—the same prevailing wisdom also holds that French food is rich, fancy, and expensive. Further, very few people can actually name more than a handful of French dishes. Almost no one wants to admit to this slightly embarrassing quandary, however, which is why I'm happy to share my own learning curve in the hope that it's enlightening.

My earliest memory of eating anything specifically described as French was the éclairs my mother bought at the A&P supermarket in Westport, Connecticut. Long, narrow soggy pastries shaped like hot dog rolls, they were filled with a gelatinous yellow pastry cream and glossed with chocolate frosting. I liked them well enough, but as my only firsthand reference, they offered little by way of elucidation about French food.

Sure, my parents bragged in the most general of terms about excellent meals they'd had during trips to Paris, and Mom occasionally made "Beef Burgundy," a stew of cubed beef with mushrooms, onions, and a short pour of Holland House red cooking wine, and sometimes even a cheese soufflé, but when we had a quiz about "Foods from Around the World" in my second-grade class at the Greens Farms Elementary School, I chewed my pencil. Italian was easy—pizza, meatball grinders, and spaghetti—and so was Chinese—the egg rolls, fried rice, barbecued spareribs, shrimp toast, and Moo Goo Gai Pan we'd get as Sunday-night takeout from the West Lake restaurant downtown. But French? I finally wrote "French toast, French dressing, and French fries," and was surprised to get my test back with a red penciled "Good!" in the margin next to my flat-footed guesses. Even though I was only seven years old, I suspected the inadequacy of my answers.

As a bookworm, I eventually gathered that French food was special and fancy, but since the French kitchen had contributed no signature dish to the repertoire of foreign foods figuring in the American diet of the 1960s, I wasn't exactly sure what form this edible elegance might take on a plate.

At some point in the 1960s, a very good cheese store opened in downtown Westport, and my father liked to stop by after our Saturday trip to the library and pick up a random assortment—random because we didn't really know what we were doing—of cheeses. We all liked Brie, which suddenly became popular in the late sixties, but the cheese that made Mom really happy was a triple crème called L'Explorateur, which had a little drawing of a rocket ship on the round gold label riding its velvety white rind. Slowly other "French" foods registered on my radar. Pepperidge Farm introduced a line of heat-and-serve croissants, which suburban Connecticut decided were a dressy alternative to Parker House rolls at the Saturday-night dinner parties that were so much a part of this era, and on hot summer days, Mom liked a bowl of Bon Vivant brand canned vichyssoise (cream of potato soup) for lunch, or she did until the night we were listening to WQXR, New York's classical radio station, and the flannel-voiced newscaster announced that a Westchester couple had died of botulism after eating said soup. "Bon vivants no more!" my father quipped when my mother told him about it. The company went out of business within a month, but Mom fearlessly transferred her allegiance to Pepperidge Farm canned vichyssoise, which seemed so smart and, well, French, with a sprinkling of freeze-dried chives.

Not long after the vichyssoise incident, I had my first French epiphany. On a lazy June Saturday, Mom drove my brother John and me into New York to go to the Metropolitan Museum of Art. On that hot day in the wanly air-conditioned museum, I could have stared at Monet's *Garden at Sainte-Adresse* for hours. A man in a waistcoat and straw boater sat in a wicker chair next to a woman hidden under a white parasol staring out at the flinty waves of the breezy English Channel—you knew there was a wind because you could almost hear the two flags in the painting snapping—and if I loved the freshness implied by this scene, I was also smitten by its elegance—the immaculately groomed garden with its scarlet swords of gladioli and banks of nasturtiums, the two well-dressed couples, several sailboats near the shore. The formality and reserve of the scene fascinated me, too. It was summertime, but no one was wearing shorts or T-shirts.

"Are either of you hungry?" Mom eventually asked, and when we said we were, I assumed we'd eat in the museum cafeteria, where the food wasn't especially good but the life-sized bronze figures skipping across the fountain basin in a reproduction of a Roman atrium made a meal special even if it was eaten from a warm, wet fiberglass tray. To my surprise, we left the museum and hailed a cab, which took us to Le Charles V, a French restaurant somewhere in the East Fifties. I was very excited when we arrived and a waiter with a thin mustache in a black jacket showed us to a table in a dining room decorated with miscellaneous medieval heraldry and wrought-iron paraphernalia.

Mom had vichyssoise to start, of course, but here with real chives scissored over the thick creamy soup. John ordered a chef's salad, and I chose champignons à la Greque. The hilarious discovery was that John's salad was topped with a hard-boiled egg, tomato, sliced Swiss cheese, and thin strips of a dark pink meat that the waiter told us was tongue. *Tongue.* A merciless tease, I stuck mine out every time my mother looked away, until she finally saw me and told me to stop it. John, a good sport, said it tasted sort of like a cross between ham and roast beef. My mushrooms—real ones, not canned—came in a tangy tomatoed vinaigrette with pearl onions and large white seeds, which Mom explained were coriander. Next, boeuf bourguignon (Beef Burgundy) for John, sole with grapes and toasted almonds for Mom, and coq au vin for me. The coq au vin came in a little copper casserole, and the meaty pieces of chicken were bathed in a glossy, winy-tasting mahogany-colored sauce. It was delicious, but what amazed me most was that I was finally eating French food, which made me feel as worldly and sophisticated as an eleven-year-old boy could be without being insufferable. The real triumph of the meal, however, was the poires belle-Hélène, pears poached in a syrup spiked with vanilla bean and lemon and served with vanilla ice cream and hot chocolate sauce, which I had for dessert. Sprinkled with slivered almonds, it was everything I'd so desperately hoped French food might be—something elevated and absolutely delectable.

Our lunch left me elated for weeks afterward. Suddenly, I was more knowing and tentatively connected to a world much larger than the one I lived in. It also made me rabidly anxious to get at some more French food, though this took a while.

We never ate at the one French restaurant in Westport. It was too expensive and apparently not very good, so my aspirations remained fallow until the beginning of the 1970s, when

two women, one of whom was half French, opened Bon Appétit, a cooking school and lunchroom, in an old brick mill
building on the muddy banks of the Saugatuck River, Westport's own rather meager little river. It quickly became a refuge
for a small but growing tribe of smart, restless women who
wanted more out of life than macaroni and cheese and meeting
their husbands' commuter trains every night.

The first time I went was after playing tennis with my friend
Clay, his mother, June, and her friend Mrs. Weinstein, whom I
remember because she'd stopped shaving her legs, a sign of her
affinity with Women's Liberation, as it was then cumbersomely
known. June and Clay talked about the years they'd lived in
Venezuela—Clay's father worked for one of the big oil compa-
nies—and Mrs. Weinstein reminisced about living in New
York's Greenwich Village as a young woman, her memories of
parties on fire escapes, little theaters, and good bread implying
that life in our small suburban town was wanting. Having never
lived anywhere but Connecticut, I had little to add to what
struck me as their knowing chatter, and so when the three of
them ordered quiche Lorraine and salad, I did, too, even though
I didn't know what it was. It turned out to be an egg, bacon, and
cheese pie—a French recipe, of course—and the accompanying
salad was a mixture of small feathery leaves and fronds that had
nothing to do with the wedges of iceberg lettuce I knew as
salad. What was even more interesting was that there were little
ceramic salt dishes on the table filled with coarse gray crystals—sea salt, June explained. Rather dim-wittedly, I wondered
how you got the salt out of the sea and also if it was clean, but I
kept my mouth shut.

The quiche was wonderful—how could anything made with
eggs, cheese, and bacon be bad?—but I was slightly disap-

pointed by its homeliness. I'd been hoping to pick up where I'd
left off at the Charles V. Mrs. Weinstein told us that the accompanying salad, which was simply dressed with oil and vinegar,
was known in French as mesclun and that one of the owners actually grew many of the little leaves and herbs in her own garden. Worried that I'd been mute for too long, I decided
curiosity was the best gambit. So I parried, "I wonder who Lorraine was?" June laughed out loud, and, after rolling her eyes,
Mrs. Weinstein explained: "Lorraine is a region of eastern
France, and quiche Lorraine is one of its specialties." Ouch. But
save for this sting, I was very interested by what she had to say,
and she must have sensed it. "Mesclun is traditionally eaten in
Nice and the south of France, where another specialty is bouillabaisse, the famous fish soup," she said, adding, "Almost all of
the regions of France have a famous specialty or two. It's one of
the great pleasures of traveling there."

Further corrections to my developing but wobbly knowledge of French food occurred when a French foreign exchange
student came to live with us for a month. Francis's father was an
oyster fisherman in Arcachon, a small seaside town west of Bordeaux that's famous for these bivalves, and he'd eat absolutely
everything, with the exception, however, of a few things he
found in our pantry. He set me straight, for example, on French
dressing—"We'd *never* put that on a salad. It would kill it"—
and French toast—"We call it pain perdu and have it for
dessert." Francis also intervened in the preparation of Mom's
Beef Burgundy, politely suggesting that the beef be marinated
overnight. He also asked her to buy some real garlic, fresh
mushrooms, and, after tasting the Holland House red cooking
wine in a Dixie cup, a bottle of real wine, which required a trip
to the liquor store. The next afternoon he was a blaze of activity

in the kitchen, and when dinner was served that night after Dad got home, the results were stunning. Though she'd been up-staged, Mom graciously complimented Francis on his cooking, though she couldn't help observing that his version required an awful lot of work.

That Christmas, someone gave us a fondue kit—a cast-iron pot to be placed on a trivet over a tin of burning Sterno (a little tin of jellylike fuel that you lit and placed under the pot, ostensibly to keep its contents warm—it never worked very well) and six long thin forks, each of which had a different-colored plastic handle—and on many Sunday nights that winter Mom made fondue, which she considered to be a useful way of using up various bits and pieces of old cheese. The cardboard box the kit came in had a skier schussing down a slope past several chalets and some styl-ized pine trees and was stamped MADE IN FRANCE. An accompa-nying recipe booklet explained that fondue, or melted cheese, was a popular dish in both the French and Swiss Alps.

I gleaned more information when I started taking French in junior high school. One of the basic pedagogical tools in class was the memorization of rather daft dialogues between imaginary people. One of them memorably took place in a restaurant in Lyon, where six Lyonnais—a boy and a girl, their parents and grandparents—were celebrating the mother's birthday. It was a grand restaurant for this family of swells, too, even if they started off with several things I found repugnant at the time—foie gras (fattened duck's liver) for the adults and frogs' legs sautéed in garlic and parsley for the children, followed by a few more things I couldn't imagine eating—the two men ordered veal kidneys in mustard sauce, the ladies, quenelles de brochet (pike dumplings) in sauce Nantua (crayfish sauce made pink with a dab of tomato paste). The kids, those little garlic lovers, had roast lamb—"Bien rosé, s'il vous plaît" ("Nice and rare, please"), the bratty little boy told the waiter—with pale green flageolet beans, which sounded delicious and were certainly a better garnish than the alarmingly green mint jelly we always had with roast lamb. For dessert, the men had cheese, the ladies île flottante (floating island, or clouds of meringue floating in crème anglaise), and the kids tarte pralinée, which Madame Barrow, my French war-bride French teacher, explained was an open tart made from crushed darkpink-colored candied almonds. She also emphasized that this was a very special meal—most of the time, French people went to bistros, which specialized in slowly simmered dishes, or brasseries, which were big busy places that usually had oyster stands out front and served steaks, fish, and choucroute garnie. "There are few things better than a good choucroute garnie on a cold day," she added, sounding pensive and a little wistful on an October afternoon in New England. I asked her what it was, and she explained that it was an Alsatian dish of gently pickled cabbage—"not like your sour American sauerkraut"—topped with grilled bacon, several kinds of sausage, and pork, eaten with boiled potatoes and mustard.

The following summer, I made my first trip to France, and the vague but eager outlines of what I knew about French food finally came into clearer focus. We went to Au Pied de Cochon, a bustling brasserie in Les Halles, the neighborhood that had once been the main food market of the city of Paris, and ate onion soup, which came to the table under a gooey molten cap of Gruyère cheese, delicious little crispy baked ribbons of which ran down the sides of the white porcelain bowl. Under the cheese, which floated on a slice of toasted bread, the soup itself was hot salty beef broth loaded with sautéed onions, and it was one of the best things I'd ever eaten. Then, filet mignon with a side dish of sauce béarnaise, a wonderful little pot of edible yellow unguent made with egg yolks, butter, shallots, vinegar, white wine, tarragon, and parsley, flanked by a dainty little log cabin of French fries and garnished with sprigs of parsley. For dessert, we had crêpes flambées au Grand Marnier, which the waiter prepared in a shiny copper saucepan over a table-side burner and then lit in dancing blue flames for a finale I felt was the height of gastronomic glamour. Another night, I ate the best boeuf bourguignon—you may have gathered that this dish obsesses me—in a Latin Quarter bistro, and the next day, an amazingly good roast chicken, a dish that was a revelation for being so stunningly simple.

By the time we left Paris to visit the châteaux of the Loire and Normandy, something vital had shifted in the way that I thought about French food. What I'd learned was that the best French food often *is* stunningly simple. Sure, we went to a fancy restaurant or two in Paris, but the places that made me happiest were the city's bistros with their hearty, homey, happy cooking based on the freshest seasonal produce.

The many years I've lived in Paris have only confirmed the truth of this adolescent awakening. Though I've had the privilege of ascending the pyramid of French gastronomy and discovering some spectacular food at its higher altitudes, in the end, it is bistro food, or rustic cooking with deep roots in the various regional kitchens of France, that remains the blessedly eternal bedrock of the French kitchen.

A recent survey of their favorite recipes reveals that the French love their simplest food best, too. So here are the ten dishes that answer the question, "What is French food?"

• *Roast chicken.* The most popular dish of all with French home cooks is a well-roasted bird. There are two reasons why it tastes so good in France. First, the French prefer good free-range chicken, and second, they never stuff the bird, rightly believing that the best way to enhance its flavor is to butter it well before cooking and baste it several times while it's in the oven.

• *Moules marinières.* Mussels cooked with chopped shallots, parsley, white wine, thyme, and a bay leaf or two, sweet and succulent.

• *Boeuf bourguignon.* As far as I'm concerned, humanity has invented few dishes that produce joy and solace at the table more reliably than this famous Burgundian beef stew.

• *Sole meunière.* After being dredged in flour, salt, and pepper, this princely fish is sautéed in hot melted butter and dosed with a bit of fresh lemon juice.

• *Pot-au-feu.* Nothing offers more primal comfort than this winter-defying dish of beef and vegetables braised in bouillon and served with coarse salt, mustard, and horseradish.

• *Choucroute garnie.* Like so many of the most ancient French dishes, this one displays a humble but shrewd gastronomic genius, since choucroute, or pickled cabbage, is rich in vitamin C and so was a perfect medieval panacea during the many months when France was greenery-deprived. It is garnished with grilled bacon, sausages, and salt pork and eaten with boiled potatoes and lashings of sharp mustard.

- *Navarin d'agneau.* The best way to experience what a godly gift the arrival of spring was for the French in centuries past is to sample this stew of lamb and spring vegetables, including turnips, tomatoes, carrots, and onions.

- *Blanquette de veau.* Veal simmered with mushrooms and onions in a white sauce of egg yolks, cream, and lemon juice. Delicate and delicious, it is usually served over rice.

- *Cassoulet.* Though there are endless riffs on this southwestern French standard, it is generally a slow-simmered combination of white beans, lamb, pork, mutton, and sausage.

- *Bouillabaisse.* As the name tells—it roughly translates to "slow boil"—this fish soup native to Marseille is simmered for hours so that the homeliest fish of the catch of the day thrown into the kettle dissolves into a rich, ruddy potion that is an honest, ancient gust of the Mediterranean.

TUILERIES, LES HALLES, BOURSE

Chez Georges

CHEZ GEORGES IS THE GASTRONOMIC EQUIVALENT OF THE
little black dress—unfailingly correct, politely coquettish, and
impeccably Parisian. This is why it was no surprise to find our-

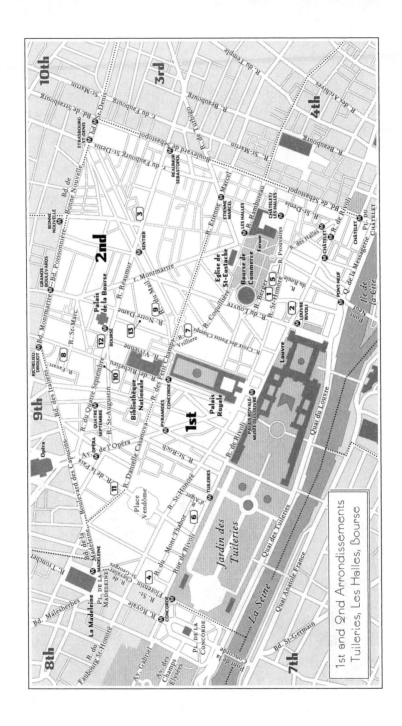

1st and 2nd Arrondissements
Tuileries, Les Halles, Bourse

selves seated next to the affable and slightly owlish Didier
Ludot on a balmy summer night. A self-described antiquaire de
la mode (antiques dealer specializing in fashion), Ludot runs La
Petite Robe Noire (The Little Black Dress) and another boutique specializing in vintage fashion in the Palais-Royal. Since
he was entertaining a customer, a stylish Park Avenue blonde
who gamely insisted that they speak French so that she "might
mend the wreckage of what I half learned in college"—much to
her credit, her French was good, and much to his credit, his patience didn't fail once during a two-and-a-half-hour meal—
Ludot's choice of a restaurant was perfect. Chez Georges is
exactly what most foreigners want a bistro to be, which is basically a place where time has stood still on a very French clock
(Parisians like it, too, but find it expensive).

Here, the menu is still written out by hand daily and then
mimeographed in lilac-colored ink. Brown banquettes uphol-
stered in what the French euphemistically call moleskin but
North Americans know as leatherette line both walls of the
long, narrow railroad-car-like dining room, and there's a little
bar just inside the front door where your bill is tallied and taxis
are called. The decor, such as it is, dates back to its founding in
the early 1900s and doesn't add up to much more than mirrors
interspersed with Gothic columns and a pale tiled floor.

The older waitresses who have ruled the roost for decades
are gradually retiring, but the younger staff perpetuate a delightful house serving style based on smiles and solicitude. And
most important of all, the menu hasn't changed an iota during
the twenty years that I've been coming here. This place remains
an unfailingly good address for a trencherman's feed of impeccably prepared bistro classics.

On a warm night, Alice, Bruno, and I raced through a bottle
of the good house Sancerre and the plate of sausages and

radishes that came with a little pot of butter as soon as we'd ordered. Though everyone and his great-aunt is staking a claim to Julia Child these days, I couldn't resist telling them about how she'd taught me to butter my radishes on my first visit to Chez Georges. Invited to dinner by the late Gregory Usher, an American who founded the cooking school at the Hôtel Ritz and a close friend of Julia's, I arrived uncharacteristically early and found Child already seated and alone. I introduced myself and watched in fascination as she buttered a radish and chomped away. Then, after a swig of Sancerre, she said, "The radish is one of nature's most underrated creations." I smiled, and she added, "It's a good thing no one overheard me. When you're my age, a remark like that could land you in an old folks' home. Still, a nicely buttered radish is just the thing to remind any cook to stay humble and simple in the kitchen. Most foods don't really need any improving."

I suspect Child loved Chez Georges for the same reasons I do. Not only is the food delicious, but it's a good spot in which to channel frivolous, flirtatious postwar Paris, the wondrous city that not only made Julia Child into Julia Child but Audrey Hepburn into Audrey Hepburn, Leslie Caron into Leslie Caron, etc.

Bruno, good Frenchman that he is, ordered a salade de museau de boeuf—thin slices of beef muzzle, a curious crunchy mix of meat and cartilage, which Alice gamely tried, and I went for a sauté of girolles, tiny wild mushrooms, which were delicious, but not garlicky enough. In fact, the microscopic bits of chopped parsley included to make it a real persillade (mix of chopped garlic and onion) alarmed me. No knife I know could have chopped that finely, so suffice it to say I deeply hope Chez Georges isn't starting to take shortcuts, like ready-made restaurant-supply-company persillade, for example. Alice had a good ruddy ratatouille, in which the eggplant cubes retained their shape but had a correctly soft texture, with the lovely addition of a handful of plump capers.

Our main courses were outstanding, too, including Alice's veal sweetbreads with girolles and Bruno's similarly garnished veal chop. Neither was as good as my grilled turbot, a big slab of meaty white fish on the bone with sexy black grill marks like a fishnet stocking. It came with a little huddle of boiled potatoes and a sauceboat of béarnaise sauce so perfect that I polished off what my fish didn't need with a soup spoon.

I couldn't resist the wobbly and wonderfully cratered crème caramel in a fine bath of slightly burnt caramel sauce, while the others ate wild strawberries and first-of-season French raspberries with dollops of ivory-colored crème fraîche, confirmation of my deeply held belief that butterfat is bliss. Just as we'd finished our coffee, the blond waitress of a certain age, a handsome woman with a severe chignon, reappeared; she'd changed out of her black uniform and white apron and was wearing a perfectly pressed pink paneled linen skirt and a matching sleeveless top. She bade everyone good night and went, Cinderella-like, into the night. When we left a few minutes later, our transformation went in the opposite direction, or silk purse into sow's ear, since after several delicious blowsy hours of la vie en rose, our beeping cell phones signaled the impatience of the world outside. This is why I hope we'll always have the delicious antidote to modernity offered by Chez Georges and buttered radishes.

· ☙ ·

IN A WORD: The perfect all-purpose Parisian bistro and a great place to hunt down impeccably made bona fide bistro classics like blanquette de veau (veal in a lemon-spiked sauce) that are increasingly hard to come by.

DON'T MISS: Terrine de foie de volaille (chicken liver terrine); harengs avec pommes à l'huile (herring with dressed potatoes); foie gras d'oie maison (homemade goose foie gras); escalope de saumon à l'oseille (salmon in sorrel sauce); coquilles Saint-Jacques aux échalotes (scallops sautéed with shallots); grilled turbot with béarnaise sauce; profiteroles (cream puffs) with hot chocolate sauce.

. . .

[**9**] **1 rue du Mail, 2nd, 01.42.60.07.11.** MÉTRO: **Bourse or Sentier.** OPEN **Monday to Friday for lunch and dinner.** CLOSED **Saturday and Sunday.** ▪ **$$$**

Les Fines Gueules

WINE BARS ARE HAVING A MAJOR REVIVAL IN PARIS, AND this one, occupying a pleasant corner just up the street from the

Banque de France, is one of the best. The best is its theme, too, since it serves only the finest pedigreed produce. The butter comes from Jean-Yves Bordier in Saint-Malo, the oysters from David Hervé in Oléron, the bread from the Poujauran bakery in the 7th, vegetables from the lord of the legumes, Joël Thiébault, and meat from the star butcher Hugo Desnoyer; all of the wines on offer are organic.

The beautiful zinc bar announces the vocation of this place, and exposed stone walls make for a mellow atmosphere. Since it's not far from the Louvre, it's ideal for a light lunch, maybe veal carpaccio with shavings of three-year-old Parmesan, a plate of charcuterie, jamón ibérico (the best Spanish ham) with Buratta, a creamy cheese from Puglia in Italy, and then maybe one of the daily specials from the chalkboard menu—cod with fork-mashed potatoes, zucchini, and pleurottes mushrooms; steak tartare made from Salers beef; or fusilli with Gorgonzola sauce. Finish up with a cheese plate, a varied selection of perfectly aged cheeses that might include a chèvre from the Ardèche, Brie, Parmesan, and Roquefort. Friendly service and modest prices add to the pleasure of a meal here, and the restaurant is open daily, although only charcuterie and cheese plates are served at lunch on Saturday and Sunday.

IN A WORD: With a very convenient location, this is an excellent example of the new breed of Paris wine bar. Perfect for lunch or a light, casual dinner.

. . .

[7] **43 rue Croix des Petits Champs, 1st, 01.42.61.35.41.** MÉTRO: **Palais-Royal, Musée du Louvre, or Sentier.** OPEN **daily for lunch and dinner.** ▪ **$$**

Frenchie

ON A MISTY OCTOBER NIGHT, I ARRIVE AT FRENCHIE, ONE of the best modern bistros in Paris, ahead of my friend David, and I decide to stroll the surrounding streets of Le Sentier, a maze of ancient lanes in the 2nd and 3rd Arrondissements that was once the garment district of Paris. As such, it's a place where the city's old stone is still pregnant with the flicker of small, cautious dreams—for generations of immigrant seamstresses, the modest hope of something better was the only way to stay sane in the face of relentlessly hard work at the sewing machines.

In recent years, Le Sentier, following the pattern of similar old working-class neighborhoods like Nolita in New York City, has begun a new chapter in its long history as creative types move in, drawn by its affordable rents, and open shops, galleries, and restaurants. Against this backdrop, it's no surprise that young Nantes-born chef Gregory Marchand hung out his first shingle in the tiny cobbled rue du Nil after stints at Jamie Oliver's Fifteen in London (where he acquired the nickname Frenchie) and the Gramercy Tavern in New York. With its exposed brick walls, factory lamps, and scuffed plank floors, this vest-pocket dining room invokes a gritty but pretty post-industrial aesthetic that feels more Anglo-American than French.

I'm sipping a chilled glass of Rueda, a Spanish white, when David comes in. A pastry chef and popular blogger, he's another Connecticut-born American in Paris and is as passionate about food as I am. He's never been to Frenchie, whereas I've been a dozen times, and so I'm really looking forward to the meal. We study the short menu: two starters, two main courses, and two desserts, all of which change daily, and David remarks,

"This is real market-driven cooking. This place could be in Berkeley or Napa. It looks good."

I was hoping David would want the beetroot, fresh chèvre, and preserved lemon starter, but on this damp night, we both ordered the cream of celery root soup, which was ladled over fresh croutons, a slice of foie gras, and a coddled egg to create comfort food at its most consoling. Next, some of the best brandade de morue (flaked salt cod with whipped potatoes and garlic) I've ever had. Marchand's version was wonderfully creamy, and came with vivid swirls of red pepper purée and parsley jus, both of which flattered the cod. David, happily, ordered the paleron de boeuf, or braised beef with carrots, and it was tender and redolent of wine, balsamic vinegar, and pickling spices, an original touch. And finally, a cheese plate, including a chèvre and a first-rate Tomme with a smear of heather-flower honey that pulled the grassy flavors out of both cheeses for me, and a chocolate tart with raspberry purée for David.

Busy with my cheese, I waited for the verdict of the chocolate-loving David on his tart. "This is really good. In fact, I love this place—it's too bad it's not in my neighborhood," he said. I feel exactly the same way, as do many other Parisians, so be sure to book well in advance if you want to sample Gregory Marchand's brilliant cooking.

. ·

IN A WORD: Talented young chef Gregory Marchand serves up delicious, inventive modern comfort food at this loft-like little bistro in Le Sentier, Paris's old garment district.

DON'T MISS: The menu changes daily at Frenchie, but dishes to look out for are Marchand's delicious cheese-stuffed gnuddi, cumin-scented lamb with chickpeas and tomatoes, and dark chocolate tart with salted caramel sauce.

. . .

[3] **Frenchie, 5 rue du Nil, 2nd,** 01.40.39.96.19. MÉTRO: **Sentier.** OPEN **Wednesday to Saturday for lunch and dinner;Tuesday dinner only.** CLOSED **Sunday and Monday. • $$**

Liza

PARIS IS ONE OF THE BEST CITIES IN THE WORLD FOR anyone who loves Lebanese food. Why? Lebanon was a French protectorate from 1922 to 1943, and the Lebanese still learn French, aspire to sending their kids to school in France, and love vacationing in Paris. Many wealthy Lebanese also fled the country during its recent cycles of turbulence and settled in Paris, which means that the capital has a large, affluent community. The French themselves love Lebanese food, especially mezze, or the assorted hors d'oeuvres that begin most Lebanese meals.

Liza is one of the best of a new generation of foreign tables in Paris that are ditching ethnic stereotypes—in terms of both decor and cooking—for edgy style and culinary authenticity. Located near the old Bourse, this place is a sexy gallery of almost invisibly contrasting tones of ecru and ivory rooms with dark parquet floors and perforated white steel tables that were imported from Beirut, owner Lisa Soughayar's hometown.

The kitchen shows off just how dazzlingly good and varied Lebanese cooking can be, with mezze and regional dishes that go beyond the usual standards. The best way to enjoy this restaurant is to come as a group, so on a warm summer night Bert and Noël, friends who live in Los Angeles, joined Bruno and me for dinner. For starters, we loved the lentil, fried onion, and orange salad; the kebbe, raw seasoned lamb, which is sort of a Near Eastern take on steak tartare; grilled haloumi cheese with apricot preserves and moutabbal (a spicy mash of avocados), and fried shrimp. The main courses were excellent, too, including roast sea bass with citrus-flavored rice and fruit sauce, grilled lamb chops with lentil puree and cherry tomatoes slow-baked with cumin, and ground lamb with coriander-brightened spinach and rice. Among the desserts we enjoyed were the rose-petal ice cream with almond milk and pistachios and the halva ice cream with tangy carob molasses.

· 🕮 ·

IN A WORD: This small, stylish, friendly Lebanese restaurant has quickly become popular with Paris's large Lebanese community and fashionable Parisians who love the decor and light, bright, authentic cooking. An excellent choice when you want something other than French food.

DON'T MISS: Lentil, fried onion, and orange salad; kebbe (seasoned raw ground lamb); grilled halloumi cheese with apricot preserves; moutabbal of avocados and fried shrimp; grilled lamb chops with lentil puree and cherry tomatoes; roast sea bass with citrus rice and tagine sauce; rose-petal ice cream with almond milk and pistachios; halva ice cream with carob molasses.

· · ·

[13]   **14 rue de la Banque, 2nd, 01.55.35.00.66.** MÉTRO: **Bourse.** OPEN **Monday to Saturday for lunch and dinner.** CLOSED **Sunday. www.restaurant -liza.com** ▪ **$$**

Aux Lyonnais

THE FIRST TIME I WENT TO THIS COZY 1890-VINTAGE bouchon (Lyonnais bistro) twenty years ago, it was staffed by kindly older waitresses in black dresses and white aprons, the beautiful Art Nouveau tiles needed a scrub, and the kitchen sent out a variety of Lyonnais specialties that the French would describe as "correct," or decent if unremarkable. I liked its homely charm, however, and the saucisson de Lyon (pistachio-studded pork sausage) served with warm potato salad and quenelles de brochet, or pike dumplings in a pale pink sauce Nantua (creamy crayfish sauce), made for a fine feed.

Then, in 2002, Alain Ducasse, now France's most ambitious gastro-entrepreneur, took it over, freshened it up, and shrewdly revised the menu to appeal to contemporary Parisian preferences for lighter, healthier food within the parentheses of traditional Lyonnais cooking. The transformation was a big surprise to anyone who knew the old place, since the very idea of reinventing a venerable old-time table like this seemed, well, like

something an American would do. In fact it brought to mind the bizarre way the traditional old farm stand in the Connecticut town I'd grown up in had been knocked down and replaced by a luxurious, sanitized, and expensive pastiche of a New England farm stand. Both replications have turned out to be a huge success, however, and Ducasse's version of Aux Lyonnais is very popular, packed at lunchtime with men in suits and international types who view the Ducasse name as the gastronomic equivalent of Chanel, and in the evening with a mixed crowd of journalists, bankers, and bourgeois couples.

As is true of all of Ducasse's satellite restaurants, this place follows a carefully devised, high-concept script, the intention being to make one of France's sturdier and most venerable regional kitchens fresher and sexier. Presentation is always important to Ducasse, which means that many dishes come in squat glass mason jars or enameled cast-iron casseroles, bread is slotted into a tan canvas pouch that hangs from the table, and wines are served by the *pot*, the thick-bottomed glass flask you find in traditional Lyonnais bouchons. Even though neither the menu nor the atmosphere approximates the real experience of a Lyonnais bouchon—they're bawdy, sleeves-rolled-up places serving copious quantities of sturdy old-fashioned food like museau de boeuf (beef muzzle) and tablier de sapeur (breaded marinated tripe), neither of which is on the menu here—you still get a very good meal and the chance to sample several classics that are rarely seen on Paris menus anymore.

Start with some charcuterie—several types of sausage, pork crackling, and cervelle de canut (silk worker's brain, a reference to the pale complexions of Lyon's silk workers), a delicious mixture of fromage blanc (fresh white cow's milk cheese), shallots, garlic, chives, oil, and vinegar. The salade de cervelas, sauce gribiche is excellent, too—thick slices of cervelas sausage (a finely textured pork sausage) and waxy potatoes served hot in a little casserole. I also like the casserole of seasonal vegetables, the coddled eggs in a mason jar with morels and crayfish, and the marinated herring. My favorite main course here remains what it's always been—pike dumplings with crayfish in sauce Nantua—and this version is exemplary. Calf's liver en persillade (bread crumbs, garlic, and parsley) is impeccably cooked, too, and the Saint-Marcellin is a runny, lactic treat. The tarte de pralines, an open-faced tart made with vividly red-colored sugar-coated almonds, is a treat, too, and the service is young, friendly, and swift.

IN A WORD: Alain Ducasse's neo-Lyonnais bouchon cleverly updates the gastronomic idiom of the famously gastronomic city at the confluence of the Rhône and Saône rivers for the twenty-first century. The satisfying richness of such hearty dishes as sabodet (sausage made from pig's head and skin) is retained, but the kitchen's subtle sleight of hand renders them lighter and more refined.

DON'T MISS: Charcuterie plate; salade de cervelas; poached eggs with morels and crayfish; marinated herring; casserole of seasonal vegetables; quenelles de brochet aux écrevisses (pike dumplings with crayfish sauce); calf's liver en persillade; navarin d'agneau (lamb stew); tarte de pralines.

. . .

[8] **32 rue Saint-Marc, 2nd, 01.42.96.65.04.** MÉTRO: **Bourse or Richelieu-Drouot.** OPEN **Tuesday to Friday for lunch and dinner. Saturday dinner only.** CLOSED **Saturday lunch, Sunday, and Monday. www.alain-ducasse.com**
▪ **$$$**

Le Mesturet

NOT FAR FROM THE OLD BOURSE (THE FORMER FRENCH stock exchange) Le Mesturet, previously a corner café and now a simple, friendly restaurant, is like a souped-up Gallic version of a New York coffee shop, an affordable, casual place where locals go for simple, tasty comfort food when they don't feel like cooking. What's made this place with wan lighting and negligible decor a big hit is generally good food for very reasonable prices and the contagiously jolly atmosphere generated by people letting their hair down.

The amiable owner, Alain Fontaine, sources directly from small producers in southwestern France, which explains the succulent confit de canard (duck preserved in its own fat and

then grilled), Rocamadour (a creamy cookie-sized cow's-milk cheese from the Dordogne), and excellent Corbières, a hearty red wine with a cherry perfume from the abbey of Fontfroide in the Languedoc-Roussillon. "In a country as agriculturally blessed as France, there's no reason you shouldn't eat well, even for modest prices," says Fontaine.

On a Friday night just before Christmas, we went as eight—five Parisians, two visitors from Chicago, and a friend from Marseilles—and this demanding octet loved the meal that followed.

Grilled eggplant topped with melted goat cheese and surrounded by a tangy tomato coulis on a bed of salad leaves was redolent of good olive oil and Mediterranean herbs, and a homemade terrine de chevreuil (roebuck) with a big lobe of lush foie gras in its center tasted of the wild—this entrée was a real surprise on the menu in such a modestly priced restaurant, since game is expensive in Paris.

Alain Fontaine's menus assiduously follow the seasons—I still remember a delicious open tart of sardines with a compote of shallots and grilled red peppers on a summer night—and mignons de biche (venison medallions) in a sauce of preserved wild blueberries and a tender civet de marcassin (braised baby wild boar) were both excellent. Though tempted by one of the better blanquettes de veau (veal, mushrooms, and baby onions in a lemon-spiked cream sauce) in Paris, I couldn't stay away from the confit de canard, duck preserved in its own salted fat, which came with pommes dauphinoise (potatoes baked with cream); the crisp skin of the bird contrasting with its melting flesh is one of the great pleasures of the French table.

While we were idling after dinner, over coffee and Vieille Prune eau-de-vie, a delicious amber spirit distilled from plums in southwestern France, Fontaine came to the table. "Tell your friends I bought them some Bénédictine," he said, reminding me that the last time I'd been in his restaurant had been several months before with friends from Seattle, who had yearned for a tot of the herbal liqueur made by Benedictine monks in Normandy. I dutifully informed Seattle and received the following e-mail: "Fontaine is a true restaurateur—he knows any good restaurant is all in the details, and his hospitality is exceptional. Tell him we can't wait to come back!" Most clients of Le Mesturet feel exactly the same way.

. 🍂 .

IN A WORD: With a menu that brims with the goodness of the best French regional produce, this amiable bistro is a perfect place for a relaxed meal that's easy on the wallet.

DON'T MISS: Coq au vin (rooster braised in red wine); sea bream with Mediterranean vegetables; grilled tuna with anise oil; Rocamadour cheese; clafoutis aux quetsches (baked custard with plums).

. . .

[10] 77 rue de Richelieu, 2nd, 01.42.97.40.68. MÉTRO: **Bourse or Quatre-Septembre.** OPEN **Monday to Friday for lunch and dinner. Saturday dinner only.** CLOSED **Saturday lunch and Sunday. www.lemesturet.com** • **$$**

Le Meurice

AS A SHY BOY LIVING IN A CORNER OF THE COUNTRY WITH long winters, I happily spent hours with my nose in a book. I was lucky enough to have an aunt who worked as an editor at a publishing company in New York, and for my ninth birthday she gave me a series of books that profiled the lives of a little boy and a little girl in various different European countries. I read the French book so many times I'd almost committed it to memory before it fell apart, and my favorite chapter was when the children's grandparents came from Nice to visit them in Paris and took them to what we used to call a "fancy" restaurant. The fancy restaurant was in a nameless hotel, but it had huge flower arrangements, glittering crystal chandeliers, candles in silver candelabra, waiters in black vests with tails, and an elaborate mosaic floor. The children, lucky things, ate langoustines, foie gras, and a poulet de Bresse en demi-deuil, or chicken cooked with slices of black truffle tucked under its skin, and wild strawberry soufflé, a meal I dreamed of for years before I finally scaled the ramparts of French haute cuisine and sampled such delicacies for myself.

Every time I go to Le Meurice, I wonder if this magnificent dining room wasn't the inspiration for the children's book

writer, too, since a meal here is everything a perfect experience
of French haute cuisine should be—exquisite cooking, impeccable waitering, a spectacular setting, and a shimmering sense
that every service here is a special occasion.

Chef Yannick Alléno is also one of the most intriguing talents working in Paris today. I first discovered his cooking when
he was chef in the dining room at the Hôtel Scribe and have had
the pleasure of sampling his ascension at every step of the way.
And as a recent tasting menu proved, he's never been better
than he is today. We were six at table, a perfect quorum for such
an experience, since all of us know and love food.

Though a first course of mackerel marinated in white wine
left several unenthused, Alléno had succeeded in transforming
this underappreciated fish into an elegant delicacy. The almost
creamy fish was served with a succulent gelée printanière, fine
aspic with a colorful dainty dice of baby spring vegetables that
was the perfect contrast with the meaty fish. "Mackerel is not
one of my favorite fishes," observed Judy, "but that was lovely."
Next, coeurs de celtuce aux grains de caviar. Celtuce, or stem
lettuce, originated in China and is often used there in stir-fries.
Alléno had blanched the tender heart of the pleasant chewy lettuce and served it in a smoky cream sauce garnished with tiny
black pearls of herring caviar to create a dish that seemed daringly rustic in such an opulent setting. With foie gras in a
sweet-and-sour sauce of honey vinegar, he veered back to the
luxury of classical haute cuisine, which he does quite well, but
then he surprised by tacking on the tongue-in-cheek cooking
that is so much his own with grilled rouget (red mullet) on a
bed of his signature risetto, a risotto-style dish made with a tiny
pasta-like orzo, garnished with shellfish and fresh basil. What
he understands better than many chefs at this altitude is that
people come to such exalted tables to be surprised and enter-

tained. Rooted in a stunning command of technique, Alléno's culinary wit remains consistently polite and polished—he likes to provoke but knows better than to shock his well-heeled international clientele.

The menu offered a choice between spit-roasted pigeon in a gossamer sauce spiked with anchovy cream and veal sweetbreads perfumed with nutmeg and served with asparagus and a mushroom fumet. Charles, a television producer visiting from Los Angeles, was ecstatic over his perfectly roasted small bird—"Juicy, succulent, just amazing!"—while I loved my veal sweetbreads, impeccably cooked to the texture of firmly set custard and a study in restraint, since the nutmeg quietly emphasized their natural richness. Our cheese course—tomme de chèvre—came with Granny Smith gelée (fine green apple aspic) and a superb salad of wild sorrel, and the pleasant acidity of gariguette strawberries under a golden cap of meringue was the perfect conclusion to this remarkable feast.

· ☁ ·

IN A WORD: Against the backdrop of one of the world's most beautiful dining rooms, chef Yannick Alléno offers flawless French haute cuisine dishes that find a perfect equilibrium between tradition and innovation. Exquisite service and one of the best wine lists in Paris add to the unfailing pleasure of a meal here. Your wallet will take a beating, but it's worth every cent.

DON'T MISS: Smoked salmon Koulbiac (smoked salmon inside a roll of fine pastry) with mushrooms and caviar; turbot with a pistou of bitter herbs, stuffed turnips, and morel mushrooms; sea bass with herbs, fava beans, baby peas, and Noirmoutier potatoes; wild salmon with sauce Choron (béarnaise sauce with tomato puree); grilled rouget barbet (red mullet) with a risetto (pasta

risotto) of shellfish and basil; roast pigeon in anchovy cream sauce; veal sweetbreads roasted with nutmeg; fraises gariguettes soufflées (strawberries capped with a meringue soufflé); vanilla, coffee, or chocolate millefeuille; transparent ravioli stuffed with red fruit and served in a Champagne cream with basil.

. . .

[6] Hôtel Meurice, 228 rue de Rivoli, 1st, 01.44.58.10.10. MÉTRO: Tuileries. OPEN Monday to Friday daily for lunch and dinner. Saturday dinner only. CLOSED Sunday. www.meuricehotel.com ▪ $$$$

Le Pur'Grill

THOUGH IT DOESN'T COMPLETELY OVERCOME THE STIGMA of being a chain hotel restaurant, Le Pur'Grill is still one of the best restaurants in the heart of Paris. Scandinavians in stone-washed denim, impatient Israeli businessmen, sleepy Asian tourists not yet in town long enough to even begin recovering from their jet lag, and Euro execs with well-groomed blonds of both sexes wouldn't at first glance appear a promising clientele for a chef as talented as Jean-François Roquette, but even these indifferent eaters are aroused by his subtle, sexy, sophisticated cooking, which constitutes some of the surest "fusion" cooking to be found in the French capital.

The dining room here is puzzling at first glance, too, with a vaguely Asian-inspired circular banquette in the middle of the low-lit, mostly beige dining room, which makes the outside tables seem like Siberia. Once settled in, though, it hardly matters where you sit, although it's fun to have a direct sight line to the very busy and well-drilled open kitchen.

On a slack winter night just after the holidays, we weren't very hungry when we settled in at our dark-stained, bare wood table, but amuse-bouches of lobster meat with potently vegetal celery gelée and a parmentier d'homard (mashed potatoes capping tender chunks of lobster in a sauce of their own coral, as lobster eggs are known) quickly brought us to attention, since these weren't the usual ho-hum hors d'oeuvres but fascinating miniatures reflecting a lot of talent and intelligence. Then a starter of thinly sliced scallops marinated in lime-infused oil with a mimosa (laser-fine slices and crumbs, respectively) of cauliflower and broccoli was simply brilliant, with the citrus spiking but not overwhelming the creamy crustacean and the crunchy texture of the vegetable garnish, situating the dish squarely in a Breton vegetable patch with an ocean view despite the Asian gloss of the lime. Likewise, turnips lacquered with maple syrup and garnished with snow peas was a deeply nuanced dish with an intriguing tone-on-tone play between the bitterness of the vegetables and the ambered sweetness of the New England syrup.

Though the zealously trained customer-service-concept-driven waiters and waitresses gave the meal a slightly hasty edge, nothing could detract from the point-blank brilliance of main courses like Breton lobster cooked in salt with three different seaweeds—laitue de mer (sea lettuce), dulse, and wakame—and Bresse chicken in a creamy sauce of foie gras with a pot-au-feu de légumes, each vegetable poached in a different liquid (the baby carrots smacked of a well-balanced vinaigrette, while the cherry-sized turnips and slender leeks had been blanched in hot bouillon), a dish so profoundly satisfying in its elegant simplicity that shavings of white truffles, though always welcome, were luxuriously superfluous.

Since Paris has generally fallen out of love with them, desserts in contemporary French restaurants are often beside the point, but Roquette did a stunning grand finale with a vacherin à la poire comice et curry "Mumbai"—poached pears with a delicate meringue globe filled with curry-flavored ice cream, and mandarine corse et cheesecake, Corsican mandarin orange slices slipped out of their jackets and garnishing a crunchy crumble-rich cheesecake. With food this elegant and erotic, it frankly seems unlikely that Roquette will remain at the Paris Park Hyatt indefinitely, so note the name and get ready for the takeoff of a major talent.

·⟨⟩·

IN A WORD: Chef Jean-François Roquette is a rising local talent, which is why this sleek hotel dining room attracts sophisticated Parisians as well as tourists and hotel guests.

DON'T MISS: Scallop carpaccio with lime-flavored oil; lobster bisque; langoustines cooked with lemongrass; Breton lobster cooked in salt with seaweed; Bresse chicken with foie gras sauce and pot-au-feu vegetables; cheesecake with mandarin oranges; vacherin with pears and curry.

. . .

[11] **Park Hyatt Vendôme Hôtel, 5 rue de la Paix, 2nd, 01.58.71.10.60.** MÉTRO: **Opéra.** OPEN **daily for dinner only. www.paris.vendome.hyatt.com** • **$$$$**

Yam'Tcha

TUCKED AWAY IN A QUIET SIDE STREET NEAR LES HALLES, this sweet and very sincere little restaurant may offer the first twenty-first-century table in the French capital. Why? Because

young chef Adeline Grattard, who trained with Yannick Alléno at Le Meurice and Pascal Barbot at L'Astrance before spending two years in Hong Kong, has coined a brilliant new culinary idiom with a healthy pulse of aesthetic and gustatory originality.

Grattard eschews fusion in favor of an elegant and very delicate gastronomic minuet between the French and Cantonese palates. In contrast to the heavy-handed mixing and mashing that often occurs when a French chef mines a foreign kitchen for inspiration, the dishes that make up Grattard's tasting menus (four or six courses, changing almost daily) are beautiful, deeply considered, and intricately composed studies in taste and texture that create their own subtle but unfailingly elegant gastronomic logic.

This intimate dining room with its soft lighting and exposed stone walls is also a pleasant place for a meal. At the service bar Grattard's husband Chi Wah Chan oversees the optional tea service—Yam'Tcha means "to drink tea"—and you can choose to sample a different tea with each course. The hospitality is relaxed but stylish and unself-conscious, and depending on where you're seated, you can also watch Grattard hard at work in the compact glass-walled kitchen just inside the front door.

My first meal at Yam'Tcha was on a mild pollen-scented spring night right after it opened, and what Bruno and I were served perfectly captured the quickening season. We began with an amuse-bouche of slivered broad beans with ground pork and sesame seed oil, followed by grilled scallops on a bed of bean sprouts in a luscious emerald-green wild garlic sauce. Next came whole rougets served on a bed of Chinese cabbage with enoki mushrooms, a slice of Cîteaux (a Burgundian abbey cheese), and finally a sublime dessert of homemade ginger ice cream with avocado slices and passion fruit. Delighted and a little awed by this meal, I knew I'd come back, and so I have, with every visit reprising the pleasure of this first discovery and yielding a dish or two I muse on for days afterward.

· ·

IN A WORD: The signature of young chef Adeline Grattard's cooking is a subtle, sensual mingling of the French and Chinese palates.

DON'T MISS: Grattard's tasting menus change constantly, but one signature dish to look for is roast duck served over Szechuan-style eggplant.

. . .

[1] 4 rue Sauval, 1st, 01.40.26.08.07. MÉTRO: Louvre-Rivoli. OPEN Wednesday to Sunday for lunch and dinner. CLOSED Monday and Tuesday.
• $$$

La Tour de Montlhéry

IF YOU'VE NEVER BEEN TO THIS BAWDY, BRAWNY BISTRO
in a side street running off of what used to be Les Halles, the
heaving main food market of Paris (now long gone), you might
wonder why a noticeable number of people seem to show up
with damp hair. I certainly did before I'd lived in Paris for several years, and eventually I discovered that this is one of the best
places in town to go after the quick shower that follows some
amorous ardors. Why? Because this ballsy old place drives any
happy couple in on itself at the same time that it provides the foil
for a really good time—the drama of waiters in black aprons
sweeping through the bric-a-brac-decorated dining room filled
with red-checked tables, the absurdly generous portions of the
sort of stick-to-your-ribs comfort food you want when you're
really hungry, and the quiet hilarity of a shared, consensual
party to which everyone's been invited.

Be forewarned that when I say the portions are generous, I
mean huge, so the daintier appetizers are prudent—maybe a
salade frisée (curly endive) with garlicky croutons, smoked
salmon, one of my very favorite and increasingly difficult to
find old-fashioned starters, oeuf en gelée, or a poached egg in
salty beef aspic with ribbons of ham or tongue.

It serves one of the best côtes de boeuf (rib steaks) in Paris,
and it comes to the table with an avalanche of hot, golden,
freshly made frites. If the onglet (hanger steak) is my hands-
down favorite, however—rare, chewy, well-aged meat with a
sauce of shallots sautéed in wine and butter—I also like the
haricots de mouton, mutton stewed with white beans, a
trencherman's dish par excellence that I recommend to anyone

suffering from jet lag or who's preparing for a move or any other exhausting and stressful event. The first time I ever tried the mutton, I'd come to the table with wet hair, and though the elderly man in a bread-crumb-dotted sweater vest at the next table seemed to be contentedly churning his memories, he eventually revealed his sly sense of humor. "J'ai faim," I'd said while studying the menu. A minute later, he leaned over and spoke, "Excusez-moi, s'il vous plaît, mais il faut vite gouter ça. L'amour vous a rendu souriant mais un peu pâle." ("Excuse me, but you must try this, since love has left you smiling but a little pale"). No cool day anywhere in the world goes by without pricking a yearning for its pot-au-feu, beef boiled in bouillon with vegetables. Sprinkled with coarse gray sea salt and eaten with tiny cornichons (cucumber pickles) and a tiny wooden spade or two of nostril-clearing mustard, it's one of the most brilliant antidotes to winter I've ever found. Oh—and dessert? I've never gotten there, but others have extolled the profiteroles (choux pastry with vanilla ice cream and lashings of hot chocolate sauce).

IN A WORD: An authentic old-fashioned bistro with a retro decor that recalls the days when it fed workers from the now-gone Les Halles, Paris's main food market, just down the street. Busy but good-humored waiters serve a jovial crowd feasting on good, sturdy French comfort food served in gargantuan portions. A great choice for a late dinner or a good dose of sepia-toned Paris.

DON'T MISS: Salade frisée aux croutons aillés (curly endive salad with garlic croutons); oeuf en gelée (poached egg in beef aspic with ham); onglet (hanger steak) with shallots; tripes au Calvados; côte de boeuf (rib steak); haricots de mouton (mutton with white beans); profiteroles.

. . .

[5] 5 rue des Prouvaires, 1st, 01.42.36.21.82. MÉTRO: **Louvre-Rivoli or Châtelet-Les-Halles.** OPEN **Monday to Friday for lunch and dinner.** CLOSED **Saturday and Sunday.** ▪ **$$**

Le Vaudeville

JUST ACROSS THE STREET FROM THE STATELY PALAIS Brongniart, a handsome nineteenth-century building that was once Paris's palace of commerce, Le Vaudeville lost many of the dapper pin-striped bankers and brokers who used to pack it to the rafters at noon when the Bourse (stock exchange) moved from this colonnaded limestone building to high-tech new quarters in the office-park-dull La Défense district outside the city, but it remains one of the liveliest and better brasseries in Paris. And this is saying a lot, since this much-loved restaurant genre, as indelibly associated with Paris as cancan dancers and the Eiffel Tower, has mostly succumbed to a rather tragic senility (see "The Rise and Fall of the Parisian Brasserie" on page 326).

To be sure, brasseries were never meant to be beacons of gastronomy; they came into being during the nineteenth century to provide a good, fast-paced feed to large numbers of people in a stylish setting. The Vaudeville still rises to this task quite respectably, and there are few places where you'll find a more diverting cross-section of Parisians than this handsome black-

and-white-marble-walled Art Deco dining room. The truth is that Parisians go to brasseries as much to people-watch as they do to eat, and this explains the popularity of this intimate place with great sight lines, as much as the menu. The gang's all here—BlackBerry-toting journalists (the offices of *Le Figaro*, France's largest national daily, are nearby), finance folks, theater people, the occasional politician or movie star, a vital dose of tourists—Paris wouldn't be Paris without them—and tousled young couples (the Vaudeville is a great spot to come with a lover).

There's an oyster stand out front, as there should be at any brasserie worthy of the name, and a plateau of freshly shucked bivalves, followed by the grilled salt cod with black-truffled potato puree, make for a mean meal. The filet mignon is cute indeed and comes with a little nosegay of watercress—its peppery bite is the perfect foil to the buttery richness of the meat—and a side of decent frites. For intrepid gastronauts and Frenchmen wanting to show off their testosterone, the menu also boldly includes tête de veau, sauce gribiche (calf's head with a sauce of eggs, vinegar, cornichon pickles, and capers), an old-fashioned dish rarely seen on brasserie menus anymore. Desserts are rarely a strong suit at brasseries, but the classic profiteroles (cream-puff-like pastries with vanilla ice cream and hot chocolate sauce) are good for a commissary-style kitchen, and anyone wanting a high-proof conclusion might enjoy a Colonel, which is lemon sorbet splashed with vodka, a nice idea on a summer night or, for that matter, on a rainy Monday afternoon when you're in a bad mood.

Unfortunately, Paris has increasingly adopted one of the worst aspects of the English-speaking world's restaurant culture, which is the obligatory reservation. Sure, it's always better to book, but sometimes life isn't that tidy and you're hungry on the spot. Fortunately, the Vaudeville soldiers on as one of those rare places where you can walk in at the last minute and still usually cop a table after a kir at the bar.

· 🔺 ·

IN A WORD: An intimate Parisian brasserie with a cosmopolitan crowd, friendly bustle, and handsome Art Deco decor. The busy kitchen sends out better-than-average brasserie classics, the waiters are appropriately saucy, and the late serving hours make it perfect for a quick bite after the theater or for anyone who'd rather surf their jet lag with a tray of oysters than fight it.

DON'T MISS: Foie gras de canard; sole à la plancha (griddled sole); grilled salt cod with black truffled potato puree; skate with capers; andouillette AAAAA (best-quality chitterling sausage); millefeuille.

· · ·

[**12**] **29 rue Vivienne, 2nd, 01.40.20.04.62.** MÉTRO: **Bourse.** OPEN **daily for lunch and dinner until 1** A.M. **www.vaudevilleparis.com** ▪ **$$**

Chez La Vieille/Lescure

THE DAY I LEARNED CHEZ LA VIEILLE HAD CHANGED HANDS and was no longer a real bistro, I was heartsick. Every time another one of these independently owned places with a good honest old-fashioned menu of traditional French dishes like boeuf aux carottes or navarin d'agneau goes under, Paris is the poorer for losing not only another piece of its gastronomic history but one of those now increasingly rare tables that have long served as the ballast of its gastronomic reputation.

Chez la Vieille was a personal favorite, too, since I actually met the original vieille (old lady), the wonderful and wily Adrienne Biasin, the first time I dined there right after moving to

Paris in 1986. If I enjoyed her teasing (my accent) and babying (realizing after several visits that I was a serious student of French food, she'd bring out a sample of a dish she wanted me to try), the real gift Mme. Biasin made me was a deepened understanding of a cooking style the French affectionately but also somewhat patronizingly refer to as "la cuisine ménagère," or "housewives' cooking"—the battery of delicious dishes that make a family happy when it gathers around the dinner table.

To be sure, Biasin's cooking was always brighter and better than that. The hors d'oeuvres cart, a Rabelaisian serve-yourself affair of heavy ceramic bowls bearing such simple vieille France standards as marinated herring, celery rémoulade, terrine de campagne, and other glories of Gaul, was truly epic; her main courses displayed an artfulness and precision that trumped even the best home cook; and her dessert cart reprised the generosity and excellence of the hors d'oeuvres. But you can be sure she never cooked with recipes—everything that came out of her kitchen was a dish she'd learned to cook as "a careless and rather silly girl."

The woman that girl became, a charmingly knowing version of an old crone who wore carpet slippers in the dining room, astutely bequeathed her baby to a kind, hardworking Corsican, Mme. Cervoni, when it was time to retire, and this savvy successor carried on admirably until very recently.

When the shock of Mme. Cervoni's departure had worn off, I was, of course, eager to know what would become of the restaurant, and a day later there I was at a table for two in front of the heavy old-fashioned bar in the ground-floor dining room. Rather improbably, because he's always worked so much higher on the food chain, the new chef here is Michel del Burgo, a tremendously talented but mercurial haute cuisine cook who streaked through the kitchens of Le Bristol, Taillevent, Le Chantecler, and others before attempting to resuscitate, unsuccessfully, L'Orangerie, a beau monde favorite on the Ile Saint-Louis. Del Burgo has always been a tough chef to plot, because he almost never stays anywhere long enough to leave a lasting imprint; I first noticed his meticulously classical but intriguingly off-center cooking style when he was at the Bristol. On a wintery night with a beautiful Minnesota-born food blogger in tow, I loved my starter of an impeccably seared lobe of duck foie gras—it had just set like a rich custard—on a bed of finely diced légumes oubliés ("forgotten vegetables," or mostly winter root vegetables that older French people still associate with the privation of wartime diets) in a light port sauce. This was followed by grilled scallops in buttermilk foam with an intriguing garnish of braised endives and crushed freshly roasted hazelnuts, and finally a pleasant runny chocolate cake with pecans and salted-butter caramel sauce. This meal had nothing to do with bistro cooking and its long-simmered casseroles based on slowly braised meat, but instead showcased highly skilled dishes from

the canon of another almost defunct genus of French cooking, which is cuisine bourgeoise, or the serious, dressed up special-occasion cooking Parisians once cherished as part of serious meals in a whole category of formal, expensive restaurants—Le Recamier and Le Vert Galant come to mind—that have since become extinct.

So while I miss what it once was, I quite like the new version of Chez la Vieille, especially since del Burgo will be regularly revising his menu. My main worry is that this peripatetic new chef won't stay put, so confirm his presence when you make your reservation. And on the off chance he's flown the coop, I'd suggest Lescure, a friendly little bistro just off the Place de la Concorde, as your backup. The same family has run this happy place since 1919, the terrine de campagne, boeuf bourguignon, and poule au pot are reliably good, the wines are very fairly priced, and proprietor Denis Lascaud is a charming host.

· ·

IN A WORD: Chef Michel del Burgo serves up delicious cuisine bourgeoise (classical French cooking) with a twist in the setting of an old-fashioned bistro near Les Halles.

DON'T MISS: Del Burgo's menus will change with the seasons, but his ravioli with a duxelles filling (finely chopped mushrooms), grilled foie gras in port sauce, and witty Gallic riff on beef Stroganoff are dishes to look for.

· · ·

[2] 1 rue Bailleul, 1st, 01.42.60.15.78. MÉTRO: Pont-Neuf or Louvre-Rivoli. OPEN Monday to Friday. Saturday dinner only. CLOSED Sunday. • $$$

[4] Lescure, 7 rue de Mondovi, 1st, 01.42.60.18.91. MÉTRO: Concorde. OPEN Monday to Friday. CLOSED Saturday and Sunday. • $$

THE FOUR SEASONS

· 〰 ·

STRAWBERRIES AND MANURE. GUSTS OF FLOWERING privet hedge—a cloying smell like perfume on dirty skin. The summer smells of France are surely one of the main reasons I made it my home. The French not only have no fear of strong smells, they prize them, relishing the sensual provocation offered by this most defenseless and instantaneous of our senses.

It's early July in France, and I'm traveling all over the country on assignment as I always do at this time of the year, which is why my nostrils are being punched into bliss. France is a country that still lives the seasons on the most ancient and intense of terms, as a suite of gifts from nature.

Outside Bitche, a forgotten corner of the country on its border with Luxembourg, the smell of ripe strawberries from the surrounding fields is so strong on a hot afternoon I almost drive off the road. Five days later, the reek of Breton pig barns packs a punch that makes my eyes water, and a week later, during a walk along the beach on the Ile-de-Sein, a tiny island off the coast of Brittany, at low tide when the sun bakes the shaggy tufts of seaweed clinging to rocks, the seaside stink is so primal that evolution never seems more obvious.

France, thank God, has not lost the seasons, and the purest proof is found in the country's markets and on its menus, where a colorful, slow-moving carousel of pleasure requires 365 days to make a full turn. The urgency and avidity of our need to bodily consume the seasons corresponds to deep things, to an-

cient animal cravings to chomp on what surrounds us for pleasure and a visceral understanding of what we need to remain
healthy, and also as a way of measuring time against the specter
of our own mortality. After winter's sluggishness, what brings
on a quickening physical gladness faster than the season's first
asparagus and its intriguing uric visiting card, the olfactory sign
of a potent diuretic purging that's a relief to sluggish gizzards at
winter's end? Can anything express the poignancy of autumn
better than the last raspberries? By living outside the seasons,
we've not only forsaken—and increasingly forgotten—centuries of nutritional wisdom as encoded in seasonal recipes and
produce, we've made our bodies mute. Historically, appetite,
the desire for one food over another, has been the purest form of
humanity's self-preserving and sustaining biofeedback.

Where Cheez Doodles, Mountain Dew, and Reese's Peanut
Butter Cups fit into this equation is hard to say, but galloping
obesity, along with the alarming rise in the incidence of diabetes
and heart disease in the United States, are sure symptoms that
something's gone very wrong in the country's eating habits.
Less egregiously, it's not right that Costco sells huge bundles of
asparagus year-round, to say nothing of peaches, nectarines,
and, amazingly enough, zucchini blossoms (I swear I saw them
recently at the Costco in Norwalk, Connecticut).

Like most Americans, I grew up guilelessly eating Chef
Boyardee canned ravioli and drinking neon-pink strawberry-
flavored milk. And then I had the same awakening as many other
lucky Americans when I went to Europe. Before, I had no inkling
that the anonymous, aseasonal produce of suburban American
supermarkets, the cellophane-wrapped iceberg lettuce and the
New Zealand blueberries on sale in January, symbolize our alien-
ation not only from what we eat but even from one another.

Living in London for a year in the late seventies, I was a flat-broke student sharing a run-down duplex with a motley crew of similarly hard-up types. They were Irish, Maltese, Australian, Rhodesian, and Scottish, which made the kitchen an interesting place. Just out the door was the North End Road market, one of the last of London's great old-fashioned street markets, and we shopped there with pooled change for whatever we could afford. During the winter we ate carrots, cabbage, leeks, potatoes, Swedes, rutabagas, Jerusalem artichokes, or whatever was cheapest because it was what was in season. In those days, there was no lettuce because lettuce doesn't grow in England in February and the Spanish hothouse stuff in the supermarkets was too expensive for us. Spring brought forth fleeting treats like Jersey new potatoes. I still remember being puzzled by the fuss over these potatoes, which was all we had for dinner one night. Then I tasted them. Nutty and sweet, glossed with butter and simply dressed with sea salt (the first time I saw its gray color, I was reluctant to try it because it looked *dirty*), black pepper, parsley, and chives, they were astonishingly good. Early summer—runner beans, real lettuce, early stone fruit. Fall—the first apples and chestnuts, which Jenny from Dublin cooked up as a casserole one night. And on a cold winter night, a gratin of parsnips with a loaf of good bread, some butter and blue cheese, and a jug of red wine was a fine feed that cost the tribe barely more than a pound. It took a year, but through privation, I discovered there was more to eating than just meat with a starch and veg, and, freed from this model of what a meal should be, I became increasingly curious about what I ate.

To be sure, I wasn't completely ignorant of how the seasons could animate a year at the table. In the summer, we'd occasionally stop at one of the farm stands once common in New England for cherries, tomatoes, and corn on the cob, and again in the fall for big glass jugs of cloudy caramel-colored apple cider made on a clanking machine surrounded by a swarm of yellow jackets that had been put into service just after the Civil War. I also had once rather reluctantly discovered what real milk tasted like because one of the best dairy farms in Connecticut was a short bike ride from our house. The gentle old farmer with his fat Guernsey cows in a tidy barn where the tiled walls were covered with faded satin rosettes—his serial farm show awards—stunned my brother and me one June afternoon by offering us mugs of milk still warm from the cow and thick with sweet-tasting cream. But most vegetables on our family table were frozen, herbs were dried, and fruit, something none of us much cared about, often came in cans. So I came home from England with what must have been an insufferable disdain for the family larder. Little did I realize how little I actually knew, however, until I moved to Paris in 1986.

That first fall, I happily lost my virginity over and over again. I had my first fresh cèpes (porcini mushrooms), my first bécasse (woodcock), and my first quince. It was a season of lavish discoveries, and best of all, it never ended. Even after twenty years, I'm still exploring the bounty of a country that has a proud and ancient consensus that eating of the moment is the key to eating well.

This is why when people who love to eat ask me what's the best time of the year to visit Paris, I tell them there's no bad time—it all depends on what you're hungry for. And if you're unsure of your cravings, tour a market or two as soon as you get to town, since they're an unfailingly good reference for what's best of season.

MY PARIS FOOD DIARY, A MEMO ON THE BEST SEASONAL eating in Paris, begins in October, when it all began for me. It's a glorious time of the year, because, depending on the weather, it offers a wonderful edible crosshatching between late summer and autumn. You'll find late raspberries and Provençal tomatoes at the same time game begins to appear, and mushroom lovers know bliss as black trompette de la mort (trumpets of death, but delicious), cèpes, and girolles come to town. October also sees the beginning of serious shellfish eating, notably scallops and oysters, and is a fine month for cheese. (Yes, in France cheese is seasonal, too.) Brie, that all-American French favorite, is ideal (it should be made with lait cru, raw milk, since pasteurizing kills off all of the friendly bacteria that give any good cheese its taste and character), and the best are labeled as coming from Meaux—my favorites are from Melun and Montereau. Chestnuts are also come into season, and a superb variety of fruit finds its way into homey desserts, including figs, pears, quinces, and apples.

On the cusp of winter, November has many consolations. The call of the wild is never stronger, including sanglier (wild boar), lièvre (hare), chevreuil (roe deer), and biche (venison), as well as the best birds—pheasant, partridge, and wild duck among them. The winter vegetables found in medieval still lifes—leeks, Savoy cabbage, carrots, and Brussels sprouts—start to appear, and any good cheese tray startles the nostrils with Époisses, an odoriferous, full-flavored cheese from Burgundy.

December is Lucullian, a time for feasting on foie gras, oysters, truffles, lobster, and langoustines, perhaps followed by a juicy Corsican clementine or two (they're at their best during the holidays and show up on many restaurant menus as part of citrus desserts), while January and February whet the appetite for some of the most ancient French dishes, many of which have a historical pedigree as a reflection of the way the Gauls tided themselves through the winter once the barnyard had gone quiet. With dusk beginning at 4 P.M., I crave pot-au-feu (beef in its own bouillon with carrots, leeks, and potatoes), choucroute garnie (sauerkraut with sausage and pork), cassoulet (white beans, preserved duck, and sausage stewed under a crust of bread crumbs), coq au vin (rooster, traditionally, or chicken in red wine sauce), and poule au pot (chicken poached in stock with carrots, potatoes, and celery). Oursins (sea urchins) provide some bracing iodine-rich punctuation to winter's stewed meats, and I never pass up the cheese tray, especially the creamy vacherin, a soft cow's milk cheese from Savoy that reaches perfection during the winter; Morbier, from the Jura with its distinctive dark gray ribbon of pine ash; Beaufort, a rich nutty cheese from the Alps; and Mimolette, a hearty, orange-colored cheese with a rind like a melon from the north of France.

March is a tease. The first mesclun, or mixed baby salad greens, reaches Paris from Provence, and the stalls at the organic market on the boulevard de Batignolles in the 17th Arrondissement, which has many of the same vendors you find on the boulevard Raspail in the 6th Arrondissement but with lower prices and a more convivial atmosphere, are often decorated with feathery sprays of lemon-bright mimosa, a signal that the grip of winter is easing. Milk-fed baby lamb from Sisteron in Provence and the Pyrenees appears on the butchers' stalls, and the fishmongers display turbot, cod, and John Dory. Toward the end of the month, there's a moment of jubilation when I spot the first asparagus, usually from Pertuis in Provence, in tight purple-headed green bunches. They cost an arm and a leg, but I fork over my euros without hesitation. Likewise, the first of a new season's chèvres (goat cheeses) have a delicious lactic tang that quickens the palate.

April brings new potatoes, slightly tart tapered gariguette strawberries from southwestern France or plump sweet ones from Carpentras in Provence, rhubarb, and occasionally even early cherries from Roussillon. At the fishmonger's, pearly pink langoustines languish on crushed ice next to glossy gray sole, and I crave small, runny Saint-Marcellin cheeses made with milk from cows that have finally gotten a little greenery back into their diets. The veal is also excellent at this time of the year.

In May and June, farm wives sell lilacs and peonies from their own gardens, and salads of peppery roquette (arugula) are part of every weekend meal. Baby artichokes, fava beans, and fresh garlic are perfect for impromptu pasta or risotto recipes, while Norman cheeses like Livarot and Pont l'Évêque are at their best, and one of the rarest French abbey cheeses, Cîteaux, from Burgundy, makes a brief but welcome annual appearance at the end of May.

The return of real tomatoes, as opposed to sad, cottony stand-ins from greenhouses in Brittany or Belgium, is cause for celebration in June and July, as is the annual avalanche of cherries. Fuzzy early peaches are a treat, as are French haricots verts (much of the year in Paris, string beans come from Kenya) and fresh almonds. And the honied perfume of melons from Cavaillon in Provence means that summer's in full bloom.

August is all about salad days—the variety of lettuce and greens on sale in Paris markets makes anyone an herbivore, plus nasturtiums, zucchini blossoms, and other edible flowers, and heirloom tomatoes. This sleepiest month in Paris also means sardines and mackerel, perfect for grilling, along with fresh anchovies from Collioure, a Mediterranean port near the border with Spain. With their tart skin and sweet amber flesh, quetsches, the yellow plums from Lorraine, are great for baking, but there's no better late-summer dessert than a bunch of opalescent Chasselas grapes.

Every September when I return to Paris from vacation, I buy a good ripe raw-milk Camembert before I even open the mail. This month is when the most emblematic French cheese is at its best, and it is hard to imagine a better lunch than a creamy wedge of perfectly ripened Camembert smeared on a torn chunk of crackle-crusted baguette and a glass of red wine. I also crave oysters and langoustines, pigeon, and buttery pears with Roquefort cheese. After languid summer days, I'm hungry for Paris.

·🕊·

L'Ambassade d'Auvergne

THOUGH MANY OF PARIS'S REGIONAL RESTAURANTS REMAIN stuck in a dulling time warp, this "embassy" of France's south-central Auvergne region is one place I desperately hope never changes. Occupying an ancient house on the edge of the Marais, this two-story restaurant's decor of dark beams, dried flowers, and rustic bric-a-brac, including copper saucepans and cast-iron cooking utensils, hasn't been touched since the Petrucci family, dyed-in-the-wool Auvergnats, their Italian surname notwithstanding, opened for business in 1968. This means that it has acquired the honest patina of a real auberge, or down-to-earth country inn. The comfortably spaced tables are dressed with pink jacquard tablecloths woven with its name, the service is well rhythmed, the welcome is warm, the prices are moderate, and, most of all, the food's absolutely delicious. In fact I can't think of many places where I'd rather end up on a cold winter's night, since its regional roster of hearty peasant dishes showcase some of the quieter treasures of the French kitchen. To be sure, it's simple,

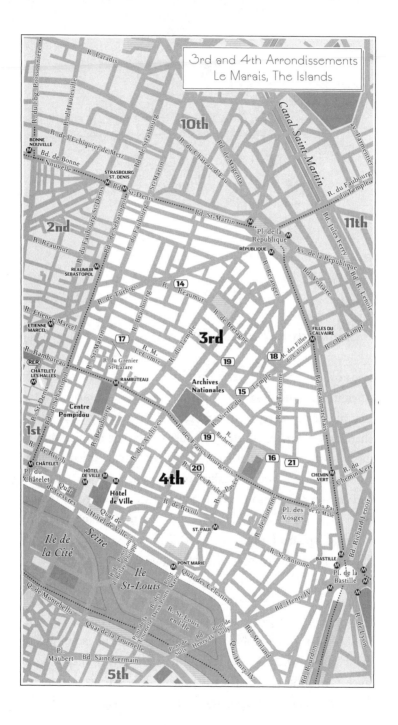

stick-to-your-ribs food, but then that's why I love it—these are dishes that have been consoling and fortifying hardworking farmers, shepherds, masons, and blacksmiths for centuries.

In a nod to its popularity with business diners, foreign visitors, and French visiting from the provinces, the menu makes a feint at contemporary preferences for lighter eating, but by all means ignore those dishes in favor of such classics as the sublime salad of brown Puy lentils seasoned with vinegar, a judicious and delicious dose of creamy goose fat (remember the French paradox, the confounding reality that the French happily consume rich and fatty treats like foie gras yet remain both thin and healthy, before you blanch), and châtaigneraie lardons (chunks of bacon). Or, if this sounds too rich, try a slice of jambon de coche de la châtaigneraie, one of the world's finest hams. Rubbed with salt, it's aged six months in a smokehouse over a chestnut-wood fire, and the result is luscious, silky, richly flavored meat that I think may be the best ham in France.

One place where the light touch works brilliantly, though, is its version of stuffed cabbage, one of the region's most famous classics. Instead of the usual mound of pork, salt pork, bread, onion, and cloves placed in the middle of a blanched cabbage and baked, this version comes as a delicate, flavorful millefeuille, where the stuffing is thinly layered between cabbage leaves and baked as a terrine. Succulent and perfectly seasoned, it's absolutely delicious, and every time I come here, I struggle to decide between the grilled sausage with aligot and the cabbage. Happily, the waiter usually offers a big dollop of aligot, one of the most irresistible comfort foods ever devised, to everyone at the table. Aligot, an Auvergnat staple, is a whipped blend of potatoes, young Tomme de Laguiole cheese, and garlic, and it provides the opportunity for a pleasing bit of old-fashioned table-side theater, since the waiter brings it to the table in a thick copper casserole and whips it a few times, holding his wooden spoon high so that you can see that it has the surprising texture of molten latex.

Dessert may seem improbable at the end of such a meal, but it'd be a shame to miss their sublime chocolate mousse. Note, too, that this place is open on Sundays and is a great alternative to the usual brasserie option.

· ·

IN A WORD: This cozy, welcoming old auberge north of the Centre Pompidou in the 3rd Arrondissement makes good on its name by being a brilliant "embassy" of Auvergnat cooking in Paris.

DON'T MISS: Chestnut soup with cèpes; jambon de coche de la châtaignerie (country ham smoked over a chestnut-wood fire); pounti (terrine of pork, swiss chard, and prunes); lentil salad; stuffed cabbage; aligot (potatoes whipped with Tomme cheese and garlic); guinea hen with braised cabbage; tray of Auvergnat cheeses; chocolate mousse.

. . .

[17] 22 rue Grenier-Saint-Lazare, 3rd, 01.42.72.31.22. MÉTRO: Rambuteau or Étienne Marcel. OPEN daily for lunch and dinner. www.ambassade -auvergne.com • $$

L'As du Falafel

EVERY DAY BUT SATURDAY, THERE'S INSTANT SATISFACTION in publicly breaking one of Paris's silliest and strangest taboos, which is the stuffy informal ban on the ambulatory snacking

that makes for great eating in so many of the world's other best cities. Here, municipal disapproval keeps Parisian streets empty of anything resembling a New York City hot dog stand or a Saigon sidewalk pho vendor, and the prevailing bourgeoisie casts a hairy eyeball on any public consumption less decorous than a picnic. But my bet is that even those sourpusses who look askance at anyone eating a cheese sandwich in a park would make an immediate exception for the falafel sandwiches sold at this hugely popular Israeli-style storefront in the Marais if they'd ever tried one. To keep the crowds at the takeout window moving, you pay first and get a chit to hand to the counterman. Then a hot pouch of the best pita bread in Paris is slit open and filled rapid-fire and generously with grated carrot; purple cabbage; cubes of golden fried eggplant; and hot, crunchy falafel. Finally the whole works is lashed with tahini and some hot pepper sauce if you want it (you do). Once you've taken possession of the city's best street food, the next goal is to find a place to stand out of the way and consume this delicious meal without covering yourself with slaw or sauce when all you have to help are a few flimsy paper napkins. Good luck.

. . .

[**20**] **34 rue des Rosiers, 4th, 01.48.87.63.60.** MÉTRO: **Saint-Paul.** OPEN **Monday to Friday and Sunday for lunch and dinner.** CLOSED **Saturday.** ▪ **$**

Au Bascou

PREDATING THE INTERNET AND THE TGV HIGH-SPEED RAIL system, which have dramatically shrunk the perceived size of France, the regional tables of Paris are a poignant reminder that even today the country is still composed of proud and distinctive regions, many of which have their own cultures and cuisines.

If the opening of the French national railway system during the nineteenth century and the ensuing massive migration to

Paris from previously poor and isolated parts of the country such as Brittany and the Auvergne originally established these nostalgic outposts in the capital, today they function as a living gastronomic library of the deep, diverse, and solidly rustic roots of French cooking.

While many of these slightly wistful tables have closed during the last few years as their owners have retired and returned to the villages from which they came, it's still possible to do an intriguing tour-de-France without leaving the capital, and this friendly, cozy little Basque table on the northern edge of the Marais is a fine place to start.

Stepping inside off the busy rue Réaumur, you could suddenly be in a little tavern in Saint-Jean-Pied-de-Port or Bayonne. Under a ceiling of exposed beams decorated with dangling strings of oxblood red Espelette peppers, wooden tables are set with Basque linens and the menu offers an excellent array of Basque country classics, including piperade, which is made from eggs scrambled with tomatoes, onions, and peppers and garnished with pieces of fried country ham, or another starter, pimientos stuffed with pureed salt cod. Then there are excellent main courses like supions (baby squid) sautéed with chorizo (spicy paprika-flavored sausage) and Espelette peppers on a bed of rice, and axoa, a Basque stew of ground veal, onions, and peppers. Desserts include beret Basque, a beret-shaped chocolate-covered, cream-filled sponge cake, and gateau Basque, a flat, flaky golden cake filled with almond cream.

Since the arrival of the new chef, Bertrand Gueneron, former second to Alain Senderens at Restaurant Alain Senderens, not only has the cooking here become more refined, but several contemporary French dishes have been added to the menu, among them a delicious chestnut soup garnished with foie-gras-stuffed ravioli, sautéed shrimp with a salad of finely sliced fennel bulb and mixed leaves, and duck breast with red pears. The red Irouleguy from Domaine Brana is a fine wine choice with this cooking, and the service by the smart, friendly young staff makes this a place you want to linger.

IN A WORD: The best outpost of Basque country cooking in Paris and a great choice for a long, relaxed lunch.

DON'T MISS: Sauté of escargots and Bayonne ham; pintade à la Bayonnaise (guineau hen with a garnish of tomatoes, peppers, and onions); grilled cod; Ossau Iraty cheese with black cherry preserves; millefeuille à la vanille.

. . .

[14] **38 rue Réaumur, 3rd, 01.42.72.69.25.** MÉTRO: **Arts-et-Métiers or Réaumur.** OPEN **Monday to Friday for lunch and dinner.** CLOSED **Saturday and Sunday.** ▪ **$$**

Breizh Café

PARISIAN PREFERENCES IN REGIONAL COOKING TEND TO reflect trends in the preferred French vacation spots of magazine editors. In the 1990s, Provençal cooking suddenly became stylish, but now, with sunbathing out of favor and real estate prices in the Lubéron well beyond the reach of most people with editorial salaries, shaggy green Brittany is getting a look in. You know what that means—crêpes, which are made from white flour, and galettes, which are dun-colored, from buckwheat.

Paris's traditional crêpe belt surrounds the Gare du Montparnasse, the gateway to the capital from Brittany and a heavily Breton neighborhood until an egregious redevelopment in the 1970s. Breizh Café, the city's best new crêperie, is a happy reflection of how much Brittany has changed during the last twenty years, since it's located right in the heart of the Marais and pokes fun at the traditional folklore of crêperies with a slick decor of slate floors, rough oak-paneled walls, and amusing Manga-style paintings of Breton women wearing coiffes, the traditional Breton lace bonnets. The Manga look and the wasabi dressing available for the house green salad also reveal the fact that the clever owner, Bertrand Larcher, had already perfected his new-wave crêperie concept not only in his native Cancale, a delightful seaside town in Brittany, but in Tokyo before opening this Paris branch. Since the French are uninspired sandwich makers, this is an ideal spot for a quick, tasty, reasonably priced lunch, too. Larcher's Japanese crêpe makers use only organic produce—flour, eggs, milk, and butter—and the results are outstanding, including one delicious galette (savory buckwheat flour crêpe) filled with a fried egg, ham, raw-milk Gruyère, and sautéed button and shiitake mushrooms, and another with ham, an egg, Gruyère, and artichoke hearts. You can add a first course of oysters if you're hungry, and do try one of the excellent dry organic ciders on the cider list (cider being the traditional drink with crêpes in Brittany). Dessert crêpes, made with white flour, include classics like one flambéed with Grand Marnier, which is brought to the table dancing with blue flame in a miniature copper casserole, and my favorite, which is drizzled with salted caramel sauce and topped with a ball of excellent vanilla ice cream. P.S. With the opening of the new TGV (high-speed train) to eastern France, my bet is that Alsatian

cooking is next up for a Parisian revival, as in, Bonjour, chou-croute!

IN A WORD: The crêpe and galette get a makeover for the twenty-first century using top-quality, mostly organic produce, and the stylish interior reflects Brittany's emergence as a newly chic holiday destination for increasingly SPF-conscious Parisians.

. . .

[15] 109 rue Vieille du Temple, 3rd, 01.42.72.13.77. MÉTRO: Filles du Calvaire. OPEN Wednesday to Monday. CLOSED Tuesday. ▪ $

Café des Musées

AS HEARD FROM A BASEMENT MEN'S ROOM, THE LEVEL OF echoing laughter and conversation may seem a very odd way to gauge the quality of a Paris kitchen, but it's a surefire measure of a place where a wonderfully diverse crowd of Parisians comes with the certain knowledge that they're going to eat well and have a good time. So when I briefly excused myself from the table at the Café des Musées, this wonderful human music heard from afar made me eager to get back upstairs as soon as possible and rejoin the fun.

In fact, this corner café with a forgettable decor might well serve as a model for what the Parisian café genus could and should become. This understandably popular place keeps the neighborhood—the western edge of the Marais, not far from the Picasso Museum—excellent company all day long, beginning with a first-rate breakfast and seguing on to lunch and dinner, with relaxed time-outs between meals when you can just swan in for a sandwich (the curried chicken is excellent) if you like.

On one of the more forlorn restaurant days of the year, New Year's Day, we met a pair of hungry friends from Boston, and our progress through the daily chalkboard menu made an already happy occasion, a reunion, even better, especially since these Bostonians love to eat but were on a budget. A half-dozen deep-sea oysters from the waters off Paimpol in Brittany were superb, served room temperature with a basket of crusty baguette and good butter, and carefully shucked so that not a drop of their delicious brine went missing. Still, these beautiful bivalves were upstaged by a terrific soup of smoked garlic and beer from the northern French town of Arleux—creamy with pureed potato, comforting with the ancient whiff of a wood-burning hearth, and celebrating the sturdy eternity of honest peasant cooking with a soft gust of garlic, along with a coarse, richly flavored terrine de campagne with a miniature salad of mixed leaves and tarragon glossed with good oil. Poulette fermière aux chanterelles arrived in a miniature black cast-iron casserole with plump pieces of barnyard fowl riding a deep, creamy bed of chanterelle mushrooms, and the entrecôte, an often problematic cut of French beef for Americans accustomed to a thicker and much more tender steak, was immaculately cooked and wonderfully chewy. It also came to the table with a generous bowl of hot hand-cut golden frites that we squabbled over and a ramekin of excellent homemade béarnaise, a real treat now that many restaurants buy in their sauces.

Two of us followed with the excellent assortment of cheeses—Saint-Nectaire, Camembert, and a chunk of ash-blackened Pyramide (goat cheese), and the others swooned over an individual serving of chocolate mousse and pears poached in red wine with cinnamon, vanilla beans, and cloves, a really lovely winter dessert.

The wine list offers a bluff assortment of good bottles, including several by the glass or *pot* (a 50-centiliter carafe), and our saucy waitress never missed a beat throughout the whole meal. Come here once, and you'll ending up wishing this place was just around the corner from your own front door for a long time to come.

. . .

IN A WORD: If only every café in Paris served food this good and reasonably priced.

DON'T MISS: Smoked garlic and beer soup; tarte moelleux (like a quiche); terrine de campagne (country-style terrine of coarsely ground pork); free-range chicken with chanterelles; entrecôte; chocolate mousse; pears poached in red wine.

. . .

[16] 49 rue de Turenne, 3rd, 01.42.72.96.17. MÉTRO: Saint-Sébastien-Froissart or Chemin Vert. OPEN daily for lunch and dinner. ▪ $$

Le Carré des Vosges

THE MARAIS IS ONE OF MY FAVORITE PARTS OF PARIS. I LOVE its often curiously named lanes (rue des Mauvais Garçons, or street of the bad boys, immediately comes to mind), most of which blessedly escaped the ham-handed Baron Haussmann when he smashed up Paris during the nineteenth century. Instead of grandiose boulevards and apartment blocks with beveled corners, this part of the city remains a dense medieval townscape that's organic yet unpredictable, intimate but filled with secrets.

I also love the Place des Vosges, an elegant urban stage where I could sit and listen to the fountain splash for hours while savoring unexpected cameos of Parisian life. The French aren't generally inclined to speak to strangers, but the last time I was here, it seemed everyone stopped to chat. I was reading *The Belly of Paris,* Emile Zola's novel about Les Halles, when a retired Bucharest-born piano teacher sat down, lamented the long gone central market of Paris, and recommended the nearby Le Carré des Vosges, a restaurant I didn't know. "We were once so poor in this neighborhood! Things are better now, but the memory of being hungry makes us a demanding public," she added. "So for me a restaurant must be better than what I can do at home."

I agree, so when my friend Robin, an American who grew up in Paris and loves her food and wine, flew in from New York, I booked here with real curiosity.

Arriving, I found this good-looking restaurant on the ground floor of a beautiful seventeenth-century mansion. As soon as I stepped inside, I knew we'd eat well, too. The welcome was cordial and the place was tellingly packed with local boutique owners. Both of us chose the lunch menu, an excellent value, and it was exceptionally good.

I started off with one of the best risottos I've ever eaten anywhere, perfectly al dente and topped with tiny pan-fried squid, and Robin had a delicious lentil salad garnished with shredded pork shank and foie gras. "This is just the kind of restaurant we'd kill for in New York. The ingredients are first-rate and there's so much technique in the cooking, but it's reasonably priced and quiet." Next, a superb daube de sanglier (wild boar stewed in red wine) for me, and cod with a crust of buttery bread crumbs and fresh herbs for Robin. For dessert we both had the beautifully made tarte Tatin.

I've since been back several times for dinner—Marc Ouvray's roasted turbot with morels in a sauce of vin jaune and millefeuille aux marrons glacés (candied chestnuts) were remarkable. All I can say is that only in a city as spoiled for choice as Paris could a restaurant this good remain under the radar of guidebooks and bloggers. And if I ever run into that Romanian piano teacher again, I'll give her a big kiss on both cheeks.

. ⁂ .

IN A WORD: Chef Marc Ouvray's restaurant is relaxed, comfortable, and quietly stylish, or a perfect reflection of the Marais. Ouvray is an imaginative perfectionist with haute cuisine training, and his contemporary French cooking is outstanding.

DON'T MISS: Cèpe ravioli with garlic cream, lentil salad with pork shank and foie gras, risotto Milanese with baby squid, roast turbot with vin jaune sauce and morels, ris de veau meunière, daube de sanglier, mille-feuille aux marrons glacés, tarte Tatin.

. . .

[21] 15 rue Saint-Gilles, 3rd, 01.42.71.22.21. MÉTRO: Chemin Vert. OPEN Tuesday to Friday for lunch and dinner. Saturday and Monday dinner only. CLOSED Monday lunch and Sunday. www.lecarredesvosges.fr • **$$**

Le Pamphlet

EVER SINCE IT OPENED TEN YEARS AGO, I'VE BEEN SENDING friends to this dark horse of a bistro in the northern reaches of the Marais. Why? Not only is chef Alain Carrère's cooking delicious, but his prix fixe menu is one of the best buys in Paris. Unlike so many other ambitious contemporary Paris bistros, where you eat cheek by jowl, this attractive dining room with gunmetal gray beams overhead and exposed stone walls is also refreshingly quiet and comfortable. The tables are large and widely spaced, and the service is more polished than at other bistros.

Carrère trained with chef Christian Constant when he was at the Hôtel de Crillon, and he's a rigorous, precise, passionate cook who remains one of Paris's underrated talents. A native of Pau, Carrère often makes a citified feint or two at hearty southwestern French cooking, but I'd be devoted to him for no other reason than the fact that he rather improbably does the best risotto in Paris.

The menu at Le Pamphlet showcases the best seasonal produce, so on a balmy June night I started with a superb risotto of asparagus and morel mushrooms. The French often not only overcook risotto but make matters worse by adding crème fraîche to it, but Carrère's version was redolent of delicious chicken stock and the rice still had a nice bite. Duck and foie gras terrine came with delicious tiny corn-flour pancakes and a bright salad of herbs, squid's ink pasta was topped with crunchy baby squid, and house-smoked salmon came with an appealing and very original tartine (open sandwich) of daikon radish slices, Granny Smith apples, and tarama (a spread made with smoked cod's eggs, bread crumbs, olive oil, and milk).

Bart and Stuart, the teenage sons of my freshman-year college roommate from Haverford, Pennsylvania, on their first visit to France, may have been laconic when it came to Versailles—"It was okay"—and Chartres—"Really big"—but they accurately described their filet Rossini—beef filet with slices of pan-fried foie gras—as "awesome," and their parents were very happy with perfectly roasted pigeon with baby peas and a juicy duck breast cooked with a homey dusting of mace, nutmeg, clove, and cinnamon. My Saint-Pierre (John Dory) was garnished with fava beans, chopped tomato, and a drizzle of excellent olive oil, and was served whole on a bed of mashed potatoes that had deliciously absorbed its cooking juices.

As outstanding as this meal was, the real pleasure of the evening was observing the culinary awakening of Stuart, one of the two boys. "Why does everything taste so much better in France than it does at home?" he asked innocently, and, needless to say, I gave him an earful, beginning with the importance of seasonal produce and the intense importance that Parisians attach to good food. "The food's been the best thing about this trip," Bart chimed in. "We've been in, like, so many museums and churches," he added, a remark that triggered a distant memory.

I told the boys about how my brother John and I, at the

same ages as these two, had burnt out on museums during a trip to Italy and how I'd finally persuaded my mother to let us go by ourselves to the Lido in Venice for the day. We'd had a fantastic time bobbing around in the warm waters of the Adriatic, staring at people in tiny bathing suits and eating pizza, and it renewed us for the rest of the trip. What I didn't mention was that the day we opted out was the one on which my mother had arranged to meet Peggy Guggenheim and have her take us through her collection, a missed opportunity I've regretted ever since. But that's another story, and the boys suddenly seemed livelier than they had during the whole meal. "But Paris doesn't have a beach," said Stuart. "No, but you could rent bikes and hang around in the Bois de Boulogne for a day," I suggested. "That would be, like, so cool!" enthused Bart. "What did you have planned for tomorrow?" I asked Alison, their mother. "Vaux-le-Vicomte." "Mom, wouldn't you and Dad like to have a day on your own?" asked Stuart, a clever kid.

So the deal was done, and desserts of sautéed Burlot cherries and tart gariguette strawberries sprinkled with crumbled meringue and freshly made raspberry syrup were excellent, too. "The chef here really rocks!" crowed Stuart over his berries. I couldn't have put it better myself, and so this meal turned out to be not only the celebration of a wonderful old friendship but what I hope was an enduringly memorable lesson in the sensuality of great French cooking.

· ⌂ ·

IN A WORD: Tucked away in the Marais, the talented Alain Carrère is one of the dark-horse chefs of Paris, and his Basque-Béarnaise-inspired cooking is unfailingly delicious. Friendly service and reasonable prices make this pleasant bistro a real find. A good choice for family dining.

DON'T MISS: Risotto with asparagus and morel mushrooms; duck and foie gras terrine; roasted oysters with watercress butter; rabbit stuffed with plums; John Dory with fava beans, tomatoes, and potato puree; duck breast with spices; partridge in wine sauce; tournedos Rossini (filet of beef with foie gras); rack of lamb with a garnish of feta cheese, cucumber, mint, and tomato; roast pigeon with baby peas; poêlée (sauté) of clementines with Grand Marnier and honey-nougat ice cream; pot de chocolat Guanaja version Carrère (baked Guanaja chocolate cream); sautéed Burlot cherries, gariguette strawberries façon Melba (with raspberry sauce) with meringue crumbs and vanilla ice cream.

. . .

[18] **38 rue Debelleyme, 3rd, 01.42.72.39.24.** MÉTRO: **Saint-Sébastien-Froissart** OPEN **Tuesday to Friday for lunch and dinner. Saturday and Monday dinner only.** CLOSED **Sunday. • $$**

Robert et Louise

GENTRY IS THE ONLY WOMAN I KNOW WHOSE IDEA OF A good time is the do-it-yourself courses offered in the hardware department at the middlebrow BHV (Bazaar de l'Hôtel de Ville) department store during the weekend—how to use a staple gun, how to tile a shower stall, and so on. Born in Hollywood, she also has the edgy "Black Dahlia" look of a heroine in a Nathanael West novel. You know, scissored black bangs, bright red lipstick, high-heeled lace-up boots, and a waist so tiny it's not much bigger than a large bunch of flowers. It's only her upturned, elfin nose that blunts the immediate certainty she's a dominatrix (she's actually a talented lingerie designer with her own Paris-based company).

We haven't known each other very long, but when I was mulling over whom I'd invite to lunch at Robert et Louise in the Marais, she instantly came to mind. Why? She's hilarious and a keen student of atmosphere, and she eats like a quarterback. Further, she knows that elegance—the apotheosis of any Parisian who loves the city's public life—is generated by rigid discipline in terms of texture, color, and line. Of course you create your own personal style, but the rules must be mastered and respected if elegance is the desired effect, and most Parisians couldn't even begin to fathom anyone who doesn't aspire to it. Gentry not only knows all of this but embraces it, which makes her profoundly Parisian. So I suspected she'd thrill to this funky

and rather dusty dining room where the cooking is done over a wood fire in a large chimney and in a tiny jerry-built kitchen under a flight of stairs and you occupy bare wood tables in a long, dim, narrow dining room under huge centuries-old beams.

For half a century, it was the lair of Robert Georget and his wife, Louise, who contentedly cooked for the northern Marais as it evolved from a run-down and slightly sad part of the city into one of the trendiest parts of Paris. Following Robert's death, his daughter Pascale joined her mother in the kitchen, and with any luck at all, this legendary old table will survive instead of meeting the too-common fate of many restaurants in gentrifying parts of Paris and becoming a clothing boutique. Just to get a rise out of her, I ask Pascale, a sturdy, friendly woman with an engagingly husky voice and ready smile, if she's planning to keep cooking or convert the space into a boutique. "Mais vous êtes fou ou quoi!" ("Are you crazy, or what!") she shouts, and then, when I tell her I was just teasing, she says, "Vilain garçon! C'est une bonne chose pour vous que je ne suis pas venu à table avec un couteau. Alors, qu'est-ce-que vous allez mangez?" ("Naughty boy! It's a good thing for you that I didn't come to the table with a knife! Now, what are you eating?")

I start with a plate of silky Parma ham, freshly sliced, and Gentry goes for snails. Then we split a massive exquisitely charred côte de boeuf for two. It comes sliced in a pool of its own rosy juices on a wooden cutting board, along with a bowl of pommes sautées and a side of salad. We ignore the salad, immediately ask for more potatoes, and continue sipping a great jammy Gigondas. "This is why I moved to Paris," Gentry announces when the steak is almost finished. "For this atmosphere, this sense of history, the consensus that pleasure is more

important than work. I've always wanted to be in this ancient
and brilliantly dowdy room," she continued, smiling. "It makes
me think of the old photographs by Boubat and Doisneau I'd
stare at for hours as a fourteen-year-old girl wishing herself far
from Newport Beach, California." All of which is to say that
having a truly good meal is always almost as much about good
casting as it is about the food, since who you eat with and where
you eat change everything.

IN A WORD: For carnivores only, this simple bistro offers the fleeting chance to sample an unself-conscious prewar Paris atmosphere, and the côte de boeuf (rib steak) for two is spectacular, too.

DON'T MISS: Marinated herring; fromage de tête (head cheese); côte de boeuf; omelette forestière (filled with wild mushrooms).

. . .

[19] **64 rue Vieille du Temple, 3rd, 01.42.78.55.89.** MÉTRO: **Rambuteau.** OPEN **Monday to Friday for lunch and dinner. Saturday dinner only.** CLOSED **Sunday.** ▪ **$$**

L'Alcazar

SIR TERENCE CONRAN, FOUNDER OF THE TRENDSETTING
Conran home furnishings stores and one of the most successful

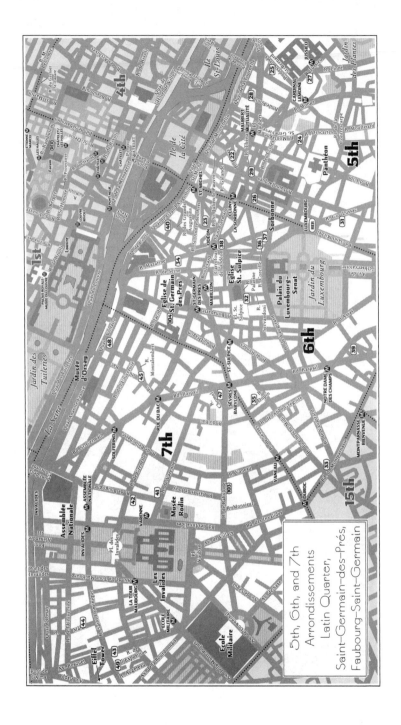

5th, 6th, and 7th
Arrondissements
Latin Quarter,
Saint-Germain-des-Prés,
Faubourg-Saint-Germain

restaurateurs in England, has always reminded me of a country schoolmaster. He often wears striped oxford shirts and bow ties, his steel gray hair falls boyishly onto his forehead, and his blue eyes are alert and bemused but kindly. I first met him ten years ago when I went to an opening lunch at the Alcazar, his audacious foray into the Paris restaurant world.

What Conran wanted to do was give something back to the country he loves so much, France, which has been the bedrock inspiration of his hugely successful group of restaurants across the Channel. And as often happens when a beloved local institution is seen through foreign eyes, his Anglo take on the Parisian brasserie was rather shrewd and he won grudging gratitude from the French for resuscitating a famous Saint-Germain-des-Prés cabaret, L'Alcazar, and giving it a new life and look—the clerestory ceiling was repaired, and a sleek mirrored dining room was created in the space where feather-bedecked dancers once strutted their stuff. But it didn't catch on.

Though the food was pretty good right from the start, the French food press gave the Englishman's table sulky reviews—it was, for many French food critics, just too much for un Anglais to think he could teach Parisians anything new about brasseries. Fast forward about a decade, and the Alcazar has become one of the more reliable and amusing last-minute choices you can make on the Left Bank, pulling not only gallery owners and antique dealers but a frisky young Sciences Po crowd (Sciences Politique is France's most prestigious graduate school) all done up in designer duds and eager to identify with London, where so many of them have worked or will work in the City.

So what changed? Paris caught up with London, so that now Parisians not only understand but like Conran's concept of a new brasserie for the twenty-first century. In truth, Sir Terence didn't stray all that far from the boilerplate—what makes this place different from, say, La Coupole, is better service, better lighting, and a more cosmopolitan menu. An example? A delicious starter of hand-chopped raw tuna, avocado, mango, and fresh herbs. Modern dishes like this one, so often an echo of the long-haul winter-sun holidays in Thailand and Mauritius that have become a fixture of European life, flank respectable riffs on French classics, including an outstanding rabbit and hazelnut terrine served with salad and warm toast. It also does excellent shellfish platters in season, and there are daily specials that reflect what's best in the local markets. Main courses include a delicious braised lamb shoulder with a crispy crust and tender, succulent meat, a fine steak with freshly made béarnaise sauce, and a fish and chips good enough to make a trip to London unnecessary. The service is smart and young, a reflection of the stylish clientele, and cantilevered mirrors hung above the crowd allow for perfect people watching. Desserts could be more interesting, but almost no one orders them—a cheese plate is a better conclusion, especially since the wine list is well chosen and very fairly priced.

· ·

IN A WORD: A stylish Saint-Germain-des-Prés brasserie from the British restaurateur and arbiter of style Sir Terence Conran. Ideal for late or last-minute dining, it has an appealingly cosmopolitan menu and serves up excellent people watching.

DON'T MISS: Wild boar terrine; house foie gras with apple chutney; steak tartare; brandade de morue (like shepherd's pie, but made with salt cod and garlic); wild duck with raisins and pistachios; sea bream with baby vegetables; Saint-Marcellin cheese; chocolate profiteroles; peach poached in lemon verbena syrup with peach sorbet.

. . .

[34] 62 rue Mazarine, 6th, 01.53.10.19.99. MÉTRO: Odéon. OPEN daily for lunch and dinner. www.alcazar.fr • $$$

L'Ami Jean

IF YOU MISSED THE GLORY DAYS OF LA RÉGALADE, THE most famous bistro to open in Paris during the last fifteen years under the founding chef, Yves Camdeborde, this brawny southwestern bistro in a polite part of the 7th Arrondissement is about as close as you can get to finding out what all of the original fuss was about. Chef Stéphane Jégo worked with Camdeborde for ten years before going out on his own, and his style remains very much inspired by that of his master.

This place also approximates the original La Régalade in terms of being a busy, bustling place with several sittings (if you come for dinner, book the second one so that you won't be rushed), a good-value chalkboard menu that changes regularly, closely spaced wooden tables, and slightly frantic waitresses.

Despite the fact that it has the bawdy atmosphere of a rugby players' canteen, it's very popular with staff from nearby UNESCO and decorous loden-coat-wearing locals, and you'll spot a lot of très 7th Arrondissement ladies of varying ages wearing Alice headbands and inherited Hermès scarves. In fact, the friendly older couple sitting next to Claire, Denis, Bruno, and me on a busy Saturday night seemed to be lapping up the rambunctiousness of this place, and when we fell into conversation, Madame accurately described Jégo's bistro as "très bon enfant," French argot for "very pleasant."

Chef Jégo sautées tiny pétoncles (scallops) in their shells in foaming butter, and once they open, he sprinkles them with sautéed shallots, a little garlic, a few branches of thyme, and several slices of grilled bacon to create a dish that's irresistible. Claire and I couldn't stay away from these sweet little morsels, while Denis had baby squid sautéed with plump white beans and Bruno was in ecstasy over his potent game bouillon with crumbled bacon, sliced chestnuts, and chives. The main courses were similarly delicious, including a perfect petit salé, a stew of salted pork and lentils; axoa, a traditional Basque veal stew spiked with red and green peppers, the quiet fire of ground Espelette pepper, garlic, and onions; and a succulent griddled daurade (sea bream) with olive oil and lemon.

Instead of dessert, I chose the Ossau Iraty cheese from the Basque country with black cherry jam, while Bruno was happy with his slice of gâteau Basque (a flat pastry cake filled with cherry jam), and Denis pronounced the rice pudding even better than that of his grandmother in Rennes. "That was a very good meal" was Claire's verdict once we'd found the calm of the sidewalk out front. "It was even worth putting up with the noise," Denis added, and he's absolutely right.

·　🐾　·

IN A WORD: Chef Stéphane Jégo's southwestern-French-inspired bistro cooking is hearty and delicious, and this sincere, happy place is one of the best buys on the Left Bank. If you're coming for dinner, book the calmer second service.

DON'T MISS: The chalkboard menu changes constantly, but dishes to look out for include baby squid sautéed with white beans; bouillon de gibier (wild game bouillon); pétoncles (tiny scallops); axoa (Basque veal stew); daurade à la plancha (grilled sea bream); petit salé (salted pork and lentil stew); sanglier (wild boar); crème de citron avec nougatine noix-pistachio (lemon cream with walnut-and-pistachio nougat); and rice pudding.

. . .

[**44**] **27 rue Malar, 7th, 01.47.05.86.89**. MÉTRO: **Invalides**. OPEN **Tuesday to Saturday for lunch and dinner.** CLOSED **Sunday and Monday.** ▪ **$$**

L'AOC

WITH ITS FLESH-TONE WALLS, BOUQUETS OF DRIED ROSES, and collection of cast-iron agricultural fair award plaques on the wall by the tidy rotisserie, this cheerful Latin Quarter restaurant could be found anywhere along thousands of kilometers of

route nationale in France. In the big city, this ruddy, profoundly Gallic tavern is a rarity, a happy place where the French come to feel good about themselves by celebrating the extraordinary agricultural bounty of l'Hexagone, as they affectionately refer to France. "I have no formal background in cooking," explains chef-owner Jean-Philippe Lattron, a strong, stout man with beetle brows, a big smile, and a reassuringly firm handshake. "My idea in opening this restaurant was to work exclusively with the best produce and let it speak for itself."

It was a great idea, too, since Lattron combs France in search of the best AOC foods and then cooks them with respectful precision to bring out their natural flavors. AOC, which stands for Appellation d'Origine Contrôlée, is the star of French agriculture, a designation that's sparingly awarded by the French government to produce that adheres to a legally defined set of qualifications that govern almost every aspect of its production and require that it come from a specifically defined geographical area. In the same way that most Americans possess a frightening store of television show trivia—almost everyone over a certain age knows the names of the Three Stooges or, more recently, the Simpsons—the French can be counted upon to offer up a reverent sigh when reference is made to such AOC products as porc noir de Bigorre, pork from a special breed of black pigs raised in the southwest French region of Bigorre, part of the Béarn. And for this reason, the menu at L'AOC is an implicit celebration of good eating and environmentally intelligent farming, a concept that couldn't possibly be more timely.

For foreigners who want more details on the various AOC labels on the menu, Lattron's delightful wife, Sophie, speaks perfect English—she lived in New York for several years—and loves to reminisce about her experience of "la vie américaine" and how much she loves the Big Apple.

On a sullen winter night when the pavement outside was glistening with rain, we settled in over glasses of white Quincy wine and shamelessly helped ourselves to the two big terrines she set down on the table—chicken liver and campagne (country style), which was unctuous and almost gamey with pork liver. With a little linen slip of Pourjaran bread, we could happily have made a meal of the terrine but went on to excellent first courses of oeufs en meurette, a Burgundian classic of poached eggs in a sublime sauce of deeply reduced beef stock spiked with red wine and loaded with chunky lardons (hunks of bacon) and baby onions, and marrow bones seasoned with Guérande sea salt and served with a small salad. Rotisseried AOC chicken from Lattron's native Sologne just north of the Loire River valley, known for the quality of its fowl, came with sautéed potatoes, and a thick slab of Bigorre pork had a crunchy skin and delicious blazes of fat and came with a mountainous side of sautéed potatoes.

Afterward we split a plate of brebis, ewe's milk cheese made by Benedictine monks in the Pyrénées mountains, served with black cherry jam, and concluded with a delightful café gourmand, espresso served with a tiny glass ramekin of hazelnut-topped rice pudding, another one of chocolate pudding, and a miniature financier cake.

All during the meal, I was distracted by the self-satisfied chauvinistic grumpiness of the neighboring table of six, clearly politicians since they spoke about how hard it is to get a "handicapé" parking place, thus confirming my suspicion that most of these reserved parking spots in the streets of Paris aren't for handicapped people at all but for VIPs with pull. Their happy ranting also took them to subjects as diverse as the quality of America's cheeses (épouvantable, or dreadful), the madness of even thinking of admitting Turkey to the European Union, and how the Germans were getting the better end of the stick when it came to the job cuts at Airbus. In almost any other setting, these snatches of overheard conversation would have rankled, but so lavishly served and well fed on such an inhospitable night, I actually felt forgiving and even a little humbled by my own good fortune in living in a city where a young couple so passionate about the quality of the food they serve would find such an enthusiastic following.

· ⟨⟩ ·

IN A WORD: This cheerful, friendly bistro in the Latin Quarter makes a welcome fetish of the finest-quality French produce, foodstuffs worthy of receiving the coveted AOC (Appellation d'Origine Contrôlée) label, and the chef, Jean-Philippe Lattron, wisely knows that food this good should be prepared simply.

DON'T MISS: Marrow bones with Guérande sea salt; terrine de foie gras; roast lamb; roast pork loin; roast chicken; crème brûlée; baba au rhum (sponge cake with whipped cream and rum).

. . .

[25] 184 rue des Fossés-Saint-Bernard, 5th, 01.43.54.22.52. MÉTRO: Cardinale Lemoine or Jussieu. OPEN Tuesday to Saturday for lunch and dinner. CLOSED Sunday and Monday. www.restoaoc.com ▪ $$

Arpège

ROGER, AN AUSTRALIAN BUSINESS LAWYER WITH WHOM I shared a shabby bedsit in London many years ago when he thought he was a thespian and I was writing mediocre poetry in the style, I hoped, of Gerard Manley Hopkins, calls from Sydney. He's coming through Paris for a night on his way to a week's work in Africa and invites me to dinner at Arpège. He hears me hesitate—time and distance have not dulled the antennae of the heightened intimacy born of the privation we shared.

"I know it's bloody expensive, but the firm's paying, and since I remarried I've become almost completely vegetarian," he explains.

Not having known about his vegetarianism, I scuttle my reluctance. It'll be great to see him, and I suspect he'll very much enjoy the many vegetarian dishes on chef Alain Passard's menu. Whether I will enjoy the meal or not remains to be seen, but frankly under the circumstances, it doesn't matter—this will be an occasion where friendship trumps gastronomy.

What I didn't tell him is that I have a complicated and often conflicted relationship with Arpège. I've had some sublime meals here, but I'm bothered by the brazenly expensive wine list, often find the service aloof, and am underwhelmed by the visual austerity of this small dining room just across the street from the Musée Rodin. Most important, I often find Passard's food so simple, even ascetic, that it fails to ignite the blaze of pleasure I expect from haute cuisine. On the other hand, I'm fascinated by the fact that Passard is such an iconoclast, and, almost more than any other restaurant in Paris, this place forces me to ruminate on what the experience of a restaurant should be at the beginning of a new century.

The last time I'd been there, I'd been intrigued but troubled by a plate of tiny new potatoes from the chef's five-acre garden in the Sarthe, an hour southwest of Paris. They were smoked in oat straw and served with a horseradish mousseline, to create a dish that was a brilliant declension of a rustic Breton taste memory—Passard is from Brittany, where they eat a lot of potatoes, and learned to cook from his grandmother, who insisted that the most important skill in the kitchen was learning to do an impeccable roast. Serving up smoky spuds in the Faubourg-Saint-Germain, the citadel of the French aristocracy, was clearly intended to shock and provoke, and it succeeded at doing both. Despite its homeliness, it was brilliant and deeply satisfying, since the sweet taste of the potatoes was amplified and framed by the sharp horseradish, and the umami (the fifth sense of taste, including tastes like sharp cheese, chicken soup, soy sauce, seaweed, cured meats, etc.) added by the smoke ennobled the dish with perfect balance. On the other hand, this dish cost 42 euros—for potatoes! In the same vein but even more extreme was a gratin of Cévennes onions with aged Parmesan. It was delicious, but ultimately I could have cooked it myself. So was this deliciousness adequate to my expectations of a great chef? I wasn't sure.

On my way to meet Roger, this spool of thought renewed itself. Making great produce eloquent is an extraordinary talent, but when it veers towards a simplicity accessible to any layman, the specter of the emperor's new clothes is uncomfortably invoked. Out of curiosity, I glanced at the recipes posted on Passard's website before going out the door, and they confirmed my confusion, or the seesaw, love-hate relationship I have with this restaurant. A recipe for carpaccio de langoustines might take twenty minutes—you just slice the raw langoustines and season them—while his famous "tomates confites aux douze saveurs," Arpège's signature dessert, wouldn't take a half hour. When it comes to cooking, the input of time doesn't always equate with ecstasy, but I think we go to restaurants of this caliber to experience something we could never hope to achieve ourselves.

Roger, already at the table, was let down by the dining room. "It looks a lot like the executive lunchroom of a gray flannel bank," he astutely observed of the curved pear-wood paneling ornamented only with a few inserts of Lalique glass. He loved Passard's signature amuse-bouche of an eggshell filled with a raw yolk, cream, and maple syrup, however, and we were both in great spirits and honestly hungry.

So we ate. He had spinach with salt butter and carrots with orange zest, a vegetable plate of snow peas, asparagus, fava beans, tiny peas, cabbage, onions, and a few other legumes, while I went for the foie gras with dates and roast chicken. And as is invariably the case, my reflexive dubiousness with regard to Arpège was eclipsed by the point-blank fact that the food is often excellent. It helped, too, that the Aussie bank popped for a superb bottle of Condrieu, and even though he described the service as "chilly," Roger and I had a hilarious time reminiscing about Monique, a friend who used to shoplift trays of pork chops at a Sainsbury's supermarket in London's North End Road for Saturday-night feasts. And thirty years after scarfing down this purloined merchandise, here we were, former turnstile jumpers, splashing out in one of the most expensive restaurants in Paris. Our collective memories formed the jolly scrim to this meal, and I held my tongue throughout—there's nothing worse than the local expert when all anyone wants to do is have a good time—but I was curious about what I knew would be his very blunt take on the place once we were outside on the sidewalk a few hours later.

"Damned good food, and it's brilliant that someone really cares about veggies, but what a bloody-minded place," said Roger, as I walked him back to his hotel. My sentiments exactly.

· ☙ ·

IN A WORD: Alain Passard is an iconoclast who thumbs his nose at the conventions of haute cuisine dining by serving delicious but often dead simple vegetable dishes, along with fish and fowl, in a rather wan dining room. Though his swooningly high prices are a brainteaser to justify, there's no denying that Passard's a superb chef.

DON'T MISS: Potatoes smoked in oak straw with horseradish mousseline; gratin of Cévennes onions with Parmesan; lobster in vin jaune (a maderized golden-colored wine from the Jura region of France) sauce; veal sweetbreads with réglisse (a licorice-tasting herb); roast pigeon with hydromel (mead); tomatoes confites aux douze saveurs (baked tomatoes with twelve flavors).

. . .

[44] 84 rue de Varenne, 7th, 01.45.51.47.33. MÉTRO: Varenne. OPEN Monday to Friday for lunch and dinner. CLOSED Saturday and Sunday. www.alain-passard.com • $$$$

L'Atelier de Joël Robuchon

TAKING A LEAF FROM NEW YORK CITY COFFEE SHOPS, JAPAnese sushi bars, and Spain's tapas counters, chef Joël Robuchon opened his counter-service-only snack de luxe just off the rue du Bac in 2004 and it's been packed ever since. I love the way Robuchon democratized great food by freeing it from its normal formal sitdown rituals, and occupying a comfortable stool at the bar here is one of the most convivial restaurant experiences Paris has to offer. Since the no-reservations policy, aside from the 11.30 A.M. and 6.30 P.M. sittings, often means a long wait, I usually pop in at the last minute at an unlikely moment, late on a rainy Tuesday night, for example, and treat myself to a luxurious if pricy feast by foraging among the many delicious small plates on offer. The innocuous black-lacquer-and-red decor has always reminded me of something you'd expect at a pole dancers' club, but this hardly matters when you're so intently focused on what's on your plate. There are some lovely things to eat here, too, including Iberian ham with pan con tomate, tomato-smeared toasts like those you'd get in a Barcelona tapas bar; a layered timbale of grilled eggplant, tomato, zucchini, and buffalo-milk mozzarella; frogs' legs beignets (fritters) with garlic cream; and the sublime merlan Colbert, a whole deboned breaded whiting delicately fried and served with fried parsley, herb butter, and a side of the world's best potato puree. And thanks to a charming Brazilian gem dealer, who recommended it so heartily she couldn't be ignored, I discovered Robuchon's elegant take on spaghetti carbonara, which is made with smoky Alsatian bacon and crème fraîche. The brilliant Chartreuse soufflé, which is spooned open and topped with a ball of pistachio ice cream, creates an elegant finale with its sophisticated contrast of sweet and bitter flavors, but every time I taste it I can't help but feel slightly wistful for Robuchon's original restaurant, Jamin, which the chef sold at the age of fifty, ostensibly to retire. Anyone as creative as Robuchon could hardly be expected to remain idle, however, and so L'Atelier was his comeback vehicle. L'Atelier is great fun, but it offers tantalizing cameos of his extraordinary talent rather than the mesmerizing full-barreled experience Jamin once did.

· ☂ ·

IN A WORD: Chef Joël Robuchon's counter-service-only snack bar de luxe is one of the most original restaurants in Paris and a delightful place for solo diners and couples (conversation becomes awkward if you're more than three). The small-plate format offers a dazzling experience of his talent that's ideal for lunch or a light dinner.

DON'T MISS: Griddled encornets (baby squid) and artichokes; Iberian ham with tomato toasts; frogs' legs beignets (fritters) with garlic cream; timbale of grilled eggplant, tomato, zucchini, and buffalo-milk mozzarella; braised duckling; merlan Colbert (boned, breaded, fried whiting with herb butter sauce and potato puree); grilled tuna belly; scallop with truffle shavings; caramelized quail; spaghetti carbonara; Chartreuse soufflé.

. . .

[45] 5–7 rue de Montalembert, 7th, 01.42.22.56.56. MÉTRO: Rue du Bac. OPEN daily for lunch and dinner. www.joel-robuchon.com ▪ $$$$

Auguste

DESPITE ITS SOMEWHAT UNLIKELY LOCATION ON AN EXclusive street in the silk-stocking 7th Arrondissement, Auguste is one of the more interesting restaurants in Paris right now. For almost twenty years, the vital middle layer of the French food chain, serious restaurants, often with a single Michelin star, has been steadily atrophying, leaving a sorry gap between the lofty summit of increasingly corporate-bankrolled haute cuisine and the bistro, which will always be the solid base of good eating in France. Now something is stirring, and Auguste is one of a few new tender shoots in this once forlorn territory.

"When I first opened, a lot of the younger French food journalists told me my cooking was too old-fashioned and that I should become more tendance, or attuned to the cooking of chefs like Ferran Adria or Thierry Marx. But I knew this wasn't what my clients wanted. So I've found my own way to be modern," says chef Gaël Orieux, a Breton who looks as if he could be Errol Flynn's grandson and who named his restaurant in honor of that grandest of classic French chefs, Georges-Auguste Escoffier.

By choosing to ignore all the Merlin-like trends of the moment, including molecular cooking and now tired bells and whistles like miniature wands of cotton candy as garnishes, he has succeeded in creating an impressive template for the modern French restaurant that's chic and comfortable, with swift, friendly service that suits busy people who want exceptionally good contemporary cooking without all of the pomp once associated with this category. "I've consciously streamlined the whole experience of a Michelin one-star table," says Orieux, who won his first star in 2007 and whose impressive résumé began at Paul Bocuse and includes stints at Alain Senderens, Les Ambassadeurs at the Hôtel de Crillon, Taillevent, and finally Le Meurice under chef Yannick Alléno.

Wintergreen walls, sleek Art Deco *Normandie*-style armchairs, and a scarlet banquette that makes me think of the huge lips in the Man Ray painting *The Lovers* make a refreshing break from the faux rustic or Louis-something settings usually favored by Paris power brokers and presage Orieux's exquisite modern cooking. He tinkers with his menu all the time, so it's hard to recommend my favorites, but on a rainy night in May, I loved his asparagus with a "gariguette" garnish made from chopped country ham, shallots poached in red wine, tomatoes, and tarragon. This condiment brilliantly teased out the natural taste of the asparagus, and I found myself wishing that I could take home a mason jar of it to use on pasta and grilled chicken. Served in a martini glass, sea snails and oysters in seawater aspic came with two crispy bread-crumbed beignets of spinach and pig's feet, and, more than any other dish, this one expressed Orieux's Breton origins, since creating elegant encounters between mer (sea) and terre (land) is one of the driving preoccupations of contemporary cooking in Brittany. "This is excellent," said my friend Michèle, a longtime resident of the nearby rue Vaneau, "but the locals are so parsimonious, I don't know if they're ready for these prices."

Two snowy filets of John Dory posed on a thick emerald green pudding of riced artichoke hearts, marinated vegetables, and pureed fresh coriander were magnificent; the gentle bite of the vegetables complemented the taut fish and the subtly acidulated tones of the sauce flattered it without masking its natural flavor. Baby lamb from the Pyrénées had a similarly delicious natural logic, since it was served on a bed of coarsely pureed rattes potatoes dotted with pleasantly chewy salty laitue de mer (seaweed) and lightly dosed with elderberry-infused oil. Though tempted by a Saint-Marcellin from La Mère Richard, a peppery blond cheese merchant in Lyon who has made this creamy Rhône valley cheese her life's work and one of the French establishment's favorite dairy treats, I finished up with a lovely composition of wild strawberries, raspberries, and rhubarb in lychee juice, and Michèle relished a private gastronomic souvenir by ordering a Grand Marnier soufflé, something she said she hadn't eaten since her First Communion lunch in the small Breton city of Quimper many years before. Chatting briefly with Orieux after dinner, Michèle politely wondered about his prices, which frankly, given the quality of his food, I find perfectly reasonable. "If I serve a lot of politicians at noon the Assemblée Nationale is just up the street, in the evening my regulars are all local, including people like François Pinault," Orieux replied, doing a harmless bit of name-dropping—Pinault, one of the richest men in France, is head of PRP, the luxury goods holding company that owns Gucci and Christie's. And, proving his implicit point that restaurants are an intriguingly accurate gauge for reading any neighborhood, we passed three Bentleys parked along the rue de Bourgogne while walking home. Clearly, this neighborhood needed this restaurant, and in Orieux, they've found a real star.

IN A WORD: Gaël Orieux is one of the most exciting young talents in Paris, and his excellent contemporary cooking has made this stylish restaurant a new address for Paris power brokers and anyone who loves good food. With its racy contemporary decor and friendly, well-drilled service, it's as good a choice for a tête-à-tête as it is for a business meal. Note, too, that it offers a great-value prix fixe lunch menu.

DON'T MISS: Asparagus with gariguette garnish; oyster and sea snails in seawater aspic with spinach and pig's feet beignets; pigeon roasted with spices; veal sweetbreads roasted in vin jaune with salsify; Saint-Marcellin "La Mère Richard"; strawberries, raspberries, and rhubarb in lychee juice; soufflé Grand Marnier.

...

[42] **54 rue de Bourgogne, 7th, 01.45.51.61.09.** MÉTRO: **Varenne or As-semblée Nationale.** OPEN **Monday to Friday for lunch and dinner.** CLOSED **Saturday and Sunday. www.restaurantauguste.fr** ▪ **$$$**

Le Balzar

THE LACY IVORY-COLORED SCRIM THAT ONCE SHIELDED saucy lunches between professors and their students from prurient eyes had gone, so that the place felt a bit nude, but coming in for supper on a cool Sunday night in mid-September it was a relief, after a long absence, to see that the exquisitely ugly Art Nouveau vases filled with funereal floral compositions of mums and birds of paradise had survived, as had the saggy-bottomed banquettes, the globe lamps, the Bakelite sign indicating a telephone downstairs by the toilet, and the soggy-looking tarte Tatin perched on the end of the bar.

The Balzar, you see, is as eternally a part of Paris as Notre Dame or the Louvre. And if the owlish maître d' who presided here for nearly twenty years has gone, along with most of the waiters, the new maestro reassures with a luxuriant mustache, a border guard's alert eye, and a generally bemused approach to his fiefdom, this famous little dining room and the brilliantly peculiar people it attracts. No, an insipid host at Le Balzar just wouldn't do, since even after falling into the clutches of Groupe Flo, a mediocre catering company if ever there was one, this snug Latin Quarter brasserie just steps from the Sorbonne remains a gloriously impregnable citadel of parisianisme, or supremely Parisian habits and behavior. Observing the culinary waltz here is, in fact, easily as much of a reward as the food you'll find on your plate, although what it serves is perfectly respectable vieille France comfort food. Or food you eat because you're hungry. Or not. One way or another, it's not food that's

meant to create a fuss. Still, the menu offers up certain possibilities that have almost become the stuff of anthropological memory. Oeuf en gelée, for example, that Fabergé treat popular on the table of Napoléon III, is a no-nonsense but very satisfying starter that has vanished from most other Paris menus—fine ribbons of boiled ham, a few leaves of flat-leaf parsley, a bit of tarragon, and a poached egg, hopefully with a runny center, all suspended in the salty amber of beef aspic. Also rare, though once common and still considered to be a signature dish of Paris the world over, is a classic gratinée, as the Parisians refer to onion soup, the reference being to the floating croutons with a few deliciously burnt peaks that keep a huge gooey cap of melted Gruyère cheese afloat.

Where you sit at the Balzar matters. I wanted either the banquette for two in the southwest corner of the room or a face-à-face banquette table in the corral near the cash register. What you don't want is to be seated near the door—too busy—or along the western wall—all tourists. Does it really matter? Well, yes, or at least it does if you'd prefer to be surrounded by Parisians and so receive the infinitesimally calibrated blessings of the better service that is always meted out to the French by the French.

As is so often true of the Balzar, there was a great crowd that night. A handsome American couple in black turtlenecks, she with a beautiful turquoise necklace, he with an electric smile and both speaking damned good French, sat with a broad-backed tweed-wrapped professor who kept them nodding most of the meal. A giggly Texan au pair being treated to a birthday dinner by the long-suffering sister of the woman who employed Miss Yellow Rose was at our left, and across the way, a table of South Africans dissing, rather unfairly, the house Bordeaux. And most memorably, to the right, a solid woman in a marled tweed suit of autumn colors—pheasant, maize, vermillion, scarlet—who ate every scrap on her plate, burped deeply and proudly without excusing herself, and paid only the most occasional notice to her faded-looking husband. After a coffee and a small Cognac, the unabashedly privileged creature belched again and then bid the waiter adieu while loudly noting that she'd certainly return again soon in the hopes of eavesdropping on such an astonishing conversation, ours, a remark of such cunningly serrated snideness it took one's breath away with admiration and horror. She made her point, though—all real Parisians know how to hunt and kill without a tremor of social mercy, and don't you forget it. Further, if there's anything the French like less than a foreigner who doesn't speak fluent French, it's a foreigner who does.

I went for the gratinée (onion soup), and Bruno ordered a salade mâche betterave (mâche garnished with cubes of baked red beet). Next, a perfect Chateaubriand with the even black scoring from a grill, hot but slightly leathery frites, sublime spinach that seemed to have been boiled in butter, and a coy little sauceboat of tepid, commercially made béarnaise sauce that was just fine. Bruno sawed away at his andouillette AAAAA, the best quality of tripe sausage around, declared it a huge treat, and I didn't even mind the occasional septic whiff that caught my nostrils when he'd pierce a new zone of his tube. The bread was good, and so was the thin house Bordeaux, a perfect example of what Parisians drank as their daily pour before Bordeaux fell out of favor and various Côtes du Rhône won the hearts of all Parisians under thirty-five. Extravagant and silly, I popped for a grainy slice of Roquefort, and then we split a portion of profiteroles, choux pastry stuffed with passable vanilla ice cream and napped with gunky, splendidly bitter dark chocolate sauce. A fine meal indeed.

· 🕊 ·

IN A WORD: An intimate Belle Époque Latin Quarter brasserie favored by professors, fashion types, and the local bourgeoisie. A perfect example of an increasingly rare genus, right down to the pleasant but unremarkable food—this place is all about atmosphere. The locals love it for Saturday lunch and Sunday supper, but it's also an ideal spot for a quick late feed on your first jet-lagged night in Paris.

DON'T MISS: Oeuf en gelée (poached egg in beef aspic); marinated herring; salade mâche betterave (lamb's lettuce salad with diced beet root); gratinée (onion soup); Chateaubriand; andouillette (chitterling sausage); profiteroles.

. . .

[26] 49 rue des Écoles, 5th, 01.43.54.13.67. MÉTRO: **Cluny-Sorbonne.** OPEN **daily for lunch and dinner. www.brasseriebalzar.com** ▪ **$$**

La Bastide Odéon

NEITHER JUDY, A NEW ORLEANS NATIVE WHO HAS LIVED in Saint-Germain-des-Prés for more than thirty years, nor I had been to chef Gilles Ajuelos's Mediterranean-inspired bistro for a long time, so, once settled in the pretty ocher-and-gray-painted first-floor dining room (more fun than the one upstairs), we reminisced about how it had created a real stir in the neighborhood when it opened in 1994. Ajuelos was one of the first

Paris chefs to do contemporary Provençal cooking, and, happily, he has avoided the curse of the successful restaurant—the slackening creativity conveyed by an unchanging menu, along with the temptation to wedge a few more tables into the dining room and the dronelike service such crowding creates. So while this place is hardly a discovery, it remains an excellent address in a very strategic Left Bank location, just steps from the Odéon in Saint-Germain.

We did our best to ignore the tetchy vegetarian from Seattle who was inexplicably making life miserable for her travel companion at the table next to us—Ajuelos does several stunning vegetarian entrées, plus a gorgeous vegetable plate, and, having once lived with a vegetarian who loves food, I know that being an herbivore is no roadblock at the table. The proof of Ajeulos's commendably green credentials is that we happily tucked into excellent starters of beautifully made terrine of grilled eggplant, ricotta, and tomatoes and a stunningly good goat cheese mousse on an artichoke heart with fresh, perfectly cooked fava beans and a lively vinaigrette. Our main courses were outstanding, too. My plump, crunchy grilled shrimp were arranged on a long rectangular plate atop a bed of saffron risotto with grilled baby leeks, and Judy's sea bream filet topped a mixture of spring vegetables and was garnished with a few small puddles of a delicious coulis made from preserved Moroccan lemons. When I mentioned to the waiter that I was happy to see the roasted free-range chicken with whole garlic cloves and baby potatoes still on the menu, which changes constantly according to Ajuelos's inspiration and the season, he brought me a meaty drumstick with a few creamy cloves of roasted garlic on the side. My cheese plate—Roquefort terrine and fresh goat cheese with an excellent chutney of dried fruit—was lovely, and Judy, who's utterly indifferent to dessert, enjoyed her Moroccan-style orange salad sprinkled with cinnamon and finely sliced candied orange peel.

It's true we had to listen carefully to hear the French speakers in the crowd, but Saint-Germain-des-Prés is incontestably the English-speaking world's favorite non-English-speaking neighborhood. That said, almost everyone in this part of Paris speaks some English these days, and the cosmopolitan mix of the crowd creates a quintessentially Left Bank atmosphere, stylish but low-key and effortlessly sophisticated.

· ⁂ ·

IN A WORD: A friendly, sophisticated Saint-Germain-des-Prés table with an international crowd and a modern Mediterranean-inspired menu that consistently delivers good eating. A good choice for vegetarians, since there is regularly a nice selection of vegetable dishes on the menu.

DON'T MISS: Grilled eggplant, ricotta, and tomato terrine; goat cheese mousse on an artichoke heart with fava beans; penne with sobrassada (paprika-seasoned sausage from Mallorca) and black olives; artichoke-and-goat-cheese-stuffed cannelloni in grapefruit bouillon; grilled shrimp with saffron risotto and baby leeks; gray mullet with wild capers, olives, tomato, and lemon; roast chicken with whole garlic cloves; cheese plate with Roquefort terrine and fresh goat cheese; vanilla millefeuille; poached pear with fromage blanc ice cream.

· · ·

[36] 7 rue Corneille, 6th, 01.43.26.03.65. MÉTRO: Odéon. OPEN Tuesday to Saturday for lunch and dinner. CLOSED Sunday and Monday. www .bastide-odeon.com • $$

Au Bon Saint Pourçain

SAINT-GERMAIN IS WITHERED-CARROT TERRITORY, WHICH is why the refrain of the locals is "God bless, François," the kindly bushy-browed owner of this small and delightfully unpretentious little bistro behind the church of Saint-Sulpice.

Solacing the hardworking bourgeoisie of the neighborhood, that anxious elegant tribe who inhabit gorgeous apartments with dated decors they either inherited or bought a long time ago—and ascetically empty refrigerators: think a bottle of duty-free vodka, an old jar of mustard, organic jam brought home from stylish corners of Europe (fig preserves from Croatia or lemon marmalade from Puglia), a few eggs no one remembers buying, and a withered carrot or two in the vegetable

drawer—is his vocation. What François knows is that the locals live for the weekend and the pretty, busy markets of the towns where they have country houses and the time to cook. During the week in Paris, they chronically get home from work too late to shop, too tired to cook. So they eat a quick plate of pasta in one of Saint-Germain's innumerable Italian restaurants, or, when they're craving real food or want to share a bona fide "insider's" address with foreign friends, they come to François.

This is why his tiny restaurant feels a bit like a club, replete with heavy velvet curtains in the doorway and a crowd of regulars who recognize one another with a smile or a nod without feeling obliged to take things any further. In fact, chatting between tables normally isn't done, because it breaks the unstated rule that this precious place is for letting your hair down with friends, not networking or preening. This doesn't mean that unknown faces are unwelcome, however—this is actually a quietly friendly spot, and the worldly regulars happily welcome the variety provided by foreigners.

François, who originally worked here as the sole waiter before buying out the owner, knows all of this, which is why he quickly pours a glass of complimentary white Saint-Pourçain and brings a saucer of saucisson (sliced sausage) when you're seated on the old moleskin banquettes, and why he wouldn't dream of taking certain things off the menu. Claire, the friend who introduced me to Au Bon Saint Pourçain fifteen years ago, always has the same meal—marinated leeks to start and then brandade de morue, salt cod with mashed potatoes and garlic. The dish I crave is the boeuf aux olives, braised beef with green olives. Such homey plats mijotées (long-simmered dishes) are the stars of the menu and are cooked in a tiny kitchen just off the dining room. Other house classics include the compote de lapereau (rabbit in tarragon-flavored aspic), tête de veau sauce gribiche (calf's head with a sauce of vinegar, eggs, cornichon pickles, and capers), and a fine tarte Tatin. It's a bit raspy, but everyone drinks the house Saint-Pourçain, a rustic red wine from the south-central Auvergne region, or, wanting something better, the very good Irancy, a light red from northern Burgundy.

· ·

IN A WORD: Just the ticket when you want a good, friendly, low-effort bistro meal in the heart of Saint-Germain-des-Prés. Cash only, no credit cards.

DON'T MISS: Poireaux vinaigrette (marinated leeks); compote de lapereau (rabbit in tarragon-flavored aspic); boeuf aux olives (braised beef with green olives); brandade de morue (shredded salt cod mixed into mashed potatoes with garlic); entrecôte; sauce marchand de vin (steak with red wine sauce); tarte Tatin.

. . .

[**32**] **10 rue Servandoni, 6th, 01.43.54.93.63.** MÉTRO: **Saint-Sulpice or Mabillon.** OPEN **Monday to Friday for lunch and dinner. Saturday dinner only.** CLOSED **Sunday. • $$**

Le Buisson Ardent

LOOK CAREFULLY AT THE PEDIMENT OF THE BUILDING that houses this delightful Latin Quarter bistro, and you'll discover the origins of its name—a poignant stone miniature of Moses and the burning bush (in the book of Exodus, Moses learns of his divine calling when he comes across a burning bush in the Egyptian desert).

Though Jean-Thomas Lopez, the charming owner of this 1925-vintage dining room, found his calling as a restaurateur in a less dramatic way—after working as a banker and a high-powered corporate director, he decided to follow his natural vocation as someone who's passionate about food and a warm and natural host by opening a restaurant—his revelation seems no less evident, especially since the talented chef, Stéphane Mauduit, is one of his closest childhood friends.

Passing through the heavy curtains at the door here, one immediately senses the relaxed, happy atmosphere of this place, where the tables are generously spaced, the service is smiling and friendly, and two large chandeliers with frosted tulip lamps overhead add intimate scale to a high-ceilinged room with red banquettes, forest green walls, winsome romantic friezes, and white wedding cake moldings.

The contemporary French menu changes often, but its guiding themes are quality, generosity, and a well-groomed creativity with cosmopolitan inspiration. Stéphane Mauduit trained with Michel Rostang, and his haute cuisine background is quickly apparent in the way he works a traditional bistro register with delicious details—the bread here is homemade—and intelligent innovation, which is immediately seen in starters such as a plump artichoke heart stuffed with fresh chèvre in a sauce vierge (a light vinaigrette with tomato cubes), white asparagus with a red-fruit vinaigrette, and grilled salmon cooked rare, garnished with dill and lime and a salad of sorrel-brightened tabouleh.

During my last meal here, the quartet of academics at the table next to me eagerly tucked into two côtes de boeuf (rib steak) Simmenthal with a grainy mustard jus and generous sides of potatoes dauphinoises, but I loved my succulent chop of free-range pork with orange, fresh sauerkraut, and pickled turnips, and I had trouble keeping my fork away from Jutta's guinea hen breast in a coral-colored shellfish cream sauce with fork-mashed potatoes. "I really like this place, Alec," she said, glorying in a visit to Paris, where she lived for many years before moving to Provence. "The food's delicious, and everyone's so friendly."

The desserts were excellent, too. Jutta had the poached pear sunk in a swirl of whipped cream colored a soft pink by Lyonnais pralin, or sugarcoated almonds, and my lychee bavarois was mounted on a crunchy disk of white chocolate, praline, and puffed rice and drizzled with hibiscus syrup. Jean-Thomas Lopez stopped by for a chat at the end of the meal and discussed his love of classical music and cooking, as well as an excellent meal he'd had at Blue Hill on the Rockefeller estate in New York's Westchester County. Discussing what makes us happy at the table, he told us that "generosity and a desire to please are what I look for in a restaurant." And they're what he offers quite brilliantly at this excellent restaurant.

· ᪰ ·

IN A WORD: Excellent contemporary French cooking, warm hospitality, good service, and a comfortable, good-looking dining room make this cozy bistro in the Latin Quarter a real gem. The reasonably priced prix fixe menu is a great buy, too.

DON'T MISS: The menu changes regularly, but dishes worth looking out for include the pissaladière, an open tart of red peppers and sardines with olive emulsion; chèvre-stuffed artichoke heart; grilled salmon with dill and lime and tabouleh with sorrel; squid risotto with Parmesan; guinea hen breast in shellfish sauce; calf's liver with spice-bread crumbs and polenta; côte de boeuf (rib steak) with grainy mustard jus and dauphinois potatoes; braised beef cheeks with green olives; chocolate mousse with candied orange peel; lychee bavarois with hibiscus syrup; dark chocolate soufflé; ice cream and sorbets from Damman's, one of Paris's best artisanal ice cream makers.

. . .

[27] 25 rue de Jussieu, 5th, 01.43.54.93.02. MÉTRO: **Jussieu.** OPEN **Monday to Friday for lunch and dinner. Saturday dinner only.** CLOSED **Sunday.** www.lebuissonardent.fr • **$$**

Christophe

ONE OF THE MOST EXCITING THINGS ABOUT LIVING IN PARIS is hearing the first drumbeats about a promising new restaurant. Though for a long time, it's been fashionable to scold the city as gastronomically stagnant, the reality is that the renewal of its culinary scene has recently been accelerating as a new generation of superb young chefs strikes out on their own. And this is what makes Paris such an incomparably wonderful city to eat in: unlike in New York or London, where many new restaurants are major production affairs with huge bankrolls and publicity budgets, the undergrowth of good eating in Paris is still created the old-fashioned way, by passionate young chefs who yearn to share their cooking with the world and who are willing to work ungodly hours and risk crushing personal debt to do so.

The simple shop-front dining room in the Latin Quarter, where the only visual interest is the black-and-white photographs on the melon-colored and lemon yellow walls, doesn't promise much at first glance, but this makes it the perfect foil for a wonderful surprise. On a Sunday night—this earnest place is open seven days a week—the dining room was almost empty when we arrived but gradually filled up. Next to us, a Sorbonne professor patiently translated the menu from French into English for a tweedy college professor from Toronto and his wife, almost a cartoon of an academic spouse, with sensibly cropped short hair and a high-collared, long-sleeved red dress. "This beef is very famous in France, like Kobe beef in Japan. It comes from Coutance in Normandy, and the assiette de charcuterie Basque is an assortment of sausage and ham from the Basque country, in the southwestern corner of the country on the Spanish border." It was a pleasure to hear his commentary, too, since he took justifiable pride in educating his guests on the myriad fine points of French produce found on the menu.

I'd heard about the young chef, Christophe Philippe, from a friend who lives near his restaurant. "He worked for Sophie Pic in Valence, and he's very talented," she told me, and our first courses more than delivered on her high praise. Fine slices of smoked wild salmon were wrapped around salad leaves and horseradish cream and served with a hot chestnut-flour waffle, while a ruddy cream of lentil soup was garnished with tiny bits of grilled bacon. Perfectly cooked duck breast from Challans, a famous poultry-raising town in the Vendée region, in a deeply reduced and perfectly seasoned jus came with ravioli stuffed with duck thigh meat, a wonderful garnish, and shoulder of lamb with aromatic spices was an elegant French riff on Moroccan cooking. Philippe had grilled the braised lamb so that its skin was crunchy and the heat released the fine perfumes of cumin, coriander, pepper, and other spices you'd find in a market in Marrakesh. The modestly priced Château Saint-Martin Côtes de Provence recommended by the friendly young waitress was a stunningly elegant wine, too.

After a sumptuous millefeuille pastry with preserved-lemon cream, we wanted to know more about Philippe and quizzed the waitress. "I'll let him speak for himself," she said, and when the chef came to the table a few minutes later, we raved about our dessert.

The boyish Philippe told us he'd grown up in Menton, a faded but genteel Riviera resort town on the Italian border. With its gentle climate, Menton was once famous for its lemons, which are still prized by France's best chefs—Alain Ducasse and Joël Robuchon among them—for their highly perfumed skin, thick pith, and low acidity. Today only a few growers still cultivate the prized citrus, but Philippe has his own source. "My mother sends me lemons, which are what makes the meeting of citrus and cream so suave in the millefeuille," he explained. "I also bake my own pâte feuilletée," he added, and, as much as the lovely tang of the lemon, it was these crunchy, almost carmelized brown leaves that astonished us, especially these days, when so many restaurants buy their desserts. So why does Christophe undertake all of this backbreaking work alone in a tiny kitchen? "I cook because it's my passion—why else would anyone work so hard?" he told us with a smile and then broke away to speak with another client, who was waiting to tell him, "C'était superbe!" ("It was superb!").

· ⟁ ·

IN A WORD: Catch a rising star at this cozy Latin Quarter bistro. Chef Christophe Philippe's contemporary French cooking is disciplined, elegant, and delicious.

DON'T MISS: Trio du cochon Basque (pork from the Basque country prepared in three different ways); langoustines au basilic (Dublin Bay prawns with basil); veal sweetbreads with potato puree; grilled sea bream; pineapple carmelized with cinnamon; chocolate mousse.

. . .

[24] 8 rue Descartes, 5th, 01.43.26.72.49. MÉTRO: Cardinal-Lemoine.
OPEN Friday to Tuesday for lunch and dinner CLOSED Wednesday and
Thursday. ▪ $$

Au Coin des Gourmets

THE FRENCH LOVED INDOCHINE THE SAME WAY THE BRITISH
loved India, as the romantic colony that curiously defined and
flattered them, and long after their imperial construct was edited
off the map, the same corner of Asia—now Cambodia, Laos,
and Vietnam—still plays Parisian heartstrings.

This affinity, and the different vintages of the Indochinese dias-
pora who have settled in Paris—first at the end of France's futile
war to prevent Vietnam's independence and then after the failed
American attempt to thwart the country's fall into the fold of com-
munism—mean that the French capital has one of the most vibrant
and complex overseas Indochinese communities in the world.
Many of those who came to Paris issued from the privileged casts in
these colonies and so often had Chinese or mixed ancestry (the
Chinese communities in all three of the Indochinese countries were
prosperous and well established enough to be the middle layer, be-
tween the colonial French and the indigenous populations).

The delightful Ta family is typical Parisian Indochinese,
since Cambodia, China, and Vietnam all have a place in the
family history, which explains the varied menus at their two
very good Paris restaurants. The long-running shop-front Au
Coin des Gourmets is in the Latin Quarter, and the newer and
more stylish branch is tucked away between the Place de la
Concorde and the Place Vendôme on the Right Bank.

Both restaurants serve delicious home-style Indochinese cooking, mostly Vietnamese, but also a few Cambodian and Laotian dishes; as a new generation of the family comes into the business, the menus become longer and more authentic, including such dishes as natin, a Cambodian specialty of ground pork cooked in coconut milk and served on puffed rice. These new temptations notwithstanding, I have a hard time passing up such favorites as steamed Vietnamese ravioli stuffed with ground pork and sprinkled with fried shallots and herbs; nems, crunchy deep-fried rolls of pork, bean sprouts, and rice noodles that you wrap in lettuce leaves with fresh mint and dip in nuoc cham, a sweet-and-savory sauce; boned, stuffed chicken wings; grilled pork meatballs with salad; and the crêpe saigonaise, a very thin crunchy omelette filled with shrimp, squid, bean sprouts, onions, and herbs.

The original Latin Quarter address is a small, convivial,

often crowded shop front with framed vintage travel posters on the walls, and it has a steady crowd of regulars running to local academics and the occasional celebrity. The Right Bank address is more dressed up and a bit pricier, with a stylish decor, fresh flowers, and a refined atmosphere, but both are excellent.

IN A WORD: The excellent Vietnamese cooking served by the Ta family offers a perfect alternative to French menus when you want something light.

DON'T MISS: Nems (deep-fried spring rolls); saucisse Laotienne (spicy Laotian sausage); soupe de crevettes au tamarin (shrimp soup seasoned with tamarind paste); Cambodian squid salad; Vietnamese ravioli; grilled beef salad; amok Cambodgien (cod with coconut milk and lemongrass steamed in a banana leaf); grilled pork meatballs with salad; boned, stuffed chicken wings; shrimp with basil.

. . .

[22] Left Bank: 5 rue Dante, 5th, 01.43.26.12.92. MÉTRO: **Saint-Michel or Maubert-Mutualité.** OPEN **daily for lunch and dinner.**

[4] Right Bank: 38 rue du Mont Thabor, 1st, 01.42.60.79.79. MÉTRO: **Concorde.** OPEN **Monday to Saturday for lunch and dinner.** CLOSED **Sunday.** ▪ **$$**

Le Comptoir du Relais

YEARS AFTER YOU'VE LEFT YOUR NAPKIN ON THE TABLE, certain meals remain revelations. My first meal at chef Yves

Camdeborde's aptly named La Régalade (the name roughly means "the good time") in 1994 overturned all of my expectations of bistro cooking. It was a sleety October afternoon, and after being tipped off to this newly opened place in an inconvenient corner of the 14th Arrondissement by Françoise, my next-door neighbor, I'd persuaded Marc to join me for lunch. We both had trouble finding the place, and he arrived in the same sour mood I did, with a dripping umbrella and a certain grouchiness over having been made to trek out to this wet, charmless stretch of pavement in the middle of the day. Then we eyeballed the chalkboard menu and our spirits lifted. "Ça a l'air bon" ("It looks good"), said Marc sort of grudgingly, and a second later the waitress thumped a heavy ceramic loaf pan of terrine de campagne on the table and told us to help ourselves. We did, shamelessly, because the loaf of coarsely ground pork and pork liver with a top crust of carmelized juices and distant hints of onion, garlic, and thyme tasted incredibly delicious. We started

with creamy chestnut soup with croutons and tiny cubes of foie gras, an amazing combination, and then Marc had grilled duck hearts with pleurotes (oyster mushrooms), which he insisted I try. New to duck hearts, I was surprised by how good they were, and my tiny scallops cooked in their shells with salt butter were superb—tender, sweet, and quietly briny, with an intriguing garnish of chopped walnuts. "This place is excellent," said Marc, now beaming, over the ewe's milk Ossau Iraty served with black cherry jam and an impeccable Grand Marnier soufflé that ended a meal that left us both awed. We'd discovered a remarkable cook, someone who'd created a sexy hybrid of gutsy southwestern French grub and refined haute cuisine dishes (Camdeborde trained with chef Christian Constant at Les Ambassadeurs).

I went back a night later and often after that, until it started to become difficult to get a reservation and the service became so rushed and frantic that it dulled the pleasure of the food. Ultimately, Camdeborde was cooking lunch and three dinner services, a debilitating pace even for a barrel of a guy with a rugby man's build and stamina, so it came as no surprise when he sold it two years ago and took some time off.

Teasing rumors of his return to the range started a few months later, and then, suddenly, he was back! The opening of Le Comptoir du Relais overlooking a pricey piece of sidewalk just steps from the Odéon was electric news, and I immediately went. It was good, too—the single set menu at dinner began with chicken bouillon with mousseron mushrooms and perles du Japon (manioc-flour pearls, aka tapioca), and continued with crabmeat gelée with a zucchini puree, tournedos Rossini (steak topped with foie gras), a good cheese tray, and a red fruit and pistachio macaroon. As flawless a performance as this was, however, I found myself missing the high-testosterone cooking that had once had the whole world mewling for a place at his table. Still, given this quality, success was ensured, and it's since become viciously difficult to score a place for dinner in this pretty Art Deco dining room.

Every other person who visits me in Paris these days wants to go, though, so I've been there often. My last meal—oxtail gelée in red wine sauce with petits pois and Parmesan, sautéed foie gras with rhubarb, Bibb lettuce, and a Xérès-vinegar-spiked jus, grilled veal steak with flat parsley; cheese; and strawberries with ewe's milk ice cream and nougatine tuiles (wafers)—was excellent but curiously dainty and very polite, an opinion that was echoed by a Frenchman at the table next to me, who pronounced it "très première communion" (very First Communion), a reference to the extravagant lunches served by bourgeois families in the provinces to celebrate this important childhood milestone. So should you go? Yes, of course, but show up with the expectation of a very nice meal rather than a revelation.

· ⁂ ·

IN A WORD: The star bistro chef Yves Camdeborde's latest place has rapidly become just as popular as his original rough-and-tumble La Régalade, but the earthy, lusty cooking of the old address has given way to a much politer and more polished cooking style. The food here is very good but will never make you moan.

DON'T MISS: The prix fixe dinner menu changes regularly, but good dishes often served à la carte at noon include a deboned pig's foot that could completely change your mind about this French favorite.

. . .

[38] 9 carrefour de l'Odéon, 6th, 01.44.27.07.50. MÉTRO: Odéon. OPEN daily for lunch and dinner. www.hotel-paris-relais-saint-germain.com • $$

La Fontaine de Mars

SINCE I WAS SENSITIVE AND SOLITARY AS A LITTLE BOY, the shy wobbly birth of a new friendship always seems to me kind of a miracle and leaves me elated. As the years have gone by, though, I experience that fine fleeting moment when the mutual recognition of two psyches ignites the reciprocal curiosity from which friendship is born rather less often, because I'm part of a couple, have many friends already, and am much too busy. Against this backdrop, I prize the rarity of a new friend even more, which is why I gave it some thought when Felisa, a new friend who lives in California, e-mailed and suggested we meet for Sunday lunch while she was in Paris.

This particular meal is always a challenge, because so few really good places are open then. I'm also definitely not a fan of brunch in restaurants—I can do that meal much better at home, where I can eat it without changing out of my usual home gear of a teddy-bear pile Ralph Lauren jacket, oversized AMHERST COLLEGE T-shirt, sweatpants, and L.L. Bean moccasins, and most of the city's brasseries, always the weakest link in the Parisian food chain, are at their worst at Sunday noon. The main reason for this is that the Sunday lunch crowd at most brasseries preponderantly orders the cheap prix-fixe menu, so owners staff their kitchen lightly and with chefs and servers who are only partially trained, making mediocre cooking worse and slow to arrive at the table.

Knowing that Felisa loves old-fashioned Paris, I booked at La Fontaine de Mars, the 1908-vintage bistro selected for a very public private dinner by President Barack Obama and his wife Michelle when they were here in 2009. Though I hadn't been to this old-timer for a while, I knew that the elegant but relaxed mis-en-scène of the place—red-and-white checked tablecloths woven with the name of the restaurant, bentwood chairs, cushy old leather banquettes, and a pretty setting overlooking a fountain on the rue Saint-Dominique—would make Felisa happy. Owners Jacques and Christiane Boudon are consummate professionals, and La Fontaine usually offers first-rate people watching and eavesdropping as well as solid well-prepared old-fashioned bistro cooking with a southwestern French accent.

So on an Indian summer day when it was cool enough to air out the mothball scent of a tweed jacket not worn since May, I set out to meet Felisa. On the cusp of two seasons and facing the stolid Sunday dourness of the 7th Arrondissement, where I lived for many years, I felt wistful for all of those things I'd never know again, and I arrived at La Fontaine de Mars feeling pleasantly melancholy after these private pensive hors d'oeuvres.

Dramatically dressed in black-and-white, with wonderful 1950s costume jewelry, Felisa, an architect with a passion for vintage clothing, was waiting for me at a terrace table, and even though we'd only met several times before, conversation was exceptionally easy as we sipped kirs and studied the menu. "There's nothing in the world I think I'd rather read than the menu of a good Paris restaurant," she said, and I agreed wholeheartedly.

Suffice it to say, we had a very, very good meal, and La Fontaine has vaulted to the top of my Sunday lunch list and found a place on my roster of favorite bistros. The stylish Felisa didn't want a starter, but I couldn't resist the oeufs au Madiran façon meurette, which are as good a reason as I can imagine to get out of bed on a Sunday before noon—two perfectly poached eggs in a sauce of reduced Madiran wine with onions and bacon. A charming Dutch woman at the table next to us had the foie gras maison mi-cuit: probably because I couldn't take my eyes off it, she kindly offered me a taste on a toast point, and it was excellent.

Next Felisa, whose petite size is strikingly misleading when it comes to her appetite, ordered steak béarnaise with homemade frites, because "the beef in France has so much more flavor that it does in the U.S.," and I had free-range chicken in a cream sauce that was generously loaded with morel mushrooms. My fowl was juicy, tender, and wonderfully infused with the taste of the morels. After Felisa put a good dent in her beautiful pile of golden frites, I greedily finished them off, using the rest of her béarnaise as a condiment, and noting it was homemade—rather sadly a rarity in Paris these days—with a lovely bite of tarragon preserved in vinegar.

Finishing up over first-rate chocolate mousse and baba au rhum, I concluded that the presidential minders had chosen well for the First Family. I also knew I'd never eat here again without thinking of Felisa and that my next meal would be imminent, because I crave both the confit de canard and blanquette de veau from this lovely old-fashioned bistro the minute the trees of Paris go nude in the night.

· · ·

IN A WORD: This well-mannered Hollywood set of a bistro is a perfect expression of the pleasantly bourgeois 7th Arrondissement and serves up fine renditions of such vieille France dishes as blanquette de veau, along with specialities from southwestern France.

DON'T MISS: Foie gras mi-cuit, oeufs au Madiran façon meurette, escargots, salade de tête de veau, blanquette de veau, boudin Basque (black pudding), cassoulet, confit de canard, steak béarnaise, poulet aux morilles, sole meunière, baba au rhum, chocolate mousse.

· · ·

[43] La Fontaine de Mars, 129 rue Saint-Dominique, 7th, 01.47.05.46.44
MÉTRO: Ecole Militaire or Pont-de-l'Alma. OPEN daily for lunch and dinner.
www.fontainedemars.com · **$$**

L'Épi Dupin

SEVERAL LIFETIMES AGO, OR SO IT SEEMS, THE NICE LADY in the post office first told me about L'Épi Dupin. I was living in the rue du Bac, and my post office, the place I most dreaded going to in the entire city of Paris due to its interminable lines, was in the rue Dupin. Then one day, a miracle—I stepped up to the counter and was greeted by a new face, a pleasant, efficient-looking, middle-aged lady with deep blue eyes and a bemused expression. Over the course of a month, she obviously eye-balled what I was sending—and receiving, too—since after the first few encounters, she asked me to recommend a good, inexpensive place in the neighborhood for lunch. I told her about Au Babylone, the simple lunch-only canteen in the rue de Babylone where much of the sales staff of the Bon Marché department store goes daily, and the next time I came in, she returned the favor. "As soon as you leave, go next door and book a table for dinner. The place just opened, and the young chef is going to be a star."

I did as told, and my first experience of François Pasteau's cooking was sublime, especially his signature starter of carmelized endive stuffed with runny goat cheese and main course of guinea hen with fennel bulb. It turned out he was a nice guy, too, a real feet-on-the-ground cook who'd been inspired by a stint in the United States before returning to Paris. The small dining room with its exposed, worm-eaten beams also reminded me of my snug, quiet apartment, part of an old stable in a court-yard overlooking a convent (how else would I know that even nuns dye their hair?). A fresh coat of white paint had replaced the grass-cloth-covered walls of the previous tenant, a Chinese restaurant, and the place had an appealing rustic feel. I went often those first few months, and then word got around and it became difficult to get a table and then basically impossible, in spite of the two services at dinner.

So I'd sort of forgotten about this place until deciding to see if I could snag a last-minute table on a quiet night in August, low tide on the calendar of Parisian life. Bingo! Arriving, it was a letdown to be seated in such a crowded, agitated dining room, and the new lemon yellow walls hardly helped. Our dinner had a balking, sclerotic rhythm, and, jammed in between two other deuces, it was impossible for the six of us to use our knives and forks simultaneously.

Pasteau's food, however, remains superb. A pâté de cèpes, a small molded timbale of eggy, probably chicken-liver-enriched custard studded with sweet, fleshy cèpes and brightened with a flat-parsley jus was sublime, a perfect example of how good contemporary French bistro cooking can be at its best. A daily special of grilled cod steak on a bed of garlicky white Paimpol beans in a veal-bouillon-enhanced sauce was well conceived, perfectly cooked, and generously served, as was a sesame-crusted tuna with eggplant and red pepper and noisettes of lamb with creamy polenta. Our bottle of white Crozes Hermitage was an excellent buy, too. But despite the kitchen's admirable skills, the meal was melancholy.

Why? Because the relentless get-'em-in-and-get-'em-out formula of this restaurant makes it almost impossible to have a good time. The dining room's overlit, too, and much of the crowd exudes the wilting smugness of the triumphant penny-pincher (many of the people who eat at L'Épi Dupin are more excited by the admittedly wonderful bargain price of the set menu than they are by the quality of their food). The waiters have also assumed a certain ironic detachment when it comes to dealing with the foreigners who dominate the place. So how to cope? Come in a group of at least three so that you can be seated at one of the comfortable round tables, and book for a late lunch or within minutes of last orders during the second dinner service.

· ⁂ ·

IN A WORD: One of the best modern French bistros in Paris but unpleasantly crowded and marred by rapid-fire table turning.

DON'T MISS: Langoustines with pineapple-ginger chutney; cod steak with spinach and Morteau sausage; grilled skate with hazelnuts and dried fruit; cumin-seasoned pork breast with carrots and baby onions; runny chocolate-pistachio cake; apple and prune tart with pepper ice cream.

. . .

[**35**] **11 rue Dupin, 6th, 01.42.22.64.56.** MÉTRO: **Sèvres-Babylone.** OPEN **Tuesday to Friday for lunch and dinner. Monday dinner only.** CLOSED **Saturday and Sunday.** • **$$**

Les Fables de La Fontaine

CHEF CHRISTIAN CONSTANT IS ONE OF THE UNDERSUNG heroes of contemporary French cooking. While he was chef at Les Ambassadeurs at the Hôtel de Crillon, he enabled a remarkable succession of talented young chefs who passed through his kitchen, including Yves Camdeborde (Le Comptoir du Relais), Thierry Breton (Chez Michel), Thierry Faucher (L'Os à Moelle), and Eric Frechon (Le Bristol), before they went out on their own and invented the modern French bistro.

Since leaving the Crillon, Constant has been gradually colonizing a charming village-like corner of the 7th Arrondissement in one long block of the rue Saint-Dominique, where he now has four restaurants: Le Café Constant, a pleasant place for lunch if you're in this neck of the woods; Le Violon d'Ingres, which I find overpriced; Les Cocottes, which specializes in casserole-cooked dishes; and Les Fables de La Fontaine, my favorite of the quartet, a relaxed and consistently excellent seafood restaurant overlooking a square stone fountain with handsome lion faces.

During the summer, this tiny place puts a row of tables outside, and when I can snag one, it's a brilliant place for some urbane al fresco dining and a fine fish feed. On a balmy night last May, some friends and I got lucky, and the four of us had a superb meal that lasted until well after midnight as we finished off our delicious white Jaboulet Crozes Hermitage, tossed back espressos and riffed on some favorite big-city preoccupations: travel (Laurent and Carole were heading off to Venice for a weekend and wanted restaurant recommendations), real estate (will Paris apartment prices keep rising, and does it make more sense to try to buy a country house somewhere within an hour or so of Paris or go for something further afield?), restaurants (see Chéri Bibi [page 412], just a few weeks old that night), and sex (Laurent extolled the deliciousness of older women, while Carole told of the time a friend had invited her to visit the set of a porn film near the Cap d'Agde, the center of France's pornography industry; between takes, the female lead had spent her time reading the latest issue of *Cuisine de France,* a cooking magazine).

To the credit of Constant's team in the kitchen, though, the main thing we talked about was our food. Everyone loved the amuse-bouche (complimentary hors d'oeuvre) of Parmesan flan with sundried tomato puree, and our first courses—meaty Gillardeau oysters, langoustines fried in phyllo pastry with basil leaves and served with a citrus dipping sauce, and freshly poached langoustines with freshly made mayonnaise were superb.

My only regret was that I got only five langoustines when, as I once learned in rough-and-tumble fishermen's canteens in Brittany where they were freshly landed and going for a song, I can eat them by the dozen. Not well known outside Europe, these pearly pink crustaceans are like miniature lobsters, with small, sweet, fleshy tails, and the best ones come from Le Guilvinec in Brittany. They're highly perishable and easily overcooked, too, which is why I was so impressed by their freshness and the precise cooking of both preparations. The main courses, which vary according to the season and the catch of the day, were outstanding, especially my John Dory filets with plump spears of Parmesan-glazed white asparagus and a delicious ragout of morel mushrooms. Sea bass with oven-baked tomatoes and chips of grilled bacon and tiny baby potatoes was outstanding, too, and the lighter eaters loved their tuna carpaccio with Parmesan shavings and saumon tartare topped with beet gazpacho, starters ordered as main courses. Desserts are simple, maybe a slice of gâteau basque (a thin pastry cake filled with black cherry jam) or a bowl of strawberries and cream, and even when you can't sit outside, the vest-pocket Pompeian red dining room has the happy, inoffensively clubby feeling of a place where everyone's having a great time.

· ☁ ·

IN A WORD: With a stylish crowd, an impeccable catch-of-the-day menu, and a pleasantly clubby atmosphere, chef Christian Constant's seafood restaurant is a hit on the Left Bank.

DON'T MISS: The chalkboard menu changes daily, but dishes to look for include langoustines with mayonnaise; John Dory with asparagus and morel mushrooms; tuna carpaccio; lobster ravioli; hake with piquillo peppers; sea bass with morel risotto; gâteau basque.

. . .

[49] 131 rue Saint-Dominique, 7th, 01.44.18.37.55. MÉTRO: École Militaire. OPEN Tuesday to Saturday for lunch and dinner. CLOSED Sunday and Monday. ▪ $$$

La Ferrandaise

SINCE IT'S NEARLY IMPOSSIBLE TO FIND A REAL NEIGHBOR-hood restaurant in the heart of the heavily touristed Saint-Germain-des-Prés, I'm half reluctant to share the name of this excellent bistro, which has the vital ballast of a loyal following of diverse Parisian regulars—it's their exigence that keeps the kitchen on course and the atmosphere quite wonderfully local. At noon, you'll dine with book editors—Flammarion is based nearby—and epicurean but pennywise senators—the French Senat is just across the street—and in the evening, hard-driving professional couples fill the place, notably whippet-like blondes who don't cook and their slightly cowed husbands. What

everyone loves is the warmth and simplicity of this place, which is created by beamed ceilings, bare biscuit-colored stone walls, and a happy, casual staff who couldn't care less about fashion or politics, the local preoccupations, but are deeply in love with good food and wine.

The friendly welcome and attentive, slightly bemused service—the staff here enjoy babying and teasing the stressed-out power brokers—give this snug dining room the style of an auberge in a small French town like Laguiole in the Auvergne, and this rusticity, a relief from the competitive pressures of urban chic, lets all present feel as though they're getting away from it all during the space of a meal. The owner, Gilles Lamiot, is in fact an Auvergnat, and he perpetuates the tradition of good food at fair prices that his countrymen brought to Paris when many of them moved here from that mountainous central French region at the beginning of the twentieth century. This explains the winsome photographs of brown-and-white Ferrandaise breed cows on the walls—this race is native to the Auvergne's Puy de Dôme region—and also the restaurant's excellent cheese plate—Bleu de Langeuille, a creamy blue; nutty Saint-Nectaire; and the delicious, and rarely seen in Paris, Fourme de Rochefort Montagne, all of which hail from the region.

Aside from scoring such a perfect Left Bank location, Lamiot's coup was in hiring Kevin Besson, a talented chef who previously worked at Gourmand. Besson's menu is shrewd, too, since it offers the comfort food that Germanopratins (residents of Saint-Germain) crave, but in a discreetly revised register that makes it lighter and healthier. His marbré (terrine) of oxtail stuffed with leeks and served with a homemade sauce gribiche (a mustard vinaigrette containing sieved hard-boiled egg, capers, and chopped pickles) is a perfect example, since the richly flavored meat is almost fat free, the leeks add a contrasting texture, and the tangy sauce gribiche lights up the combination. On a more modern note, his crab-filled ravioli in a ruddy ocher reduction of étrilles (tiny crabs) are superb, and escargots de Bourgogne en meurette (red wine sauce) is a brilliant idea.

Cloves spike the bed of white coco beans on which braised shoulder of lamb is served, and pistachios add richness to the creamy polenta that accompanies a perfectly cooked filet of sea bream. Chaignot's pot-au-feu (beef poached in bouillon with winter vegetables) is quite simply superb, and the frites that come with the poire de boeuf, an exceptionally flavorful and tender steak, are first-rate. Among the desserts, the millefeuille minute, baked and assembled to order so that the fragile pastry leaves remain crisp, is filled with delicious vanilla cream, and the grapefruit terrine with tea sauce is perfect if you want something lighter.

Lamiot's wine list is one of the friendliest on the Left Bank, too. He serves a fine white Côtes du Rhône by the glass for €4, for example, and all of his bottles—a well-chosen selection that includes a fine Chorey-les-Beaunes 2004 by Claude Maréchal, an excellent Morgon made by Marcel Lapierre, and a nice Graves de Vayres Château Toulouze 2005, all very affordably priced—come from producers who work in "l'esprit bio," which means adhering as closely as possible to organic methods of traditional winemaking.

Finally, though I'm happy to have shared this little-known Saint-Germain gem with you, let's keep it between us so that we can always get a table.

. ☙ .

IN A WORD: A friendly, very experienced Auvergnat restaurateur has created an excellent traditional French bistro in the heart of Saint-Germain. Very popular with the locals, it hasn't yet been discovered by tourists and so is as good for savoring a Saint-Germain state of mind as it is for the delicious comfort food served up by a talented young chef.

DON'T MISS: The menu here changes regularly but dishes to look for include oxtail marbré stuffed with leeks; fricassee of wild mushrooms; escargots de Bourgogne en meurette; crab ravioli with sauce étrilles (crab sauce); cod with mashed potatoes; pot-au-feu; pintade (guinea fowl) with gratin of macaroni with Parmesan; poire de boeuf (steak) with frites; braised lamb shoulder with coco beans; cheese plate; millefeuille minute à la vanille de Madagascar; roasted pineapple flambéed in rum; grapefruit terrine with tea sauce.

. . .

[37] 8 rue de Vaugirard, 6th, 01.43.26.36.36. MÉTRO: **Odéon.** OPEN **Monday to Friday for lunch and dinner. Saturday dinner only.** CLOSED **Sunday.**
▪ **$$**

Le Florimond

THE HOPEFUL, RACING EXPECTATIONS BEFORE TRYING A new restaurant are one of the great pleasures of city life, especially in Paris, where the odds of success are solidly better than they are in other cities. I'd heard about Le Florimond from the friendly Auvergnat (from the south-central Auvergne region of France) owner of my local wine shop. "Nasty weather," he'd said a few days earlier when I had stopped by for a few bottles of his wonderful and inexpensive Colombelle, a Gascon white. "If I weren't stuck behind this counter, I'd hurry across town for the best stuffed cabbage in Paris. Now, that would taste good today." He grinned.

"So where would that be?" I said.

"Do you like stuffed cabbage?"

"It's one of my favorites."

"Then you'd really love this place, but I'm not sure if I remember the name." He was like a cat with a ball of yarn, and it took a few minutes more of this teasing before he'd had his fun

and jotted down "Le Florimond" on a notepad. I booked for lunch the next day. I've loved stuffed cabbage, one of the Auvergne's signature dishes, ever since I first had it at Jean-Yves Bath's excellent restaurant in the south-central Auvergnat city of Clermont-Ferrand fifteen years ago.

The welcome when I stepped in off the pavement was so warm it almost startled me—Parisians have finely embroidered manners but are not demonstrative, especially with strangers. Then, not a minute after I'd settled at a corner table waiting for my English friend Sue, a plate of nutmeg-scented gougères, or tiny cheese puffs, came to the table. I usually ignore such nibbles—the pleasure they offer never equals the calories they pack—but in this case I was tempted. These were hot and, from their soft, eggy consistency, obviously homemade, a good omen. The small butter yellow dining room was attractive, too. The banquette was covered in poppy-colored velvet, and there were

Delft-style serving plates on the table and more Delft displayed on the walls, all of which created the sort of prosperous, scrubbed, comfortable interior you find in Vermeer's paintings. Sue came in with Tally, a taffy-colored Labrador, and we opened our menus.

"This is tough. I want everything," said Sue, a talented chef who once had a cooking school in Paris.

I agreed. Finally we ordered, and then we got down to talking about where and what we'd eaten since we'd last seen each other. She was on meal four out of ten she'd had during a recent trip to Barcelona when our first courses came: a terrine of mushrooms and Morteau (pork sausage from the Jura) on a beautiful salad of tiny tender green-and-garnet-colored leaves in a pale garlic cream dressing for me and terrine of boudin noir (blood pudding) and chestnuts with a nice waft of mace and clove for her. She went first, and her shoulders slumped.

"Oh, my God, this is absolutely delicious. This is real food," she said. My terrine was also stunningly good, the soft hash of the mushrooms a perfect foil to the smoky, chewy cubes of sausage. In fact, I felt a twinge the moment it was gone, knowing it had already been committed to that mental repertory of dishes I'll permanently crave between servings.

When the storied cabbage came, it was glistening in a pool of brown gravy so lush it had already skeined on its way to the table. Eyeing it, I instantly yearned for a boiled potato or two to mash into this unctuous bath with the back of my fork. So I asked, because I'd understood that this was a place where any reasonable request is fulfilled with pride and pleasure. The waiter returned with a thick square of pommes dauphinoise, too rich to go well with the cabbage but a lovely gesture. Sue and I mumbled during the meal. She was preoccupied with her home-made sausage ("I love sausage, all kinds of sausage"), veal steak, and plump white Tarbes beans from the southwestern French city with the same name in a sauce related to my gravy, and I was stunned by the elegance of my cabbage, a rustic work of art. Its delicate and perfectly seasoned stuffing of pork, veal, onion, cabbage, and Swiss chard was interleaved with parboiled cabbage leaves to create a sublime version of one of the most ancient and profoundly satisfying of all European winter dishes (some version of stuffed cabbage exists in almost every continental kitchen). We gorged ourselves and laughed out loud when the charming waiter asked if we wanted cheese. No, no cheese, but a vanilla millefeuille with two forks—the one I'd seen going by earlier had looked too good to resist. It was, and so is this bistro, easily one of the best in town.

"How was the stuffed cabbage?" my wine man asked me a few days later.

"Incredible."

"I knew you'd like it, but please don't give this one away . . ."

Happily, he doesn't speak English, and you won't tell anyone who sent you either.

· 🐌 ·

IN A WORD: Aristocratic loden-coat-wearing locals with dachshunds tucked under their tables mix it up with the occasional well-advised tourist, UNESCO types, and top military brass with intimidatingly perfect posture (the École Militaire is just down the street) in this warm, welcoming neighborhood bistro, a place that's well worth traveling across town for. Some of the best home-style bistro cooking in Paris, with several outstanding Auvergnat specialties, makes this a great address for a hungry tête-à-tête or a quartet of friends who love to eat together.

DON'T MISS: Terrine of mushrooms and Morteau sausage; terrine of boudin mignon of pork braised with figs and sweet onions; stuffed cabbage; duck sausage with foie gras; gâteau (cake) of carmelized crêpes with grapefruit sections; vanilla millefeuille.

. . .

[46] 19 avenue de La Motte-Picquet, 7th, 01.45.55.40.38. MÉTRO: École Militaire. OPEN Monday to Friday for lunch and dinner. Saturday dinner only, except for the first and third Saturdays of every month. CLOSED Sunday. ▪ $$$

Les Botanistes

THE CHATTERING CLASSES ON THE LEFT BANK HAVE A complicated relationship with food. Jean-Paul Sartre and Simone de Beauvoir may be gone, but the conundrum at the core of the couple—the steely struggle for control of the axis of Eros on which life between the sexes turns in France—still shows up vividly at the table. To wit, the handsome blond woman with the horsey face at the table next to us at this charming little bistro on one of the most fashionable little streets on the Left Bank tasted each plate as it was served, eagerly told the lupine gent with salt-and-pepper hair across the table that it was excellent, and then left it untouched as she twirled a necklace of vanilla-colored pearls and watched as the wolf ate every scrap on his plate. They spoke little as he knifed and forked, but when he was through, he gently chided her for eating so little, and she brushed imaginary crumbs from her ribbed mocha-colored cashmere turtleneck and said that she wasn't hungry. Then he polished off the rest of her plate. I'd like to think she made a huge bowl of spaghetti for herself when she got home, but I doubt it.

If half of this intriguingly stilted clientele goes home hungry, their ostentatious privation adds some sizzle to a dining room where some very good food is served and the owner, Bernard Arény, who formerly ran Le Grizzli on the Right Bank, once one of the best bistros in Paris, presides as one of the more genial hosts in Paris.

This snug little room, entered by stepping through the heavy flowered curtains at the door, has a quiet chic reminiscent of the decor in the country houses where much of its clientele spend their weekends. A harlequin floor in terra-cotta and ivory tiles, country floral fabrics, black-and-white photos on the walls, low lighting, bare wood tables set with crisp napkins, and expensive stemware create an atmosphere of assured good taste, and service is soigné and good-humored.

The menu changes regularly, but with any luck, you'll find the sublime mushroom terrine with garlic cream I had one night last winter. A mixture of ground button mushrooms and reconstituted dried cèpes, cream, and eggs, it's light but superbly earthy. A delicious riff on the food of the mountainous Jura region of eastern France, Judy's starter was a delicious composition of poached Savoy cabbage leaves and slices of smokey Morteau sausage in a sauce made with nutty Beaufort cheese. Since I could eat mushrooms at every meal I have for the rest of my days, it wasn't overkill for me to order the fricot de veau avec champignons sauvages, a tender veal stew made with dried cèpes and morels. This dish had always been one of my favorites at Le Grizzli, and I was delighted to find it again, which I mentioned to the owner when he stopped to pour our wine. "My grandmother used to make it with mushrooms she'd dried and gathered herself, and if mine's good, hers was incredible," he said with a smile. Judy's tuna steak was perfectly seared and came with an appealing basquaise garnish of sautéed tomatoes, peppers, and onions. Hazelnut crème brûlée was outstanding, as was Judy's dark chocolate tart.

Chef Jérôme Catillat trained at the Crillon and has a real talent for creating dishes that are at once homey and chic, exactly the kind of food Parisians love. I've eaten here many times and always come away with the quiet elation of being profoundly well fed, which is why this place is not only a great neighborhood address but a table worth traveling for.

. ☙ .

IN A WORD: Hidden away in one of the most fashionable little streets on the Left Bank, this bistro is a charmer with a chic clientele of locals and a few smart tourists.

DON'T MISS: The menu changes regularly, but dishes I've liked recently included the salade de lentilles aux pieds de porc et foie gras (lentil salad with deboned pig's foot and foie gras); cream of chestnut soup with cèpes mushrooms; chipirons (baby squid) sautéed in olive oil with a risotto made with their ink; terrine de champignons avec crème à l'ail (mushroom terrine in garlic cream sauce); cabbage stuffed with Morteau sausage in Beaufort sauce; perdreau (partridge) with buttered cabbage; fricot de veau avec champignons sauvages (veal stewed with wild mushrooms); tuna steak with Basque vegetables; dark chocolate tart; hazelnut crème brûlée.

. . .

[47] 11 bis rue Chomel, 7th, 01.45.49.04.54. MÉTRO: Sèvres-Babylone. OPEN Monday to Friday for lunch and dinner. CLOSED Saturday and Sunday. ▪ $$

Joséphine "Chez Dumonet"

DINNER AT JOSÉPHINE THE OTHER NIGHT LEFT ME FEEL-
ing optimistic about the future of France. First of all, after an
absence of six years, nothing about this Left Bank bistro had
changed, a truly blessed expression of the French talent for
leaving well enough alone. The cracked tile floors, extinct brass
gas jets, zinc-topped service bar, and custard-colored nicotined
walls survived as one of those precious Parisian decors that instantly, almost tauntingly, promises a good meal with the confidence of a place that's been a setting for pleasure for more than
eighty years.

Dorie, a cookbook writer who divides her time between
New York and Paris, and I sat side by side on a brown-vinyl-
covered banquette and talked our favorite subjects, books and
food and books about food. Since I'd had a rich and rather
soulless lunch in Reims, my appetite for the evening was more
about seeing her than eating, or so I thought. Dorie's an interesting woman, with an intelligence and ambitiousness that's
hidden by her easy laugh. Dining with her is a rare exception to
my aversion to meals with people who have a professional relationship with food. Why? Eating shouldn't be competitive.
Cooking can be good or bad, but taste is subjective because its
original function was instantaneous biofeedback, an instant re-
action based on our own personal taste memories of pleasure
and aversion.

The last time I'd been here was at the invitation of a rich industrialist who'd made one of my closest friends his mistress.
That night, the crowd had a Gaullist smugness that didn't sit
well with me, and the metal-bending tycoon not only toyed

with my friend, a brilliant and beautiful woman, but made a miscalculated man-to-man assumption that I'd join him in his game. Though the food was delicious, there was no pleasure at our table, and a week later I had only a vague memory of what I'd eaten. Looking at the menu with Dorie, however, my appetite stirred.

Unusually for Paris, you can order half portions of most starters and many main courses, but we went whole hog. It was a good decision, too, since her house-smoked salmon was superb and my thick slab of coarsely ground, beautifully seasoned terrine de campagne was lusciously enveloped in a sticky brown aspic of carmelized meat juices. When you're not very hungry, really good food not only comes as a brilliant surprise but seduces with real power.

Dorie was detailing the latest romantic travails of a mutual friend when a short, rough-looking, unshaved young man came in, sat at the bar, ordered Champagne, and got busy on his cell phone. A few minutes later his friends arrived, and I found myself thinking about how much younger and hipper the clientele at Chez Joséphine had become. The trio sat next to us and included a light-skinned black man in layers of oversized but carefully laundered stone gray sweat clothing. He wore a cap embroidered with an NYC emblem, the international don't-mess-with-me symbol, cocked sideways, and a massive, expensive wristwatch that looked as if it could run a NASA launch. I'm not much of a fan of rap music, but I recognized him anyway—Joey Starr, the most famous French rapper and the former lead singer of a group called Nique Ta Mère, or F——Your Mother.

Our main courses were served, and they were superb. Dorie had a millefeuille de pigeon, a brilliant creation of the young chef-owner, Jean-Christian Dumonet, golden layers of pommes de terre Anna interleaved with boned rare pigeon in a silky dark brown sauce. My boeuf bourguignon came in an enameled poppy-colored Le Creuset casserole and was lush; beef, pearl onions, and button mushrooms were suspended in a rich sauce redolent of wine and meat. Meanwhile, Joey Starr was tucking into a thick slab of foie gras and clearly enjoying it. Just as our cheese course arrived, a lovely assortment from Quatrehommes just down the street in the rue de Sèvres, a massive grilled andouillette (pig's intestine sausage) was served to Starr. I filled Dorie in on our neighbor, his music, and all of his drug convictions, and, as a big-city girl, she was fascinated.

We dawdled over our cheese and had just finished our Bordeaux when an aproned waiter brought Starr a perfect Grand Marnier soufflé, which he accompanied with a snifter of Darroze Armagnac. By now I wasn't surprised when I overheard him say something about the Michelin guide. After all, he'd just scarfed down the same sort of rich, well-constructed meal you'd expect to see served to a priest or a notary.

We paid our bills at the same time, but the rap trio stood up first. Starr glanced at us and flashed the shy smile appropriate to the occasion of our being the last clients left in the restaurant. "Bonsoir, Madame, M'sieur," he said, and stepped into the night. Sometimes even the French forget that few things are more civilizing than good food and good wine, and walking home I couldn't imagine a more hopeful vignette of the country's future than the gourmet meal consumed by the dapper and surprisingly polite rap star.

· ·

IN A WORD: A venerable and much-loved Left Bank bistro has evolved with the times by attracting a younger clientele and adding new dishes to the menu. Perfect for a first or last night in

Paris, since the atmosphere is almost as smooth and thick as the foie gras. Also good for business meals, tête-à-têtes, and solo dining. A great address for game lovers, too.

DON'T MISS: Foie gras; salade de mâche; pommes de terre et truffe (lamb's lettuce, potatoes, and truffle shavings, in season only); boeuf bourguignon; millefeuille de pigeon (boned, rare pigeon in flaky pastry with a sauce of its pan juices); cheese tray from Quatrehommes, one of Paris's best cheese shops; soufflé au Grand Marnier.

. . .

[33] 117 rue du Cherche-Midi, 6th, 01.45.48.52.40. MÉTRO: Duroc. OPEN Monday to Friday for lunch and dinner. CLOSED Saturday and Sunday.
▪ $$$

Les Papilles

THE LATIN QUARTER HAS A SPECIAL STATE OF MIND. IT'S perenially young, inquisitive, iconoclastic, creative, and cosmopolitan, but as rising real estate prices have pushed students and academics out of the neighborhood and seen many of the cafés where they once gathered converted into clothing shops or fast-food places, this bohemian groove has become increasingly elusive. Happily, there are still a few places where you can channel this delicious sensibility, and one of the best is Les Papilles, a wine shop and épicerie (grocery) cum restaurant that quickly became a local favorite after its opening in 2004.

The genial owner, Bertrand Bluy, worked as a pastry chef at Troisgros, Marc Veyrat, Taillevent, and the Hôtel Bristol before deciding to get out of the kitchen, and he's the perfect host, cheerfully explaining the set menu, a single four-course meal that changes daily, and the wines he stocks on shelves that line the attractive brick red dining room. The atmosphere's homey, friendly, and fun, and I often choose this place when we'll be four or more.

We were five the last time I was here, among us Corinne, a professor of architecture who spends a lot of time in Japan and who gave Bluy a hand by translating the menu for a table of Japanese students next to us. This slightly drowsy quartet—it was their first night in town, and they'd read about this place in a Tokyo paper—were astonished to find a Frenchwoman who spoke their language, but on any given evening, this is the kind of place where you might meet an expert in Renaissance brick-work or listen in on friends plotting a trip up the Amazon.

Our meal was superb, too. We began with a tureen of arti-choke soup to ladle over oval scoops of foie gras mousse in the bowl each of us was served, a beautifully subtle taste pairing, since the faint sweetness of the artichoke was the perfect foil for the earthiness of the liver. Next, two copper-plated casseroles arrived with the main course—poitrine de porc, or pork belly, with a crunchy crust and meltingly tender meat, and baby pota-toes, mushrooms, black olives, and oven-dried tomatoes. A side dish of emerald green pistou sauce was the perfect vibrant herbal finish for this rich meat, too, and our cheese course, a runny Saint-Maure chèvre with a small salad and a tapenade-spread tartine was also excellent. Bluy's previous métier was ap-parent in a delicious panna cotta (Italian-style baked cream custard) with a tart, willow-green coulis of Reine Claude plums. Suffice to say that my papilles (taste buds) always look forward to any meal at this delightful restaurant.

· ⸙ ·

IN A WORD: In the heart of the Latin Quarter, this friendly, good-value épicerie-wine-shop-and-restaurant captures the special atmosphere of the neighborhood that's the brain of Paris and serves a single four-course chalkboard menu daily to a happy crowd of epicurean locals.

DON'T MISS: Favorites from the changing menu here include beetroot gazpacho; artichoke soup with foie gras mousse; velouté de carotte (creamy carrot soup) with coriander, cumin, and grilled bacon; poitrine de porc (grilled pork belly) with baby potatoes, mushrooms, black olives, dried tomatoes, and pistou sauce; hanger steak with carrots and spring onions; roast cod with olive oil and mashed potatoes; chocolate and coffee pudding; panna cotta with Reine Claude coulis; citrus salad with Campari gelée.

. . .

[31] 30 rue Gay-Lussac, 5th, 01.43.25.20.79. MÉTRO: **Cluny–La Sorbonne or RER Luxembourg.** OPEN **Monday to Friday for lunch and dinner. Saturday dinner only.** CLOSED **Sunday.** ▪ **$$**

Le Petit Pontoise

WHEN YOU LIVE IN PARIS AND DISCOVER A WONDERFUL new restaurant, you're faced with an instant dilemma: to share or not. The reason, of course, is that a review can completely overwhelm a promising table before it's even had a chance to find its groove. When Le Petit Pontoise opened six years ago, we decided this was one to keep under our hats. Why? Not only is it open daily, but the food's delicious and the wine list carefully composed and well priced. Alas, our coterie broke ranks, but despite its popularity with a transient and often gastronomically conservative international clientele, this snug butter yellow dining room remains one of the best bets in the Latin Quarter, an otherwise challenging place to find a good French feed.

On a Sunday night, our quartet was coming from two different Easter lunches and one Passover celebration in different corners of France, so we were surprised to find ourselves eating

with real relish. Starters included a superb salad of poached fresh haricots verts (string beans) with meaty crayfish tails; a gratin of tiny dauphinois ravioli, from the mountainous south-central Dauphiné region of France, no bigger than a postage stamp and stuffed with cheese; a first-rate terrine de gibier (game terrine); and a spectacular tarte Tatin d'artichauts. Though I don't like it when the names of specific dishes are used generically—there's a sorry tendency in Paris right now to describe everything stuffed and tubular as "cannelloni," for example—the "Tatin" more or less warranted the name as a brilliant spring dish of young artichoke quarters on a bed of rustic ratatouille on a nice crispy pastry base. (What made it a Tatin, in case you're wondering, is that the vegetables had been braised under the same pastry crust, which became the base of the tart when flipped over.)

At a neighboring table, an adolescent boy from Winnetka, Illinois, refused all attempts by his parents to get him to taste what they were eating and so clearly enjoying, shutting down further entreaties with a warning: "All I wanted was a pizza."

"Okay, but you don't know what you're missing," his mother replied. I love pizza, too, but Mom was right. The parmentier de canard avec foie gras was spectacular—savory shredded duck under a generous cap of panfried foie gras came on a bed of mashed potatoes lashed with a lush mahogany-colored sauce. Scallops in a light saffron sauce, a veal chop sautéed with a branch of fresh rosemary and garnished with marrow bones, and roast chicken with mashed potatoes were similarly carefully cooked and satisfying. Desserts like baba au rhum (pastry sponge soaked in rum with whipped cream) and île flottante, big white tufted pods of meringue on a shallow sea of custard, tasted rather standard issue, and prices have climbed a lot recently, but the service remains outstandingly friendly—

it had been a long time, too, since anyone had been so welcoming as to offer me a complimentary glass of white wine while I waited to be seated, and overall this place remains very reliable.

· ☙ ·

IN A WORD: A quality bistro with good traditional French cooking and a nice wine list in the Latin Quarter. Don't be surprised to run into someone you know.

DON'T MISS: Poêlée de grosses crevettes et asperges vertes (sauted shrimp and green asparagus); parmentier de canard avec foie gras (shredded duck and foie gras with pureed potatoes); bar rôti à la vanille (sea bass roasted with vanille); soufflé chaud à la vanille (hot vanilla souffle).

. . .

[**28**] **9, rue de Pontoise, 5th, 01.43.29.25.20.** MÉTRO: **Maubert-Mutualité.** OPEN **daily for lunch and dinner.** · **$$**

Au Pied de Fouet

WITH VISIONS OF THE SNOWY PEAKS SURROUNDING Geneva and the vineyards of the Beaujolais in the snow looking like a tidy patchwork of white corduroy still in my head, I arrived back in Paris from a trip to Switzerland on a smoking cold night last winter and went to meet my friend Judy for dinner at Au Pied de Fouet, a hole-in-the-wall in the Faubourg Saint-Germain, just down the street from my old apartments on the rue du Bac and the rue Monsieur. When I lived in the neighborhood twelve years ago, I never frequented this place, famously known as one of Jean Cocteau's favorite restaurants, because I found the welcome gruff, the food too plain, and the service rushed. But I'd heard it had recently changed owners, and a friend who lives nearby had been raving about the pot au feu, which is exactly what I was hoping to find on the chalkboard menu that changes daily as I walk down the rue du Babylone listening to the crunch of frost beneath my heels. Stepping inside the tiny place, I had a booming "Bonsoir" from the owner behind the bar, and Judy was waiting at a table covered in a red-and-white-checked cloth. Sitting next to her at the same table—you share here—was an elegant older man in a gray flannel jacket with a paisley ascot. He glanced up from his carefully folded *Le Monde* when I sat down and said "Bonsoir," too. There was no pot au feu that night, but we ate a delicious salad of lentils in shallot vinaigrette, crispy confit de canard with crunchy sautéed potatoes, and apple cobbler washed down with a pleasant Côtes du Rhône served in a carafe. The meal was briskly served but delicious, and in a break with the past, you can now have coffee at the table (previously it was only served at the bar to make way for waiting customers). Later, I realized I had finally mastered both the French language and the more arcane rites of Paris well enough to appreciate this place for what it is, a charming little hole-in-the-wall serving very good home-style comfort food in one of the city's most aristocratic and so most pecunious neighborhoods.

I've since been back many times, including this gorgeous April day, when I popped in alone and polished off oeufs mayonnaise (hard-boiled eggs dressed with mayonnaise), asparagus vinaigrette, and chicken in a lemony chive sauce on tagliatelle. Solitary diners are welcomed, and I ate this excellent lunch sitting across from a perfect stranger who broke my musing on why oeufs mayonnaise, one of the homeliest of all French comfort foods, is always served as three halves of egg when he charmingly told me that I could finish the rest of his wine if I liked.

If an anthropologist was looking for the ideal setting in which to study the way that the French relate to each other and food in public settings, he or she could do no better than this place, where everyone is skilled at the art of creating both privacy and conviviality in a small, shared space. Otherwise, it's just about as close as you can get to tasting homey old-fashioned French home cooking without being invited to dinner by a Parisian. And if I'm still some years out of port from being invited to take advantage of the rond de serviettes, or wooden napkin rack where the regulars once stored their napkins between meals, I've graduated to being greeted by the harmlessly ornery waitress as "Notre ami americain" ("our American friend"). P.S., they've recently opened a branch restaurant in the 6th Arrondissement, and it has a similarly winning atmosphere and solid, tasty French home cooking as the maison mere.

· ✿ ·

IN A WORD: A meal at this tiny cubbyhole in the Faubourg Saint-Germain is like having a comforting pantry supper prepared by an old family retainer—think the real vieille France cooking favored by the local aristocrats.

DON'T MISS: lentil salad; duck gizzard salad; oeufs mayonnaise; confit de canard; sautéed chicken livers; crème caramel.

· · ·

[103] 45 rue de Babylone, 7th, 01.47.05.12.27. MÉTRO: Saint-François-Xavier. OPEN Monday to Saturday for lunch and dinner. CLOSED Sunday.
▪ $

[104] 3 rue Saint Benoit, 6th, 01.42.96.59.10. MÉTRO: Saint-Germain-des-Pres. OPEN Monday to Saturday for lunch and dinner. CLOSED Sunday. ▪ $

Le Pré Verre

A FEW BLOCKS FROM THE SORBONNE, LE PRÉ VERRE IS AN excellent and very popular restaurant that pulls a more authentic Latin Quarter crowd than almost any other in this most famous neighborhood of the 5th Arrondissement. A scattering of solitary local diners is always a good sign, and here there are more than a few earnest types taking time off from their doctoral studies over a good meal with *Le Monde* for company, folded like origami flanking their plates. Worldly wise soixante-huitards, or "68ers," as the French call the rebellious students who hurled paving stones in the Latin Quarter in 1968 and ushered in a new era in Paris sociology and sensibility, dominate this dining room, a lightly redecorated corner café with limestone floors, nubby orange-and-gray-tweed banquettes, and some modern art on the walls. Unknowingly at the time, these young rebels ushered in a decisively fructive transformation of French cooking, at once insisting on les produits du terroir, organic traditional French produce, and the spices and flavors they'd discovered while backpacking through Asia and North Africa, and more than any other restaurant in Paris, Le Pré Verre has reset the pendulum on soixante-huitard culinary sensibilities to create some really superb contemporary French food.

What I love about Philippe and Marc Delacourcelle's restaurant, though, is that in addition to the hippie priorities of health, wholesomeness, and exoticism, they've booted up this politically correct food with a sassy attention to texture and a playful use of contrasting tones of acidity, much of it originating in

Philippe's deep knowledge of Asian cooking. If my Scottish friend David's warm watercress soup with crab was first-rate comfort food during my last meal there, my blanc-manger aux asperges was really brilliant, a small white disc of curdy lactic cream and crumbled cheese with the bite of wine-marinated mustard seeds, an asparagus aspic, and fine shavings of asparagus punctuated by a sundried tomato. Our main courses were first-rate, too—David had a lamb filet, cooked perfectly rare and served with a vivid garnish of preserved North African lemon and that most PC of grains, the high-protein Peruvian quinoa, which is often offered as an explanation for the genius of Incan engineering. My pièce de boeuf, or steak, was rare and delicious, with a topping of finely diced ginger, a lemony garnish of Swiss chard, and a delicious sauce of deglazed pan drippings. We loved our desserts, too—his, olive oil and almond essence ice cream with dried fruit; mine, a truffade of dark chocolate (a fudgelike cake) with molasses ice cream. Chewy, yeasty slices of baguette from Eric Kayser's nearby bakery filled the regularly replenished bread basket, and from an excellent and very fairly priced wine list, we started with a glass of sparkling Vouvray and then moved on to an excellent Beaume de Venise. I only wish that this restaurant was within walking distance of my apartment in the 9th Arrondissement instead of on the Left Bank, so that I could be a regular.

· ·

IN A WORD: This popular Latin Quarter bistro offers a regularly changing chalkboard menu of excellent contemporary French dishes, a first-rate selection of fairly priced wines, and swift, friendly service. The Latin Quarter sensibility of the liberal, well-traveled, cosmopolitan clientele is reflected by the frequent and innovative use of organic produce and foreign ingredients.

DON'T MISS: Blanc-manger aux asperges (fresh cheese flan with asparagus); escabèche de sardines (marinated raw sardines) with eggplant; roast suckling pig; marinated salmon with ginger and poppy seeds; potato and foie gras pressé (layered foie gras and potatoes); cod with cassia bark and smoked sweet potato puree; roast duck with tamarind and fennel; lamb filet with quinoa and preserved lemon; pièce du boeuf with ginger and Swiss chard; roast figs with olives; olive oil and almond essence ice cream with dried fruit; truffade of dark chocolate (fudgelike cake) with molasses ice cream.

. . .

[29] 8 rue Thénard, 5th, 01.43.54.59.47. MÉTRO: Maubert-Mutualité. OPEN Tuesday to Friday for lunch and dinner. Saturday dinner only. CLOSED Sunday and Monday. www.lepreverre.com ▪ $$

L'Epigramme

THOUGH I OFTEN TELL FRIENDS THEY'LL HAVE TO TRAVEL from their preferred Left Bank perches to outlying arrondissements to find really good, well-priced bistros in Paris, many of them persist in thinking that there must be a wonderful little bistro just around the corner from their hotels in Saint-Germain-des-Prés. The sorry reality is that the gentrification of this most mythical part of the city has made it impossibly expensive for talented young restaurateurs to set up shop here and that the locals, including innumerable foreigners with infrequently occupied pied-à-terre apartments in the neighborhood, are often happy to settle for some conveniently close sushi or a plate of pasta.

Just steps from the Odéon, L'Epigramme is a happy exception, which is why I chose it as the venue for two very different recent lunches. The first was a meeting with the president and the alumni director of Amherst College, my alma mater, and the second was as the setting for one of the invariably strange if always tender lunches I have with a Gaul who taught me to eat.

On a soft Indian summer afternoon the day after *Gourmet* had closed, all I really wanted to do was stay in bed with a good novel and a cup of tea. The abrupt silencing of an American cultural icon and the magazine for which I'd so happily worked for ten years had been a blow, and I wasn't feeling especially social. The appointment with President Marx and his colleague had been made weeks earlier, however, and respectful of their busy visit to Paris, I put on the hair shirt of a prickly tweed jacket—a matter of small New England liberal arts college oblige—and set off for lunch.

Within a few minutes of arriving at this cozy little place with upholstered chairs at well-spaced tables, and exposed stone walls decorated with contemporary art, I found my spirits lifted by the warm hospitality of owner Stéphane Marcuzzi, a real pro who previously worked for Guy Savoy, and the nourishing conversation of a pair of warm, literate, friendly Americans. Marcuzzi immediately offered us an hors d'oeuvre of a savory game pâté, the debut of an excellent meal that included a delicious broccoli soup; pig's feet croquette on a bed of lentils with red peppers; braised duck with sauerkraut and pollack with a fennel bulb compote. Since I wanted a good meal that would prove the ongoing gastronomic credentials of Paris without making too much of a hole in the college's finances, L'Epigramme was just the ticket.

Two weeks later, I was back for a meal with the psychiatrist from Orléans who'd been my landlord for the five years I occupied one of my favorite Parisian homes, a large, draughty apartment with creaking floors, some stunning antiques, and a prehistoric kitchen on a chic street in the 7th Arrondissement. I'd rented through an agency and never given any thought to the owner until a chilly September night when the doorbell rang and I found a short blond woman in a well-tailored tweed suit who explained she was in Paris for the apartment's co-op meeting. I'd been sitting by the fire sipping sherry and reading Céline's *Voyage au Bout de la Nuit* when she interrupted me.

Her head cocked when she saw the book. "You read Céline?" "I'm trying," I replied, and I was, in the hopes of improving my French and because my grandmother had liked him. "Very admirable, and you're drinking good sherry, too," she said and smiled as if she hadn't really noticed me before. "If it's not too presumptuous, might I invite you to dinner after our meeting is over, perhaps in an hour's time?" Fortunately, I didn't then know she was a psychiatrist, or I might have found the courage to say no, especially in view of my rather rickety emotional state in those days.

Instead, during the first of our occasional meals together, I discovered tripes à la mode Caen (cooked in cider) in a charming but now defunct bistro and listened, intrigued and horrified, as Madame explained why she despised her mother and was divorcing her husband. "The greatest pleasures in my life are good food and good wine," she said when we were served, and it was on the foundation of these shared passions that one of my oddest but most interesting friendships was founded.

Mme. Shrink, as she is amused to call herself, doesn't like to spend a lot of money but is a demanding epicurean, so for our last meeting I booked dinner at L'Epigramme. She'd already eaten all of the pork rillettes and radishes by the time I arrived, and then we feasted on young chef Aymeric Kraml's pig's ear terrine with lentils, artichoke velouté, suckling pig with pickled turnip slaw, wild sea bass with baby vegetables, Saint-Nectaire cheese, and Grand Marnier soufflé. Then the shrink passed her verdict. "That was very good, and it's à la minute (cooked-to-order food). Almost no one does cuisine mijoté (simmered dishes) anymore, and oh do we need it these days, because it's maternal and loving. Unfortunately, it takes time, and almost no one can afford that now. Still, I'll be back. I like this place very much." And so do I.

· 🐟 ·

IN A WORD: A very good modern French bistro in the heart of Saint-Germain-des-Prés where young talent Aymeric Kraml, who trained with Bocuse, Ducasse, and Piège, does an appealing, regularly changing market menu.

DON'T MISS: The menu changes often, but I've loved the carpaccio of tête de veau, fresh mackerel with leek terrine, artichoke velouté, grouse with autumn fruits, roast cod with fork-mashed potatoes, and pain perdu with poached fruit.

· · ·

[23] **L'Epigramme**, 9 rue de l'Eperon, 6th, 01.44.41.00.09. MÉTRO: **Odéon.** OPEN **Tuesday to Saturday for lunch and dinner.** CLOSED **Sunday and Monday.** ▪ **$$**

Le Ribouldingue

THE NAME OF THIS AMIABLE LITTLE BISTRO IN ONE OF THE prettiest streets in the Latin Quarter means "The Binge," but this binge is decidedly French, since the menu offers an offal feast that tends to gall those who aren't Gauls. Think extreme eating, as in groin de cochon (the tip of the pig's muzzle, or the fleshy bit with nostrils), tétines de vache (thin, panfried slices of cow's udder), brains, kidneys, liver, and other organs likely to cause even some adventurous eaters to shudder.

To be sure, chef Guy Bommefront and Nadège Varigny, who worked for many years at La Régalade when it belonged to chef Yves Camdeborde, wouldn't stay in business long if everything on their menu promised an Outward Bound experience on a plate. When my friend Peter, a Scottish antiques dealer whose father was a butcher in Glasgow, came to town with his wife, Violet, she reacted with almost delirious relief and then with real pleasure to her main course of beef cheeks braised in red wine and served with macaroni—from her point of view this was the least horrifying dish on the menu. "This is delicious, although I can barely stand to sit at the same table with the two of you. I mean, really, you can't pretend you actually like eating all of that rubbish, can you?" Well, yes. Peter has no fear of any part of any animal, and though I was hardly to the gizzard born, over twenty years of living in France I've developed a taste for such proverbial nose wrinklers as brains, kidneys, and liver.

If you're more in Violet's camp than mine but vaguely curious, this is the best place in town to lose your offal virginity, since the quality of the produce is impeccable, and it's perfectly cooked and brilliantly seasoned. Interested? Even a little? Let me suggest two delicious dishes that are unlikely to cause a bloodcurdling scream: a starter of carpaccio of calf's head with a nicely made sauce gribiche (a tangy vinaigrette with chopped hard-boiled egg, cornichons, and capers) and perfectly roasted veal kidneys with a side of gratin dauphinois (potatoes baked with onions and cream). You can revert to chicken breasts when you get home, so why not take a walk on the wild side while you're in Paris? And if more encouragement's needed, the tarte Tatin is sublime—"I'd even willingly fight my way through some of the nasty business on the menu for another slice of this" was Violet's judgment—as is the homemade pot-de-crème, a light, creamy chocolate custard.

. . .

IN A WORD: The best place in Paris to eat something offal, as in kidneys, tripe, liver, brains, and other bits and pieces inhospitably described as offcuts.

DON'T MISS: Carpaccio of calf's head; roasted veal kidneys; beef cheeks braised in red wine; sautéed lamb's brains; tarte Tatin; pot-de-crème.

. . .

[30] 10 rue Saint-Julien-le-Pauvre, 5th, 01.46.33.98.80. MÉTRO: Saint-Michel. OPEN Monday to Friday for lunch and dinner. Saturday dinner only. CLOSED Sunday. • $$

Le Timbre

EVEN IF THE MANCHESTER-BORN CHEF CHRIS WRIGHT'S cooking weren't so good, who'd ever forget having a meal in the same tiny dining room as Marianne Faithfull? On a beautiful spring night, the rock-and-roll goddess occupied a corner table in this minuscule place—*le timbre* is French for "postage stamp," and after all of us had been listening to a sozzled American stewardess recounting a torrid layover in Barcelona, the legend's table mate had a word with her.

"It all sounds delicious, dear, but unless you're making a public confession, you might want to lower your voice."

Midway between Montparnasse and Saint-Germain right in the heart of the Left Bank, Wright's place is ideal for a relaxed, homey meal of first-rate market cooking. His blackboard menu of four starters, four main courses, and four desserts changes weekly, and he prides himself on the quality of his produce—his fish comes from the famous Poissonerie du Dôme in Montparnasse and sparingly used foie gras and truffles from Le Comptoir Corrézien, a speciality shop in the 15th Arrondissement that furnishes many of the city's top tables with these two signature luxuries. Wright also hunts down unusual wines, including the deliciously flinty white Argentinean bottle we chose to accompany first courses of smoked duck breast salad with a citrus vinaigrette and green asparagus in an anise-spiked cream sauce with a few drops of balsamic vinegar and Parmesan shavings. Main courses of daube de boeuf au vin rouge (beef braised in red wine) and trout topped with shavings of country ham and garnished with fava beans were equally satisfying and had a similar homemade sincerity. In a nod to his native Albion, Wright serves excellent cheeses from Neal's Yard in London, including Stilton and Cheddar, and desserts run to fruit crumbles and soups or purees of fresh fruit. All told, a charming place for a relaxed, affordably priced feast.

· ⸻ ·

IN A WORD: This is an intimate bistro de chef that pulls a stylish, young, international crowd with a friendly atmosphere and homey but imaginative cooking.

DON'T MISS: Brandade de haddock (haddock shepherd's pie); tartines de légumes (country-bread toasts topped with fresh vegetables); guinea hen with tomato and pineapple chutney; millefeuille with vanilla cream; strawberry soup.

. . .

[39] 3 rue Sainte-Beuve, 6th, 01.45.49.10.40. MÉTRO: **Vavin.** OPEN **Tuesday to Saturday for lunch and dinner.** CLOSED **Sunday and Monday. www .restaurantletimbre.com • $$**

Le Voltaire

SOMEONE DESERVES A GOOD-SISTER AWARD. "DAD, HE loves you, it's just that he doesn't love your life, and I hope you don't mind if I say this, but instead of just cutting off his allowance, I think the best thing might be to invest in his furniture-making business like a disinterested partner," said the beautiful young blonde, a modern Gibson girl, dining with her parents at the corner table next to us. "That's a constructive idea, darling," said Mom, which left Dad cornered. "Well, maybe. Let me think about it. I just can't get my mind around the idea of anyone dropping out of college to make furniture in the middle of nowhere in Maine," said Dad, serving himself another glass of Bordeaux, a libation that made me optimistic for the wayward New England woodworker.

Few places in Paris offer a more intriguing sociological tapestry than this silk-stocking bistro on the Left Bank of the Seine in Saint-Germain. It's a clubby old place with wood-paneled walls and faded raspberry velvet banquettes, but the global gratin who love it are the same cast who made Truman Capote their lapdog and who tolerate miscellaneous deviance as the necessary fodder for that most essential of social lubricants: gossip. And thanks to these cultivated, tolerant types, most of whom are American, this place has an indestructible buzz, which comes from the fact that everyone feels comfortable here.

When I was a writer working in the Paris office of Fairchild Publications, I was a semiregular, and I never come here without thinking of the dinner or two I had here with Mr. Fairchild, one of the shrewdest old-fashioned newspapermen I've ever met and a daring judge of character with a curiously bashful Machiavellian streak. A bad boy with good manners and famous social antennae, he could never resist pulling the tail of any passing sacred cow and was never afraid to call a spade a spade. In his wake, we staffers frequented this place in search of the casual social crumbs that might make good copy, but during these meals as stalker, I rarely noticed the food. In fact, it wasn't until I'd left the fold and came back here on my own that I realized how good the kitchen actually is and how much fun it is to dine here.

To be sure, you don't come to Le Voltaire for cutting-edge dining but rather first-rate old-fashioned French comfort food, a great crowd, and superb old-school service. If the Italian equivalent of this place is Harry's Bar in Venice, the only American restaurants I've ever been to that approximate it are what Lock-Ober in Boston was when I was a child or, in New York, the now-defunct Gloucester House, the New York Athletic Club, and the Four Seasons restaurant in the Seagram's Building, but if the Gloucester House served better-than-average seafood and the Four Seasons has its moments, none of this quartet has a patch on the Voltaire as a purring, flattering machine that creates evanescent luxury.

The oeuf mayonnaise on the menu at 90 centimes may be its tongue-in-cheek equivalent of a John D. Rockefeller shiny ten-cent tip, but during my last meal here, I pounced on the poached eggs in sorrel sauce, a vieille France dish I first experienced when I was invited to Sunday supper by my landlady, a turban-wearing French countess, and landlord, a retired British diplomat, when I lived in the rue Monsieur, a short, chic street in the 7th Arrondissement where Rockefeller would have felt right at home. It's basically baby food, but I loved the sour metallic taste of sorrel, and the perfectly coddled eggs were glazed with a pellucid layer of Gruyère. My antique-dealer friend Olivier had beet and apple salad, which arrived in a pretty, round fan, and then we went for the meat. My sublime filet of beef with real béarnaise sauce came with pureed potatoes and carrots, nursing home fodder that I ignored while plundering the perfect shoe-string fries, some of the best in Paris, that came with Olivier's pert pyramid of steak tartare. The waiter brought us more frites without our asking, and when I finally took a stab at the tartare, it was impeccable, with high notes of Worcestershire sauce and Tabasco and discernible chunks of caper or cornichons (puck-ery French gherkins). Fat black cherries poached in red wine with vanilla beans, orange slices, cardamom, stick cinnamon, and mint were succulent and delicious, and the waiter gra-ciously gave both of us plates and silverware even though only Olivier had ordered them. The wine list here is a bore, and the bread should be better, but this reflexively chic hospitality means that I always look forward to a meal here.

Walking home on a balmy night, I mused on the odd but eternal connection between bohemia and the bourgeoisie sig-naled at Le Voltare by the amiably ugly and now priceless fifties-vintage Vallauris ceramics hanging on the back wall and was delighted to have found that this place is what it's always been, which is a bistro wearing Mary Janes.

· 🔺 ·

IN A WORD: Not only does this Left Bank bistro in business for more than sixty years have a stainless-steel chic created by soigné service and a stylish international clientele, the food is surprisingly good. Whether you're casting a romantic tête-à-tête, casual dinner with friends, late lunch on a rainy afternoon, or important business dinner, this place is a perfect one-size-fits-all Paris restaurant. Just come prepared for your plastic to take a beating, and don't expect gastronomic revelations but rather a solidly good Gallic feed.

DON'T MISS: Salad of haricots verts, artichoke hearts, and foie gras; salad of button mushrooms in lemon and olive oil vinaigrette with Parmesan shavings; poached eggs with sorrel; beef bouillon; crab salad; sole meunière; filet mignon with béarnaise sauce; tête de veau (calf's head); poached cherries with fresh mint; peaches poached in wine; chocolate mousse.

· · ·

[48] **27 quai Voltaire, 7th, 01.42.61.17.49.** MÉTRO: **Rue du Bac.** OPEN **Tuesday to Saturday for lunch and dinner.** CLOSED **Sunday and Monday.**
· **$$$**

Ze Kitchen Galerie

CHEF WILLIAM LEDEUIL IS NOT ONLY MOVIE-STAR HANDsome, he knows how to cook, which is why his offbeat Left

Bank restaurant with an unfortunate franglais name is an ongo-
ing hit with the gratin—antiques dealers, artists, book editors,
journalists, and celebs—of Saint-Germain-des-Prés. In fact, on
any given night, the crowd looks as though it could have just
moved en masse from a local gallery opening just a few minutes
earlier—think women with severe haircuts and lots of large ethnic jewelry and men with close-cropped beards and the classic
outfit of the good-boy, bad-boy Gallic playboy, a well-cut blazer
with a white shirt, jeans, and expensive shoes. Ledeuil adds further visual interest to the scene in the loftlike dining room with
an open window on the kitchen by employing many Frenchmen
of color—in a silk-stocking Paris neighborhood like this one, it
is still surprising to see a nonwhite face, which is revealing of
the way the French capital remains sociologically cloistered.

Settled at your rust-colored steel table with a sound-
blunting block of foam affixed beneath, you'll relax into an af-

fluent contemporary take on bohemian Paris with parquet floors, exposed pillars, and contemporary art on the walls. Ledeuil's menu is as refreshingly unconventional as his dining room, since it's organized with original and slightly puzzling subheads—instead of the traditional slugs of starters, main courses, and desserts, the menu here is organized according to Les Bouillons (soups), Les Pâtes (pastas), Les Poissons (fish), and so on.

What these menu categories don't tell is that Ledeuil is obsessed by the flavors of Southeast Asia and is one of the most accomplished practitioners of bona fide fusion cooking in Paris today. After winning a hot reputation as the launch chef at Les Bouquinistes, one of chef Guy Savoy's original and very influential "baby bistros" (offshoot tables of haute cuisine chefs that animated Parisian dining in the eighties) next door, he struck out on his own a few years back, to emerge as one of the nerviest chefs in Paris. Consider a starter of maloreddus (rolled durum-wheat flour Sardinian gnocchi) in a foam of coconut milk scented with lime leaves and sprinkled with shredded Spanish chorizo sausage and Mimolette cheese from the north of France. This is a fascinating and successful dish, since the sweetness of the coconut milk meets the lactic freshness of the cheese, with the al dente pasta offering a lot of mouth feel, unexpected at stylish Parisian restaurants, where pasta textures often run to mashed and molle (soft). Similarly, another starter of chewy bulots (sea snails) in a lemongrass-and-basil-spiked broth also offers a meaty mouth feel at pleasant odds with the gentle flavors most often associated in Thai cooking with noodles or braised seafood and fowl. Ledeuil's ravioli filled with pork, coriander, and galangal root (a rhizome that's a relative of ginger) and garnished with a condiment of artichokes and wasabi are a brilliant mixing of Asian metaphors, as is octopus with a marinade of green apple juice and fennel and superb veal cheeks with udon noodles and a Thai jus made with lime leaves, ginger, and lemongrass.

Not all of Ledeuil's ideas work—if scallops on a skewer of lemongrass are delicious, "tamarind-lacquered" veal sweetbreads lack the astringent punch that the gum from these seedpods usually offers. There's also no cheese course, for me a serious shortcoming in a country as gifted in the art of milk as France, and desserts are less interesting than the starters and main courses. Still, the wine list is excellent, and Ledeuil continues to push out the boundaries of contemporary French cooking with a fascinating hybrid kitchen that's all his own.

· 🙂 ·

IN A WORD: When a classically trained French chef develops a passion for Asia, the result is contemporary French fusion at its very best. Stylish, relaxed, and a lot of fun, this is a perfect address for anyone who wants a meal off from traditional French cooking.

DON'T MISS: Gazpacho of red beets with ginger; shrimp and cucumber with Thai herbs; moloreddus (pasta) in coconut milk with chorizo sausage and Mimolette cheese; green asparagus with Buratta (a creamy cheese from Puglia in Italy) croquettes; grilled lamb with lemongrass jus and kumquats; cappuccino of strawberries, pistachios, and lemongrass.

. . .

[40] 4 rue des Grands-Augustins, 6th, 01.44.32.00.32. MÉTRO: Saint-Michel. OPEN Monday to Friday for lunch and dinner. Saturday dinner only. CLOSED Sunday. www.zekitchengalerie.fr · $$$

TABLE FOR ONE

LEARNING TO EAT ALONE IN PUBLIC WAS ONE OF THE
hardest but most valuable things I've ever done. Why? Because
it freed me from the pitying or censorious judgments I once
projected into the eyes of total strangers ("Gosh, what a loser
that guy must be to be having dinner alone," etc.), and now
there's not a restaurant in the world that's off limits to me.
Growing out of the self-consciousness of being alone in public
isn't easy, but if I can do it, so can you. All it takes is a sense of
humor and lots of practice.

The first time I ate alone in a restaurant wasn't by choice. I'd
been traveling in Europe with a friend when he was called back
to New York a few days early to audition for a play.

At first I panicked—maybe I'd go home early, too. Then the
embarrassment of having everyone know I'd chickened out of
traveling solo shamed me into staying behind. As someone who
cares passionately about food, what really worried me, though,
was how I'd eat. Aside from many forgettable meals in fast-food
places and a New York City coffee shop or two, I'd reached my
early twenties without ever having had a meal alone in a real
restaurant. In fact, the idea was about as foreign as anything I
could imagine. If there was any way to avoid it, who in his right
mind would go to a restaurant alone?

Since I had friends in Paris, I was reprieved until I got to
Brussels, from where I was flying home. Maybe for the sake of
his own fun—many good hoteliers are voyeurs with a repressed

streak of sadism—the portly desk clerk with the wiry mutton-chop sideburns at the Hôtel Metropole, a looming old pile near a railroad station, put me in a honeymoon suite. It was a strange netherworld of rooms with an expectant erotic promise that I never lived up to, conveyed by a flesh-tone decor, lots of mirrors, and an Art Deco boudoir with pink lights. After the porter heaved my hated houndstooth-check tweed-sided American Tourister suitcase onto a luggage rack and left, the first thing I did was check the hotel information to see if they had room service. They did. But not on weekends. So I wandered around the city in a light drizzle eating all the street food I could find—crêpes, paper cones of frites (fries) with curried mayonnaise, and a nasty withered hot dog. After the Musée des Beaux-Arts, it started to pour, so I went to a movie, noticing as I went in at 6 P.M. that it was a three-hour film. My wobbly French meant I'd miss a lot, but I was buying time and vaguely hoped a jumbo bucket of popcorn would be the excuse for skipping dinner.

Two hours later, bored and hungry, I bolted out of the theater with salt-stung lips and became a stalker. Under an umbrella with two shot struts, I cruised by restaurant after restaurant, sizing them up and trying to summon the nerve to go in and ask for a table. Instinctively, I knew better than to try crowded, busy places, which meant, on a Saturday night near the Grand Place, that the pickings were slim. Cold, wet, and ravenous, I almost took the easy way out with a Chinese restaurant, a neutral option since I'd be a foreigner waited on by other foreigners, but I craved one of the Belgian specialties, maybe carbonnade de boeuf (beef braised with brown sugar in beer) or waterzooi (chicken and vegetables cooked in a cream sauce), that I'd salivated over in my guidebook. So I kept circling, and circling, until one of the barkers in a narrow pedestrian lane packed with ratty-looking Greek restaurants laughed at me, probably because he'd already seen me six times within an hour and recognized my predicament. I legged it down a side street and, peering through the tendrils of straggly philodendron in a diamond-paned window, I saw a man sitting alone at a table. I went in immediately.

"Une table pour une personne," I said to the bosomy hostess in a buttoned-up brown cardigan. She smiled vaguely and seated me along the exposed brick wall, lighting the candle in the middle of the table before handing me a menu. I almost snuffed the taper, which seemed to advertise my solitude, but then realized that it gave me something to focus on. I didn't dare look around until after I'd ordered my waterzooi, but when I did I was reassured by the sight of the other solo diner, an older man reading a magazine as he ate. Then I noticed that the table in front of him was also occupied by a solitary diner, as was one by the coat rack. As far as I could see, there was only one couple in the entire place. Everyone else was alone. I laughed out loud.

When he poured my wine, the waiter read my thoughts. "Eh oui, Monsieur, les gens seuls sont très bien chez nous." Since "seul" can mean either solo or lonely, I wasn't sure which he meant, but since I was well and truly both it didn't matter. What did was the way the sturdy rituals of the meal framed and tamed my anxiety. And then, as I settled in, it occurred to me that as far as everyone else in the room was concerned, I was doing something perfectly sensible, if maybe a little dull, which was to go into a restaurant and have a meal when I was hungry.

The food was unremarkable—I think the vegetables in the waterzooi may have even been canned—but everything else about that meal delighted me, including a fleeting linguistic puzzle. After the waiter had served my waterzooi, he shifted from French to the English he was likely studying and asked, "Have you any feather washers?"

"Feather washers?"

"Yes, feather washers."

"I'm sorry, I'm afraid I don't understand."

"I would like to satisfy your feather washers." Oh dear, things seemed to be taking a turn for the kinky. I smiled, shook my head, shrugged my shoulders.

"I really am so sorry. I don't understand."

Fortunately, he wasn't fazed. He wrote down the phrase on his pad and showed it to me: Further wishes.

"No, thank you very much, no feather washers." We shared a chuckle, but the dunce cap was clearly on my head, which was fine. I'd have been miserable if he'd been insulted or felt diminished.

In fact, I loved the seriousness conveyed by his black waistcoat and white apron, folded into sort of a cummerbund at the waist, and the way he promptly refilled my perforated metal bread basket and the reflexive "Bon appétit" that followed the arrival of each course. He greeted my decision to have cheese as proof of my admirable sagacity, and when I ordered a Cognac with my coffee, he summoned the hostess, who followed him to my table with a bottle and waited while he carefully centered a snifter the size of a goldfish bowl on a dopey little lace doily. Madame poured, and, after cocking her head to see that she'd been fair, she added another pour and trilled "À votre service" when I thanked her. What all of these cues taught me was that we were complicit in attempting to accomplish something we'd decided was of mutual importance—my pleasure at the table. Dining alone, I discovered on that rainy night in Brussels, was civilized and civilizing, and though I usually prefer company, there are times when I'm glad for the silence that allows the self-absorption that is one way of amplifying the pleasure of good food and wine.

As is true of most public pleasures in France, eating alone is an art to be learned and perfected. I wish I could claim that my Belgian triumph had left me prepared for a fresh round of solo supping when I arrived in Paris twenty years ago, but since the solution to solitary eating in most American cities remains sitting at a counter, I had to pick up where I'd left off. This time I knew no one and was living in a hotel without a restaurant, so aside from the takeaway lunches from a wonderful but now long-gone traiteur (a French take on the delicatessen) in the rue Cambon, across the street from where I worked—I still crave its delicious céleri rémoulade and succulent slices of the braised ham the owner roasted in the chimney of her girlhood home in the country on the weekends—I was up against it.

I had the major consolation of an expense account, however, and, after a few furtive suppers in cafés, I bought a guidebook and a new jacket, my college-vintage blazer being on its last legs, and doggedly set out to eat my way across Paris. I learned a lot of things about how to eat alone.

For starters, always make a reservation, dress well, go armed with a sense of humor, and never refuse the suggestion of an apéritif before dinner. If you don't want a glass of white wine or a flute of Champagne, order a Perrier (the French never drink hard liquor before a meal)—in Paris, by the way, this famous *eau* is drunk as an apéritif, not with food, *bien sûr*, because its large bubbles are reckoned to disturb the digestion. By having a drink you signal your server that you're not a skinflint and invite better service. Don't mumble or fidget, either—you're the rightful occupant of your table, and don't let anyone rush you. Bring a book or a magazine if you like, but stop reading once you're settled in and enjoy the show any decent restaurant also provides. Admittedly, single women can attract unwanted attention, but if someone tries to chat you up and you're not interested, send him packing by saying "Dégagez!" ("Get lost!"), and if that doesn't work, try "Je suis la cousine de George Bush." Refuse to be bullied, short-shrifted, or patronized, but be generous with smiles and compliments.

Ultimately, mastering the art of dining alone depends most upon cultivating the pleasure of your own company—good mental hygiene under any circumstances—and remembering that the Latin world generally casts a kindly eye on anyone in public pursuit of benign pleasures.

LA MADELEINE, CHAMPS-ÉLYSÉES

L'Abordage

ONE OF THE REASONS I LOVE LIVING IN A GREAT CITY IS that they're so propitious for unexpected encounters. This morning, I was sitting at my keyboard in an old T-shirt when my friend Charlotte, an Englishwoman who's been living in Bangkok and elsewhere in Asia for twenty years, called. She was en route to a funeral in the north of England, had the middle of the day free between planes, and wanted to know if we could have lunch. "Since I don't have much time, I'd like a fierce dose of Paris," she said, so I immediately booked us at L'Abordage and told her I'd be waiting on the terrace.

Across the street, the chestnut trees in the Parc Bergson had shed their white flowers, leaving only a long green wick at the center of the flat corsages formed by their serrated green leaves, and I found myself thinking that it was a view of this same lovely European greenery that the great French food critic Maurice Curnonsky enjoyed as he rested his gizzards and

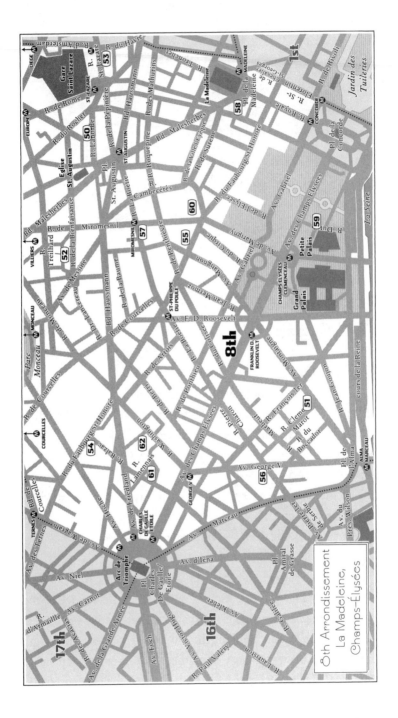

8th Arrondissement
La Madeleine,
Champs-Élysées

penned his jaunty, insightful reviews. As a bronze plaque indicates, the "prince des gastronomes" lived in a house across the way for many years, and I also couldn't help thinking that were he alive today, Curnonsky would surely have been a regular at this wonderful bistro just out his front door.

Arriving, it's not much to look at—just a long bar inside a dimly lit room with a cracked tile floor, some antique winemaking paraphernalia perched on the room divider, and then a second dining room that's equally plain if a bit brighter, but as I waited for Charlotte, it rapidly filled up with one of the sexiest crowds of power brokers to be found anywhere in Paris; bankers, brokers, politicians, newspaper people, PR and advertising people, almost all of them, both men and women, wearing beautifully cut suits. At noon, in fact, this place functions almost as a club of sorts, which is why I prefer to come on Wednesday, the only night it serves dinner and when it becomes the calmer province of discreet bourgeois couples; but I knew that Charlotte would find it fascinating, and there are very few places in town that do a better version of the basic primer of traditional French dishes.

As I rather expected, Charlotte, swathed in filmy Sri Lankan silks and wearing long, dangling Malaysian earrings, caused a stir when she arrived, and the waitress was plainly flabbergasted by her impeccable French. Desperate to get at some good French grub, she ordered marinated herring and grilled calf's liver, while I went with the chicken terrine and an entrecôte. "I say, isn't this a spot," she said, registering the human scenery. "All of these handsome men, a chalkboard menu, the smell of fried potatoes and good bread. This is exactly the Paris I miss when I'm sitting by the pool eating mangoes in Bangkok." She loved her marinated herring, and my chicken terrine, fresh and clearly homemade, was superb, with thick chunks of chicken and sliced carrot suspended in an aspic perfumed by fresh tarragon. Charlotte's liver came pink as ordered and was deglazed with Xérès vinegar, and my steak was tender and beautifully grilled. I almost never order entrecôtes in Paris, because they're often tough and fatty, but this was superb beef, full of flavor and very tender. We finished up with a brilliant baba au rhum, again homemade, for me and a Paris-Brest for Madame. "That was heaven," Charlotte said afterward while we walked to the café where she was meeting another friend, a Laotian princess, for coffee. "Exactly what I wanted, true French food with its proud quality and genius for simplicity," Charlotte concluded, and I'm certain that Curnonsky would have wholeheartedly agreed with her assessment of L'Abordage.

· ·

IN A WORD: With no decor to speak of, this clubby workaday bistro excels at a menu of French classics, which is why it's packed with one of the most intriguing Parisian power crowds in the city noon and night. Very few places take the basics as seriously as it does, with impeccable quality and cooking.

DON'T MISS: Oeufs mayonnaise; terrine de campagne; terrine de poulet; marinated herring; saumon tartare; côte de boeuf (rib steak) for two; côte de veau (veal chop) for two; calf's liver; entrecôte; Paris-Brest; crème brûlée; baba au rhum.

· · ·

[50] 2 place Henri-Bergson, 8th, 01.45.22.15.49. MÉTRO: Saint-Augustin. Lunch served Monday to Friday. Dinner only on Wednesday. CLOSED Saturday and Sunday. · **$$**

Alain Ducasse au Plaza-Athénée

APRIL, AND THE FALLEN APPLE BLOSSOMS ON THE SMALL terrace in front of the borrowed Provençal farmhouse where I've come from Paris to work look like pink confetti. If I'd had a pocketful of these pastel dots, I'd have thrown them around the dining room of Restaurant Alain Ducasse last week in Paris, because it's been a long time since I've had such a spectacular meal.

To be blunt, I've known Ducasse for years, and if I've al-

ways respected his professional acumen, recently I've been ag-
onizing over his transformation from chef into sort of a mega-
lomaniacal global gastro-entrepreneur. I didn't mind when he
came to Paris to duel with Joël Robuchon, whose three-star
restaurant Jamin was then considered the best table in town, or
when, after opening his instantly successful haute cuisine table,
he followed with Spoon, his once nervy showcase for contemporary cooking. He clearly had the resources and the talent to
run the Louis XV, his ethereal home base in Monte Carlo, and
take on Paris too, but as the empire grew, I started to have my
doubts.

In Reims last winter, a cabdriver confided that the locals
were feeling flat over the fact that both of the Champagne capital's most acclaimed tables were staffed by Ducasse-trained
chefs. "In a small city, you don't want to eat just Ducasse," he
explained, and I agreed with him. Albeit higher than highbrow,
how is Ducasse's organization, which now runs tables in London, Las Vegas, Tokyo (two), Mauritius, Beirut, and New York,
among other compass points, really any different in its basic
aims from McDonald's or Kentucky Fried Chicken? Aren't all
of these organizations gunning for the same end result—an unfailingly reliable, highly recognizable, quality product?

Perhaps my greatest uneasiness came from the way the Ducassian enterprise seemed to play large with the handmade traditions of what it means to be a chef. I kept thinking of brilliant,
passionate chefs like Pierre Gagnaire in Paris, Michel Bras in
the Auvergne, Sophie Pic in Valence, and Olivier Roellinger in
Brittany, and how they break backs and brains daily in their own
kitchens in a quest for originality and excellence. Isn't this what
it means to be a chef? Is a Manet a Manet if it was painted by a
student of Manet? Of course not. But on the other hand, with-

out a great general, an army is just a crowd of frightened men. . . .

And then last Wednesday, when I went to lunch at Ducasse's Parisian outpost at the Hotel Plaza-Athénée, this tetchy internal debate of mine was snuffed out for good as I finally understood the genius of the Ducasse academy, and it really is an academy. Denis Courtiade, solid, gallant, and knowing, which makes him the best maître d'hôtel in the city, led us to our table under the deconstructed Tinker Bell chandeliers of the designer Patrick Jouin (individual pieces of cut crystal suspended on invisible threads surround a classical chandelier, creating a sort of magical luminous wake overhead), and what followed was a meal so exquisite that four hours disappeared with stunning alacrity— why does life always move so quickly when you're enjoying it most?

First, the service, a true palace-style service, or service du palais, as the French call it, but softened by the fact that in this post-Freudian age, decent people subscribe to the democracy of lives, which means acceding to the idea that the person serving you is your equal. At Ducasse, this is strung just right, too, since the smart, good-looking waiters have the posture of cadets and the emotional acumen of therapists. Ducasse understands that modern luxury is customized service, invisibly and instantly tailored to suit the occasion without ever losing its precision or the vital element of a certain reverential reserve; graduates of the Ducasse academy get this just right, which is why the experience that Bruno and I had at lunch was entirely different from that meted out to the airplane builder Serge Dassault, presiding opposite the Saudi Arabian ambassador at a long table across the dining room. They were accorded the reverence and distance appropriate to important dignitaries, while our waiter was warm, gracious, and entirely complicit in our desire to have a superb meal.

To accompany the Champagne, a Ducassian classic: langoustines napped with a lick of cream and a dainty dollop of Ossetra caviar. The message of this dish was simplicity, since this miniature in tones of sweet and saline met the faint maltiness in the Cuvée Spéciale Alain Ducasse with a delicacy that quietly underlined all of these flavors. Then, a gustatory spring posey from chef Christophe Moret, a Ducasse protégé who worked at Spoon before donning one of the most prestigious toques in Paris and taking over the kitchen here two years ago. Served in a martini glass, the royale, or fine custard, of asparagus was capped with buttery foam and miniature matchsticks of truffle, a teasing garnish that hinted at the layer of truffle puree below. Quiet, refined, rich, almost neutral, but profoundly nuanced, it was the perfect bridge between seasons, the end of winter and the welcome, racing arrival of spring.

Having decided to drink by the glass, we gave the sommelier carte blanche, and his first choice, a Muscat Sec Domaine Peyronnet, was brilliant for adding the missing floral notes to Moret's posey. It also met a first course of alabaster-like scallops in curried coconut milk beautifully, elongating the curry and adding a tropical freshness to the coconut. I was surprised by this dish, which seemed, in the context of French haute cuisine, daringly exotic. It was delicious, but was it selling? "People are surprised by it, and that's the idea," replied Courtiade. "Our menu is composed in the hope that everyone will find their pleasure. There are haute cuisine classics, and there are more contemporary dishes." Of course, a perfect diplomat always lets you draw your own conclusions, and my supposition that the classic preparations were more popular was met with a Mandarin's grin.

Bar de ligne, line-caught wild sea bass, came in a pretty green spring robe of asparagus emulsion, petit pois jus, and tiny fava beans, and it was sweet and lovely like a crush on a grade school teacher. A square chunk of sole with an added spine of garlicky crumbs running its length sat in a silky marine-tasting marinière dotted with tiny clams, whelks, barnacles, and squid carved into tiny rolled "flowers" thrilled with its taut flesh and frank taste. I thought of the famous French cook Escoffier, who said, "Cooking becomes genius when things taste of what they are," and the famous Parisian food critic Curnonsky describing the superiority of Lyonnais cuisine: "Here cooking reached the apex in art, that is to say: simplicity."

More than any Parisian chef, with the possible exception of Joël Robuchon, Ducasse understands the chimera of simplicity. For him, culinary simplicity has a seriousness, an urgency, and a complexity that goes way beyond his oft-quoted and rather glib media mantras, "Fusion leads to confusion" and "More than four ingredients in a dish, and it becomes confused." Ducasse, like Robuchon, is a composer. Following Ducassian logic, a dish should be composed in much the same way that a song or a painting is composed, which is by allowing the imagination to be guided by the discipline of good taste—in culinary terms, the natural equilibrium of taste as dictated by our palettes and olfactory sense. This may sound obvious, even simple, but delivering someone to the highest plane of culinary pleasure is anything but. For this to happen, a meal must be profoundly well composed on both the micro and macro levels. An amazing feat for any restaurant when the master himself is present daily, it's even more spectacular when the master makes only an occasional appearance. To wit, Alain Ducasse is surely one of the most brilliant teachers of gastronomy who's ever lived.

Consider the segue of our lunch by Christophe Moret, Ducasse élève extraordinaire. After the fish course, I had a ris de veau à la ménagère (cooked as a housewife would, which is to say seasoned with salt and pepper, rolled in flour, and sautéed in melted butter), a sublime dish coyly masquerading under a name implying homeliness and modesty, since the veal sweetbread was crispy without and creamy within, no mean feat. Bruno had a still life of Limousin lamb, a few ribs, and a miniature saddle, surrounded by doll-sized spring vegetables. Cheeses by maître fromager Bernard Antony, a giggly man who lives in a tiny town in Alsace with a perfect climate for aging cheese, and the Parisian cheese merchant Marie-Ann Cantin couldn't be passed up, and the sommelier was instantly on hand to serve a small pour of vin jaune and suggest that it should be sipped with the Vieux Comté, an extra-aged Comté, a nutty cow's milk cheese from the eastern Jura region of France. The combination caused such a potent shudder of pleasure in a public place that most people would have blushed; I didn't.

I hope it isn't unseemly for me to confess that I'd been looking forward to a single dessert, my favorite one in the whole world, throughout the entire meal. In French: caillé de brebis, caramel poivré, miel d'arbousier (fresh ewe's milk cheese, peppered caramel, strawberry tree honey). If you've ever sniffed your way around an old Pall Mall club, you'll know these scents—leather, tobacco, must, musk, and the skin of a very elderly man or a newborn baby, all of which turn up in this dessert, which is a breathtaking constellation of tastes. Simultaneously prim and primal, this dish offers exactly the sensual equilibrium one dreams of finding at the end of a long and very expensive meal.

Often when I read about other people's wonderful meals, they stop before describing the part of the experience I consider almost as vital and nearly as much fun as the actual event—the wake of the meal, the Cinderella-like aftermath during which you tease over the details of everything you ate, committing the best to permanent memory or puzzling over some evanescent trail of taste. Sitting at my computer at dusk on a pale lilac-colored southern French evening, I contemplate supper—a few spears of asparagus I found growing wild in the apple orchards that surround me and a jar of Jean Martin brand pistou heated and poured over some pasta—and though I'm sure it'll be fine, what I'm really craving are the three purloined caramels—salted caramel, pistachio and saffron, and apricot and passion fruit—that rode off the premises of Restaurant Alain Ducasse in my coat pocket. Not only will they be delicious, they'll prove that this wonderful meal actually happened.

· ☙ ·

IN A WORD: The model for French haute cuisine in the twenty-first century. As perfect a setting in which to propose marriage as it is to launch a more lowly but hopefully fructive corporate merger. To wit, come here for the great occasions of life, and the great occasions of business.

DON'T MISS: Langoustines with crème fraîche and Ossetra caviar; coquilles Saint-Jacques snackées coco-curry (scallops in curried coconut milk); araignée de mer (spidercrab) with emulsified coral; ris de veau jus garniture truffée (veal sweetbreads in truffled pan juices); turbot aux crevettes grises (turbot with gray shrimp); caillé de brebis, caramel poivré, miel d'arboustier; baba au rhum comme à Monte Carlo (sponge pastry in rum syrup with whipped cream).

. . .

[51] Hôtel Plaza-Athénée, 25 avenue Montaigne, 8th, 01.53.67.65.00, MÉTRO: Alma Marceau. OPEN Thursday and Friday for lunch and dinner. Monday, Tuesday, and Wednesday dinner only. CLOSED Saturday and Sunday. www.alain-ducasse.com ▪ $$$$

La Cave Beauvau

ON A NIGHT WHEN AN AUTUMN RAIN HAS APPLIQUÉD THE shiny black trottoirs (sidewalks) of Paris with slippery but beautiful golden and bronze leaves, I arrive at La Cave Beauvau before my friends, order a glass of pleasantly flinty white Touraine wine and a small plate of Serrano ham at the bar, and savor a private moment of leisure in public, indulging in the pleasure of people watching and paddling around in my own random, idyllic thoughts. On this Friday, the front bar is lined with short dark men in dark suits with that pinched and uncomfortable-looking French cut that comes from small, high armholes; a couple of bawdy types in tweed jackets and corduroy trousers, whom I correctly guess to be winemakers; and a single pair of women, both with blond bobs, hair bands, and Hermès scarves (gallery owners).

What surprises me most about this mise-en-scène, however, is that I'm part of it. When I first moved to Paris, I'd walk by similar happy, busy, slightly bawdy bistros and as much as I yearned to, I didn't dare to insinuate myself into such profoundly French places. Twenty years later, my timidity's burned off, my French is pretty good, and nothing could keep me away from such rustic places, which worryingly have become as rare as pearls.

La Cave Beauvau also casts a nostalgic spell, because absent the stink of cigarette smoke, it still looks and smells like the city I moved to so long ago. Best of all, no one designed it this way, it just happened. With its stone-paneled copper-clad bar up front and the swirling Bordeaux-bordered cut-out ceiling that could be part of a set for Cocteau's film *Orpheus*, the ancient cash registers, and the straw-lined tray of temptingly runny cheeses on a counter, this place speaks of an eternal France that respects thrift and treasures conviviality over more strident versions of modernity.

Eventually I fall into conversation with owner Stéphane Delleré, who's one of the best bistro-keepers in France. Cheerful with a pair of winemaker pals, he sighs deeply after they leave, and after making sure everyone else who's sipping and nibbling on either side of me has been well looked after, he stops for a chat.

Tonight, he's rattled by family problems on his home turf in La Sarthe and wearied by the Herculean effort necessary to keep a small, honest, independent, and really good bistro going. (He would throw himself in front of a train before he used any industrial shortcut food products.) Delleré always remembers me in a blur, which is fine with me, because a certain anonymity is crucial to the way I work. Still, I'm flattered that something in him comes to life when we start talking, urgently and passionately, about food and wine.

The next thing I know, he is serving me a saucer of bulots (sea snails), anxious for me to try them. So I pick a first spiraled crustacean out of its shell with a sharp pin and pop it in my mouth. Chewy but crunchy and a little creamy, this tiny iodine-rich sea beast is redolent of real old-fashioned court bouillon, or broth made with white wine, carrots, celery, parsley, and other seasonings, and deliciously dredged in the rouille (spicy mayonnaise) Delleré served with them. Though just bar nibbles, the bulots speak volumes about his attention to detail.

When my friends arrive, we move to a booth with brown leatherette banquettes in the cozy if wanly lit back dining room, and begin a long, happy bacchanalian feast. We pore over the menu, which is an anthology of bona fide bistro cooking, and decide to start with jambon persillé, the Burgundian classic of shredded ham in savory parsleyed aspic, oeufs à la mayonnaise, and two homemade terrines, chicken liver and pork, both of them outstanding and served with good bread and a fine bottle of Crozes-Hermitage.

"He makes his own mayonnaise!" a friend says with delight,

and we order another round of the eggs while waiting for our main courses, steak tartare, steak au poivre, and andouillette (chitterling sausage), all of which are excellent. "I have a friend who works at the Elysée Palace (just across the street) who eats lunch here every day, and now I know why," adds my pal Anne. "C'est vraiment fabuleux!"

Before stepping out into the night, I tell Stéphane Delleré I've decided he reminds me of Asterix, the iconic French comic-strip character (a little blond Gaul with a winged helmet) who resists the Roman occupation, and he blushes. "C'est très gentil," he says, before slipping away to top up another customer's glass of Morgon. I'm glad, though, that he instantly knows what I mean, which is that he's very much a keeper of a certain precious French flame.

.   .   .

IN A WORD: This is a bona fide, old-fashioned bistro, so don't come expecting anything fancy. If you love simple, traditional, meat-oriented bistro cooking, good wine, and a lot of atmosphere, however, you'll probably be very happy here.

DON'T MISS: Terrine de campagne, terrine de foie de volaille (chicken liver), jambon persillé, andouillette, steak tartare, steak au poivre, onglet aux echalottes (hanger steak with shallots cooked in red wine), Saint-Marcellin cheese, baba au rhum.

. . .

[60] La Cave Beauvau, 4 rue des Saussaies, 8th, 01.42.65.24.90. MÉTRO: Miromesnil or Champs-Elysées—Clemenceau. OPEN Monday to Wednesday and Saturday, until 8 p.m. Thursday and Friday until midnight. CLOSED Sunday. • $$

L'Angle du Faubourg

L'ANGLE DU FAUBOURG, THE LITTLE BROTHER OF TAILLEVENT
just around the corner, is a quietly chic modern restaurant that
showcases contemporary French cuisine at its best. One would
expect nothing less from the late Jean-Claude Vrinat, the gallant
founder of Taillevent and one of the best restaurateurs in the
world, but it's still surprising and interesting to see how bold
he's been in creating a successful satellite table to one of the
monuments of French gastronomy.

L'Angle succeeds by being très Parisien, but not in the museum idiom of Art Nouveau subway entrances or gilded domes.
No, this restaurant offers a perfect snapshot of modern Paris,
which is a sophisticated, cosmopolitan, prosperous, and very
bourgeois place with a cautious taste for innovation and creativity that's tempered by a reflexive reverence for the past. At
noon, it's packed with a high-powered corporate crowd—this is
justifiably one of the most popular business dining addresses in
Paris—but at night its personality changes as it becomes the setting for tête-à-têtes between stylish professional couples and
also attracts a lot of famous faces looking for a discreet, comfortable place to have a good meal and let their hair down.

I've eaten here many times, but my favorite meal at L'Angle
was with Deborah, a charming literary friend from San Diego
with whom I share my four most public passions: food, wine,
reading, and France. She's also a brilliant conversationalist, in
the most old-fashioned sense of the word, since her curiosity is
boundless and her sense of humor seditious without ever leaving scratch marks.

We met for lunch on a beautiful Indian summer afternoon when the leaves on the trees lining the stone-cobbled streets in this elegant Haussmannian quarter of Paris had turned almost the same color of terra-cotta as the walls inside the restaurant, and both of us were really hungry. I loved watching Deborah's doelike eyes darting around the menu and was curious to see what she'd choose, since she really knows how to compose a meal. She went with chestnut soup with a royale (flan) of chicken livers, followed by cod with romaine cream and Avruga caviar. I started with onion-filled ravioli garnished with grilled bacon and then chose beef cheeks braised in red wine.

Just after Deborah had given me a full rundown of all the meals she'd just eaten in Provence, our first courses came, and they were sublime. Deborah's dish perfectly captured the changing seasons with a soft, rustic, autumnal spectrum of flavors, and mine was delicate but consolingly homey. Her cod was a gorgeous piece of perfectly cooked fish, and its vaguely sweet vegetal sauce highlighted its impeccable freshness, while my beef was fork-tender and accompanied by a sublime gratin of macaroni and artichokes. We had cheese—Ossau Iraty, a sheep cheese from the Béarn, for me and Banon, a runny goat cheese tied up in a chestnut leaf with raffia string, for Deborah—and then dessert, a delicious soft pineapple macaroon and superb lemon cannelloni, and our meal eddied away like a leaf on a pond until we were the last people left in the dining room. Even if a relationship is chaste, eating with someone is a sensual communion, which surely explains why tables of businessmen can sometimes look so uncomfortable together and why this was such a memorable meal for me.

· ⌂ ·

IN A WORD: The late Jean-Claude Vrinat, a brilliant restaurateur and the owner of Taillevent, has created one of the best
contemporary French restaurants in Paris with this casually chic
and more moderately priced annex to the grande dame around
the corner. Excellent cooking and service, plus a spectacular
wine list, make any meal here a special occasion.

DON'T MISS: Langoustines with citrus sauce; chestnut soup
with a royale (flan) of chicken livers; onion-stuffed ravioli with
grilled bacon; cod in romaine sauce with Avruga caviar; spelt (a
nutty wheatlike grain grown in Provence) "risotto" with seasonally changing garnishes; beef cheeks braised in red wine
with an artichoke and macaroni gratin; lamb shoulder with
potatoes and garlic; foie gras sautéed in sweet Banyuls wine
from Languedoc-Roussillon; soft pineapple macaroon; runny
chocolate cake with lemon verbena ice cream.

. . .

[54] **195 rue du Faubourg-Saint-Honoré, 8th, 01.40.74.20.20.** MÉTRO:
Charles-de-Gaulle-Étoile, George V, or Ternes. OPEN **Monday to Friday for
lunch and dinner.** CLOSED **Saturday and Sunday. www.taillevent.com** ▪
$$$

Le Bristol

"IT'S THE HARDEST LEVEL TO COOK AT, BECAUSE AT ITS BEST,
all of its complexity should be invisible," says Eric Frechon,
rolling an empty espresso cup between his large, meaty hands.

He's referring to traditional French haute cuisine, and he's right. Within the last ten years, the Spanish have reconfigured global expectations of high-wire European cooking, which is now meant to startle and delight like a magic show, leaving the endless cycle of hard work necessary to achieve and sustain a classical French haute cuisine kitchen profoundly unknown and underappreciated. Consider that the Bristol makes all of its stocks—fish, shellfish, chicken, veal, and beef—from scratch every single day. As Frechon explains, "Fresh, perfectly made stock is at the core of my cooking." Does the flavor really change all that much from day to day? "Yes." Wouldn't it be easier to make large batches every couple of days—I mean, who'd really know? "I'd know, and actually, I think you would, too."

I've known Frechon for a long time, ever since he first thrilled Paris with some really ballsy but elegant cooking—until he came along no one knew that food could be refined and high testosterone at the same time—at the eponymous bistro he opened in the remote 19th Arrondissement in 1995. The Bristol recruited him in 1999, and he shut down the bistro to take a chance on haute cuisine. On this particular Monday night, Frechon joins us at one of the last tables in the winter dining room of Paris's most discreet luxury hotel, Le Bristol, and we have a gab. I compliment the stunningly good food I've just eaten, especially his tête de veau, calf's head, which he serves in two different preparations—a crispy croquette of skull meat spiked with anchovies and capers and then a hunk of head, or a square of gelatinous tête (calf's head removed from its skull), with a traditional ravigote sauce (a vinegar-based sauce with onions, capers, and herbs).

Delicious though Frechon's is, I'm honestly not a big fan of tête de veau. What gave me a frisson was finding it on the menu of one of the world's most elegant and exclusive dining rooms. As an ancient, hairy-chested stable hand's sort of a treat, offering it here is smart, gutsy, and provocative, since it surprises the French ruling class clientele (the Bristol is one of their favorite tables), at the same time that it appeals to their culinary chauvinism and not so subliminal nostalgia for a lost, idyllic Gaul of happy villages, crowing cocks, and ruddy good eating just a step from the barnyard. This knowing earthiness has always been Frechon's signature, and, like the honest, hardworking craftsman he is, he hones it lovingly, constantly, and carefully while knowing exactly when to break to über seriousness with a slingshotted conker of gastronomic irreverence.

A perfect example is his "cochon fermier," or farm- as opposed to battery-raised pork, parsed out in four declensions—pig's feet, pig's trotter, fatback, and sausage, a potent piggy quartet on one plate. The dish that stunned me that night, however, was sea bass in a thin, glossy gray coat of minced oysters with fork-mashed baby potatoes sauced with flat-parsley jus. What made it so spectacular was the tone-on-tone maritime theme, with the iodine-rich shellfish teasing every bit of flavor out of the more subtly flavored fish by framing it so potently.

After Frechon's earthy acrobatics, desserts are wily, ambitious, and bold—in season, try the fresh Victoria pineapple with a miniature tarte Tatin and lemongrass sorbet or, in the fall, the flambéed Mirabelle plums with almond ice cream.

While my last dinner here was served in the sumptuous splendor of the Bristol's winter dining room—oval and paneled with Hungarian oak, lit by glittering crystal chandeliers, and thickly carpeted—during the warm months, the restaurant moves to a palmy gray-and-white-striped tented patio dining room overlooking a huge magnolia tree and splashing fountains in the hotel's courtyard garden. This romantic aerie is one of the most glamorous and intimate places for a meal in Paris during the summer, and the Bristol is the only hotel in Paris where such a luxurious seasonal migration takes place.

· ·

IN A WORD: The Bristol not only is discreet and chic but has one of the hardest-working and quietly sensual chefs of any top-flight restaurant in Paris. Come here to dwell on the riddle of a sexy dichotomy: one of the best places in Paris for a top-flight business meal is also one of the city's best addresses for romantic dining. This is also a lovely place to treat yourself to a spectacular meal if you're traveling alone, since the service is absolutely impeccable and tables are well spaced and have very comfortable sight lines. Don't be surprised to spot a famous face or two in the crowd, too, since the surrounding neighborhood is dense with French ministries and this dining room is a favorite retreat for power brokers, along with celebrities who honestly don't like the limelight. Note, too, the spectacular wine list and the fact that it serves one of the best breakfasts in Paris, a sort of early-bird splurge with a groaning buffet of delicious treats with which to start the day.

DON'T MISS: Macaronis farcis d'artichaut; truffe noir et de foie gras (pasta tubes packed with black truffle, artichoke heart, and duck foie gras and then glazed with Parmesan); poitrine de canard challandais au sang (duck breast in blood sauce); filet d'agneau de Lozère rôti aux branches de thym (lamb roasted with thyme); pigeon farci aux foie gras (pigeon stuffed with foie gras and garnished with black pudding made with apples and hazelnuts, carmelized onions, and a sauce of its own blood); homard breton et gâteau au foie blond avec taglierini (Breton lobster with a cake of chicken livers and baby clams); ananas et banana en compote et flambés aux vieux rhum (fresh pineapple and bananas baked and flambéed in aged rum); soufflé chaud au Grand Marnier (hot Grand Marnier soufflé).

. . .

[55] Hotel Bristol, 112 rue du Faubourg Saint-Honoré, 8th, 01.53.43.43.00. MÉTRO: Miromesnil. OPEN daily for lunch and dinner. www.lebristol paris.com ▪ $$$$

Le Cinq

EVEN THOUGH SOME OF THEM ARE STUNNINGLY BEAUTIFUL, hotel dining rooms in Paris used to be dispiriting places for anyone who loves good food. Heavily patronized by an Anglo-American clientele wary of garlic and other menaces, they became the refuge of timid types who were content with white fish in white sauce in the company of potted palms and somnolent waiters. To be sure, the Hôtel de Crillon has long had a line of superlative chefs and one always ate well at the Ritz, but it wasn't until the Bristol shook up the scene by hiring chef Michel del Burgo away from Taillevent that the conventional wisdom about hotel food started to change, slowly at first and then at such a gallop that every luxury hotel in Paris today that's worthy of the adjective now has a serious talent in the kitchen.

When the Four Seasons George V reopened after a multi-million-dollar renovation in 1999, it instantly aimed for a place at the top of the local food chain by shrewdly hiring chef Philippe Legendre away from Taillevent, and studiously recasting the experience of grand hotel dining for a new century so successfully that Le Cinq, its restaurant, has now become one of the best tables in the French capital.

Some twenty years later, a meal at Le Cinq is among the most unfailingly exultant experiences Paris has to offer. Chef Eric Briffard is one of the most talented classically trained chefs in France, and perhaps only Jean-Jacques Rousseau could have imagined a better hybrid of New and Old World, here expressed by the ballet-like service in this elegant Wedgewood-inspired dining room.

The visual drama of the dining room comes from its spec-

tacular flower arrangements, an idiom of single blooms placed at rakish angles in dramatic vases, which are the widely copied work of Jeff Leatham, a former male model from Utah who discovered his floral genius while working at the Four Seasons in Beverly Hills. When I arrived for lunch on an autumn day, the entrance to the dining room contained tall vases of long-stemmed roses of such an elusive and hauntingly beautiful color, they stopped me in my tracks. A dark dusty pink like an old woman's memories of being a young girl, they were some of the most magnificent flowers I'd ever seen.

My friend Enrica Rocca, who runs a popular cooking school in Notting Hill, London, was waiting for me on the banquette. A Venetian who lived in Cape Town for many years after graduating from the Lausanne Hotel School, Enrica has one of the most discerning palates of anyone I know, and she'd said she wanted food she couldn't get in London. As we studied our menus, Enrica's eyes were darting everywhere. "I'm starting to panic," she said. "There are so many things I'd like to try."

At last we threw the dice, and we were thick in conversation when a complimentary starter began the meal—an exquisite miniature terrine of wild mushrooms garnished with several slices of grilled cèpe and a dribble of parsley-and-shallot vinaigrette. "This little display of Gallic prowess gladdens my heart, but the acidity of the rivulet of dressing is a distraction from the earthy tones of the terrine," Enrica correctly observed.

This tut-tut-ing didn't worry me, though. If Briffard's cooking can be so disciplined and polite it occasionally seems academic, his talent shines when he unleashes his imagination and lets it guide his encyclopedic knowledge of culinary technique, as was made perfectly clear when our first courses arrived. Enrica's duck foie gras roasted with citrus fruits and garnished with sliced pear and a gingerbread crumble was sublime. "The citrus punctuates the richness of the foie gras, and the sweet garnishes elaborate the liver's buttery taste." My veal carpaccio with shavings of white Alba truffle, fresh chestnut, and aged Parmesan came with warm potato purée, a ravioli filled with sautéed onions, a shot of ginger broth, and an egg yolk—a magnificent composition of subtly, sensually interacting flavors and textures. Knowing that eggs, potatoes, and truffles comprise a umami trinity, Briffard quietly lit up this trellis of tastes with Parmesan and then shrewdly rode the gustatory brake a bit with the ginger broth, which I'd guess was there to disrupt the perfect flow of pleasure so that it could be so thrillingly renewed a few seconds later.

Then, almost as an answer to our curiosity about how to design dishes that will not only satisfy but titillate a worldly international clientele, our main course arrived, a stunningly beautiful Pithiviers, or golden pastry case, named for the town in the Loiret region an hour south of Paris and filled with succulent pieces of gray pheasant, wild duck, and grouse that had been cooked in chestnut honey with autumn fruit, including quince and grapes. The waiters displayed it to us before they served it tableside with great art, a performance that had Enrica swooning. "C'est magnifique, c'est vraiment magnifique," she raved as they went about their work, deftly slicing the tender pastry and serving it in tidy slices with a jus pressé à l'Armagnac.

After we began eating, it was some time before we spoke, since my mind took off on a flight of solitary pleasure, mulling over the idea that this Pithiviers could easily have found a place in one of those meticulous medieval Flemish still-lifes of the feasts of prosperous burghers in Bruges. The faint fumes of Armagnac in the sauce had the effect of scaring a whole flock of wild birds to life every time I ate another mouthful of this dish, and I was also dumbstruck by the quality of Briffard's pastry, which was just plain sumptuous. "I think he must have cooked all of the birds separately before boning them and then quickly sautéing them before enclosing them in the pastry case," said Enrica, more engrossed in her plate than I've ever seen her. We both ate quite a bit of the Pithiviers, but a good third of the dish remained when we were sated. "Caro," Enrica said, and motioned for me to lean forward. "I think the couple next to us are on their honeymoon. Let's offer them the rest of the Pithiviers." Indeed I had noticed the fresh-faced young couple who were obviously fascinated and perhaps a tiny bit appalled by our recent moaning and mewling. They politely refused our offer, we adamantly insisted, and our waiter promptly served them.

Now Enrica came clean. "To tell you the truth, tresoro, I wasn't expecting much from this meal," she confessed. "I thought it would be very corporate, but instead it was fabulous." Knowing that it usually contains a sublime Beaufort millésime I couldn't pass up the cheese trolley, and then we were delivered to quiet bliss by our desserts, a Sambirano black chocolate soufflé with chunky pineapple preserves and a coconut-milk emulsion for Enrica, and baked Reinette apple with saffron pistil ice cream, green-apple sorbet, and a rosemary honey meringue for me.

"Excuse me, Sir, Madame." It was the young man to whom we'd given the rest of our Pithiviers. "I just wanted to thank you for the best thing that's happened on our honeymoon." Like a wolf eyeing a lamb, Enrica lifted her eyebrows and cocked her head. "*The* best thing?" "Well, one of the best things," he replied, his cheeks blazing.

· ·

IN A WORD: Le V is the hole in one of Paris haute cuisine restaurants, a place that's as perfect for a marriage proposal as it is to ink a major contract, and chef Eric Briffard is one of the most consistently original but stunningly refined chefs in Paris.

DON'T MISS: cèpe risotto with eggplant; duck foie gras roasted with citrus fruit and served with pears and a gingerbread crumble; veal carpaccio with Alba truffle, fresh chestnuts, Parmesan, and potato purée; frog's legs with watercress in vin jaune sauce; sea bass with shellfish, wasabi, and Granny Smith apple juice; Pithiviers de gibier; veal chop cooked en cocotte with capers; roast shoulder of lamb with cocoa beans and sundried tomatoes; Sambirano black chocolate soufflé with pineapple preserves and a coconut-milk emulsion.

. . .

[56] **Hôtel Four Seasons George V**, 31 avenue George V, 8th, 01.49.52.70.00. MÉTRO: George V OPEN daily for lunch and dinner. www.fourseasons.com • **$$$$**

Dominique Bouchet

I LOVE TO COOK, WHICH IS WHY ONE OF THE MOST INTER-esting days I've ever spent in Paris was with chef Dominique Bouchet when he was head chef at the Hôtel Crillon. I arrived in the immaculate kitchens after a very early breakfast and proceeded to shadow Bouchet all day as he inspected the daily delivery of produce, met with his sous-chefs, worked on some shellfish stock, and ate a quick slice of cheese before the lunch service started. He personally inspected every plate, tweaking a whisker of chive here, blotting up an errant dot of sauce there, before it was sent upstairs by dumbwaiter to the opulent dining room. Perched on a stool in a corner to stay out of the way, I was fascinated by the coordination and concentration required to produce haute cuisine. By the end of the day, I'd found my culinary mantra, too, as I listened to Bouchet good-naturedly telling his staff again and again, "Great food tastes of what it is." This may sound obvious, but in fact it took a long time for top

Paris chefs to dare to do simplicity, and few do it better than Bouchet.

Even though he has an impressive résumé—he worked at Jamin before Robuchon arrived, then at La Tour d'Argent and in his own restaurant in the Charentes region on France's Atlantic coast before becoming head chef at the Crillon, and he trained Eric Ripert, one of New York's star chefs, at Le Bernardin—Bouchet is the quiet man of the Paris restaurant scene, much happier in his kitchen than he is in front of television cameras. He's an old-school cook's cook, and this explains why his eponymous restaurant, which opened in 2005 after he left the Crillon, quickly became a hit with both Paris power brokers and epicureans.

Not only is this a handsome adult restaurant with exposed stone walls, a relaxed decor of beige and brown, and an open kitchen, but Bouchet's brilliant restraint when working with first-rate French produce leads to some quietly spectacular cooking. Consider his delicious warm terrine of Beaufort cheese, artichoke hearts, and country ham, for example. Instead of trying to transform these ingredients, he has created a harmonious composition of taste and textures that makes each one distinct and delicious, and this subtlety, which comes from a desire to respect the natural tastes of food, is Bouchet's signature. Likewise, his charlotte of crabmeat, tomatoes, and basil, a starter, makes all three of these ingredients sing, and his roasted cod on a bed of tomatoes and red peppers in a luscious jus de poulet (reduced chicken stock) is a magnificent marriage of the sea and the barnyard. I also love his spit-roasted pigeon with raisin-studded polenta and a honied jus, and pasta stuffed with lobster and mushroom puree and sauced with a jus made from its own carapace is superb, too.

The last time I was here, I overheard a woman from Atlanta complaining that the food was "too simple." I suspect that she's one of the many people who still expect French food to be elaborate, when what's guiding it at the beginning of this new century is the elegance of simplicity. One way or another, her husband, who'd ordered the pigeon (she had steak) wholeheartedly disagreed, and Madame seemed wildly happy when her orange and raspberry soufflé arrived, although I also recommend the poached peach with Champagne granite and raspberry gelée.

· ·

IN A WORD: This stylish, well-mannered adult restaurant has two distinct clienteles: bankers, brokers, and politicians at noon and chic bourgeois couples in the evening. What makes everyone happy is chef Dominique Bouchet's brilliantly simple and understated contemporary French cooking.

DON'T MISS: Sautéed cherry tomatoes with foie gras ice cream; terrine of Beaufort, artichokes, and country ham; charlotte of crabmeat, tomatoes, and basil; roast cod with tomatoes and red peppers in a jus de poulet; pasta with lobsters and mushroom puree in lobster jus; spit-roasted pigeon with raisin polenta; aile de raie (skate wing) with capers and lemon on a bed of baby potatoes; roasted duck with turnip confit; raspberry and orange soufflé; poached peach with Champagne granite; raspberry gelée.

. . .

[52] 11 rue Treilhard, 8th, 01.45.61.09.46. MÉTRO: Villiers or Miromesnil. OPEN Monday to Friday for lunch and dinner. CLOSED Saturday and Sunday. www.dominique-bouchet.com ▪ $$$

Garnier

RIGHT IN THE HEART OF PARIS, I CAUGHT A SURPRISING WHIFF of leaf meal, the winey rotten-apple smell that means summer's over. It was a perfect Indian summer day, with the chestnut tree leaves just starting to curl bronze at the edges, but the surest sign that the seasons had shifted was that the stainless-steel banc à huîtres (oyster stand) on the stone-paved sidewalk outside Garnier was filled with mounds of crushed ice, tassels of bumpy brown seaweed, and big plump oysters from all over France. After a summer of salads, I wanted a real lunch.

The success of any meal depends on good casting and clear intentions. In this case, I was meeting Melissa, a clever writer from Dayton, Ohio, now living in India, and the plan was to treat ourselves to a really fine feed. This is why I chose Garnier—it's one of the most reliably satisfying restaurants in Paris.

We were seated on the glassed-in sidewalk terrace at a large round table covered with a crisply starched white tablecloth, and menus were presented by the stout, silver-haired waiter in a black vest with a long white apron. We ordered flutes of Champagne rosé to start and provoked a first sign of interest from the waiter. Sitting opposite us, a pretty older woman with her meringue hair swept up in a chignon gave us a pursed smile when the bubbly arrived; in no other city in the world do people take more pleasure in observing others in search of same than in Paris.

We studied our menus and picked tiny sea snails, a complimentary hors d'oeuvre that rewarded our Champagne, out of their shells with long steel pins. The salty marine taste of the crustaceans met the remote floral edge of the Champagne with a thrilling elegance we both noticed; I knew Melissa would love Garnier, and few things are more fun than sharing a favorite restaurant. We ordered a half-dozen spéciales Gillardeaux and a half-dozen fines de claire No. 2 from the Charente-Maritime, both among the finest French oysters, plus a bouquet of crevettes roses (boiled red shrimp). Afterward, I took the cod steak with girolles mushrooms and Melissa chose a charlotte d'avocat et de tourteau, avocado cream with crabmeat, a starter, as her main course. We drank a fairly priced Quincy, a nice Loire Valley white wine, and some Chateldon, the mineral water favored by Louis XVI. From the muscle tension that grew in his lower lip as he scribbled down our order, it was obvious that the waiter thought we had constructed an admirable meal, the results of which were little attentions like finger bowls, which weren't offered to a table of Germans across the way.

"What's with the decor, though?" Melissa asked, as I knew she would. I explained that in Paris, restaurants are invariably remodeled just at the precise moment when their decor-to-be-destroyed is teetering on the brink of becoming charming, camp, vintage, or, in the case of Garnier, all of the above. Until a few years ago, this curiously overlooked fish house—it's just across the street from the Gare Saint-Lazare, the busiest train station in France, but almost no one knows about it—had a winsomely weirdo appearance that came from a unique hybrid between its original Art Deco interior and a ham-handed seventies makeover. What did the seventies look like in France? Visit any RER station (the RER is the suburban train network that compliments the Métro) in the Paris area to feast on oddball ceramics, extruded aluminum ceilings, and dumpy color schemes like orange and brown or yellow and cobalt blue. At Garnier, the minuscule oyster bar just inside the front door, one of my favorite places in Paris for the world's best fast food—a dozen oysters and a glass of Muscadet—previously had massive grooved half-glazed brown tiles on the wall, and the last time I saw them I remember commenting on how winningly ugly they were. Tragically, they vanished during the summer of 2001, but at least the little oyster bar survived, and in the main dining rooms, French colonial furniture and a silly parquet floor just became the last visual layer of a restaurant that always seems to be trying too hard, which is completely unnecessary, since it serves the best oysters in Paris. The young chef, Ludovic Schwartz, who learned on star chef Joël Robuchon's knee, is a brilliant fish cook, ably riffing on classics like sole meunière by adding a garnish of preserved North African–style lemon or spiking a tempura of langoustines with Espelette pepper from the Basque country.

It's tough to be a good fish cook, since the best are utterly self-effacing, correctly obsessed with proper timing, and parsimonious but creative with the garnish that brings the natural tastes and textures of a first-rate catch of the day into perfect focus. The baba au rhum, a sponge cake dosed with excellent Saint James rum from Martinique and slathered with vanilla-speckled whipped cream, is the only possible way to end a meal here.

· ⁘ ·

IN A WORD: Open daily, this is a first-rate fish house with a motley clientele and decor right across the street from the Gare Saint-Lazare. As suitable for a business meal as it is for a tête-à-tête, it's also perfect for solitary dining, either at the oyster bar just inside the front door or in the main dining room.

DON'T MISS: Oysters, crab, shrimp, mussels, and clams from the stand out front; langoustine tempura; cod with girolles mushrooms; sole meunière with preserved lemons; turbot cooked with seaweed; baba au rhum (sponge cake soaked with rum and topped with whipped cream).

. . .

[**53**] **111 rue Saint-Lazare, 8th, 01.43.87.50.40,** MÉTRO: **Saint-Lazare.** OPEN **daily for lunch and dinner.** ▪ **$$$**

Ledoyen

AT NOON ON A WARM APRIL DAY, I'M SITTING IN THE WORLD'S most elegant tree house, the olive green dining room of Ledoyen. Heavy Bordeaux velvet curtains frame picture-window

views of the crowns of the flowering chestnut trees in the gardens of the Champs-Élysées, and every breeze sends a few brief sprays of tiny white blossoms into the air from these fleeting floral torches, a natural confetti that couldn't possibly be a more accurate portent of the lunch to follow.

I'm on time for a change, which means that I have the luxury of some woolgathering while waiting for Alain and Margaret. For several minutes I muse on how lunch is unfailingly the better meal at any haute cuisine restaurant. Not only does it favor leisurely, gentle digestion, but by boarding the long, luxurious cruise of an extraordinary meal in the middle of the day you make a serious commitment to its specialness since it's an experience that can't and shouldn't be hurried. I also think most kitchens are in peak form at noon, when the brigade is as fresh and bright as the produce they're about to prepare. It's also obvious that midday dining rooms have a very different intrigue from what they become in the evening, when many Parisian power brokers are at home eating scrambled eggs or order-in sushi in front of the television.

To my right, the ambassador to France from some Spanish-speaking country and the sommelier are having the sort of elegant verbal duel that makes restaurants such unfailingly intriguing places to eavesdrop. They parry ideas about the perfect wine for the meal that's just been ordered, and I savor this civilized and satisfying exchange that advances according to keenly observed signals, where the suspense comes from the reciprocity of their mutually menaced egos. Their voices grow lower and lower before a happy truce is reached and the diplomat hands the heavy tome back to the sommelier. Later, I'm not at all surprised to see a superb bottle of Vosne Romanée, an excellent choice for a festive but important lunch on a spring day, on the table. To my left, two elegant young Japanese women with obviously new Louis Vuitton handbags (the zippers are still shiny yellow brass) methodically photograph each dish as it arrives at the table, and the only word I understand from their conversation is "Chanel." Otherwise, aside from a jolly quartet I'm not surprised to later learn are from Mougins on the Côte d'Azur—one woman was wearing silver leather shoes, the other gold—the dining room hums with the diligence of corporate dining punctuated by the laughter of special occasions.

I've just been thinking about how well decorator Jacques Grange's Napoleonic decor, a tented ceiling and lovely motifs of Pompeian inspiration painted onto the wood-paneled walls, has stood the test of time since I first saw them more than a decade ago, when Margaret, one of my favorite tablemates, arrives. A native Londoner and natural wit who's lived in France for many years, she not only knows and loves her food but takes a childlike delight in the luxury of haute cuisine. When natty Alain is seated, we're served hors d'oeuvres with our flutes of Champagne rosé, and instantly I see how much chef Christian Le Squer has grown since my last meal here. These are brilliant little Fabergé bites—two mauve globes of beet meringue stuck together with horseradish cream, an exquisite bonbon of foie gras encased in buckwheat wafers and topped with tangy passion fruit gelée, and green-drizzled white globes on wooden spoons that turn out to be mozzarella skins filled with mozzarella water and a few drops of pesto, a mouthful as stunning in its technique as it is deliciously simple in its suave lactic burst of taste.

We order, and the meal begins with the slow, thrumming, luxurious anticipation of an ocean liner leaving port. It has taken us a while to negotiate our meals among ourselves—the three of us love to eat, often do so together, and have evolved our own unstated code for creating a successful meal, beginning with the minuet of who's-having-what. We never order the same thing, because forks usually fly among us, and so we take turns letting the other go first, which means you should always have a backup choice if your first one is taken.

So it was a surprise when the charming maître d'hôtel, Patrick Simiand, arrived with a complimentary first course that none of us had been tempted by—smoked eel topped with chopped beets, a dish of curiously central European inspiration from a Breton chef. The sweetness of the beets with the subtle smoke of the eel worked brilliantly, though, and the play of textures was curious but exquisite. Next, Alain's plump, snowy langoustines, two grilled in their split shells and three wrapped in a crunchy brown crust of kadif, the same fine golden pastry threads used to make Middle Eastern sweets, came with a superb citrus foam. We agreed that Margaret's medley of spring vegetables in red radish jus looked like an illustration from a Beatrix Potter book and was lovely, but though my lobster tail was beautifully cooked, I was underwhelmed by the pistachio ice cream that melted in a pale green puddle around it; the meeting between the taste of lobster and pistachios was intriguing, but I didn't much care for the contrasting temperatures.

So often in haute cuisine restaurants, the flirtatious starters are followed by main courses as solid and solemn as great-uncles, but the middle ring of Le Squer's circus is the most interesting. I first ate Le Squer's food when he was chef at the gorgeous and now sadly extinct Restaurant Opéra, a Napoléon III dining room in the Grand Hôtel with stunning views of the Opéra Garnier, and have been a fan ever since because he's one of the most gifted seafood cooks in Paris. My darne de bar poché was a perfectly poached rolled sea bass filet delicately stuffed with spring vegetables and served with grilled carmelized pink grapefruit slices and crunchy green asparagus, and Margaret's perfectly roasted pigeon stuffed with dates in a pan sauce brightened by Moroccan spices and preserved lemon was succulent and elegant. Happily, Alain had chosen the most curious dish on the menu: jambon blanc, morilles, parmesan aux spaghettis. What arrived was a small coffer made of spaghetti filled with morel mushrooms in cream and topped with a thatch of melted Parmesan and several chunks of ham, an elegant and unusual echo of the food children like best. It was delicious, but, startlingly priced at the euro equivalent of $130, it launched a brief discussion of the alarmingly vertiginous prices of haute cuisine dining in Paris. The three of us agreed that the sums required for the finest French dining are reaching an altitude that risks tipping the whole category into irrelevance, since it's become an exercise in casuistry—the science of difficult moral issues—to justify spending so much money on a single meal.

Le Squer, a pleasant man with an elfin face, stops by just in time to discover us in ecstasy over a dessert of grapefruit mille-feuille, a refreshing composition of candied grapefruit rind, pink grapefruit, and carmelized pink grapefruit sections. He explains that the spaghetti coffer was created to cater to foreigners timid about the wilder reaches of French gastronomy represented by eel and veal sweetbreads and says his greatest pleasure is cooking fish and shellfish. "My earliest memory is of walking on the beach in Brittany with the strong clean smell of the sea in my nostrils, and this purity is what I try to communicate when I cook fish," he says. Twenty minutes later, as I'm walking past the beds of sentrylike tulips in the gardens leading to the Place de la Concorde, my newest memory, that of a perfect lunch in Paris on a beautiful spring day, starts to emerge from the immediacy of recent experience, and as it takes form, I know it's one I'll treasure.

· ·

IN A WORD: With one of the loveliest settings in Paris, a beautifully decorated Napoléon III pavilion in a grove of trees just off the Champs-Élysées, this excellent restaurant is a perfect choice for a well-dressed splurge. The gifted chef, Christian Le Squer, remains a dark horse on the Paris scene, but he's one of the best fish cooks in France.

DON'T MISS: Langoustines in a citrus-flavored olive oil emulsion; smoked eel with chopped beets; hare terrine with meat jelly; truffe en croque au sel, quenelle onctueuse de foie gras (black truffle cooked in salt with Jerusalem artichokes and foie gras mousse), gujonettes de sole (strips of sole in bread crumbs) with vin jaune sauce; turbot with truffled potatoes; sautéed suckling pig with gnocchi and dried tomatoes; roasted pigeon with Moroccan spices; grapefruit millefeuille.

. . .

[59] **1 avenue Dutuit, 8th, 01.53.05.10.01.** MÉTRO: **Champs-Élysées-Clemenceau.** OPEN **Tuesday to Friday for lunch and dinner. Saturday, Sunday, and Monday dinner only. www.ledoyen.com • $$$$**

Le Maxan

THE DECOR MIGHT SAY IBIZA, BUT THE KITCHEN DELIVERS France in the most elegant and delicious of ways at this little charmer steps from the Élysées Palace (home of the French president). Think white walls decorated with concave plaster dots the size of cookies and a ceiling installation of white flannel flaps, or Euro disco lounge par excellence. But just wait for what the kitchen sends out and you'll see why such dark-suited big-name politicos as Dominique Strauss-Kahn, a former French finance minister, and many of the country's most important money men have ignored the lounge music and party-time setting to make this one of the most discreet noontime power canteens in Paris (it's much quieter, and more diverse, at night). These powerful gents like to eat, and chef Laurent Jazac, a talent with deep roots in the best traditions of disciplined French gastronomy, delivers big-time.

Jazac, who previously cooked with Gérard Vié at Les Trois Marchés in Versailles, Alain Dutournier, and the late José Lampreia when the Maison Blanche first opened, is a poignantly sincere, feet-on-the-ground chef with a vast technical knowledge of the produce he works with. The first time I ate here, I was astonished by his tartare of foie gras and summer truffles, one of the sexiest dishes I've eaten in Paris in a long time, and, unlike many other chefs, he makes good on his tantalizing starters with brilliant main courses like a classic pithiviers de canard, a flaky, buttery pastry filled with chopped duck meat and gizzards and topped with thin panfried slices of foie gras. Simpler dishes like his veal chop with potato gnocchi and sole sautéed in salted butter and served with wilted leeks and a citrus jus are also superb.

Desserts are excellent, too, including a wonderful pineapple and ginger sorbet with fresh chopped pineapple and a vanilla sabayon and a stunningly good crème caramel for two with home-baked financier cookies.

I often despair of finding a good affordable meal in the 8th

Arrondissement, which is parsed out between astronomic expense-account tables and silly fashion-driven places that never last more than six months, so when anyone asks for a solid address in this flighty part of Paris, I always recommend Le Maxan, a confidential address that never fails to deliver.

· ·

IN A WORD: Chef Laurent Jazac is an up-and-coming talent, and the delicious and imaginative contemporary French cuisine served at this relaxed, friendly restaurant has won him a well-heeled clientele.

DON'T MISS: Depending on availability, tartare of oysters and scallops; sautéed foie gras with pears; crab with a watercress velouté; croustillant de queue de cochon (deboned pig's tail meat in a crispy pastry wrapper) with potato puree and truffle jus; mont-blanc with chestnut cream and vanilla mousse.

. . .

[57] **37 rue de Miromesnil, 8th, 01.42.65.78.60.** MÉTRO: **Miromesnil.** OPEN **Tuesday to Friday for lunch and dinner. Saturday dinner only. Monday lunch only.** CLOSED **Sunday. www.rest-maxan.com • $$**

Pierre Gagnaire

BEING USHERED TO TABLE AT PIERRE GAGNAIRE SETS OFF a surge of serious high-voltage anticipation, which comes from the imminence of being indoctrinated into a select sect of epicureans, those who dare the outer limits of taste. You're not drubbed into the role of aspiring acolyte, however, but re-

ceived with velvet charm and the respect due to anyone who has both the means and the curiosity to undertake a voyage of gastronomic initiation. Pierre Gagnaire is probably the most innovative chef working in France today—a bold, brilliant, restless, and endlessly curious cook who ceaselessly pushes back the frontiers of gastronomic experience. Ever since he opened his first restaurant in the south-central industrial city of Saint-Étienne, Gagnaire, who trained with Jean Vignard in Lyon and then Paul Bocuse, has stunned and dazzled—and occasionally flummoxed—the clubby summit of French gastronomy.

Why? Gagnaire's ambition is to recoin the idiom of haute cuisine, the highest form of gastronomic pleasure, for a new century. Every dish he creates is a profoundly reasoned and studied construction rather like a Fabergé egg—beautiful to behold, intricately wrought, and unique.

I've eaten at his restaurant a dozen times since he moved from Saint-Étienne to Paris in search of a more receptive clientele, but my last meal was the one I most enjoyed. I went alone to lunch and so finally had the occasion to muse over every seed, drop, foam, and frond during the course of what was a truly spectacular meal. I'd even go so far as to say that dining solo, or at most as two, is the best way to experience Gagnaire's cooking, since conversation is a distraction from the wonderment that every course brings on. There's quite simply no other chef in Paris who demands such intent concentration at the table, an experience that's a revelation in itself, since usually we briefly register the taste of what we're eating and then resume our conversation.

Consider my starter, the aptly named "Insolite" ("Unusual"). It was listed on the menu in a four-line description:

Tsarkaya oysters, culatello ham, broccoli, and agria
(potato) with smoked eel
Galette of canaroli rice and sumac berries, sautee of
espardeignes (sea cucumbers) with parsley
Violet shrimp and red tuna, interleaved
White turnips with koktxas (hake cheeks) with crispy garlic

Each layer of this stunningly beautiful and delicious dish parsed out a different refrain on one main theme, which is the contrast of flavors from the sea and flavors from the earth. The silky culatello ham, for example, amplified the marine flavors of the meaty Tsarkaya oysters, so named because this variety of oyster was the favorite of the Russian czars, with the sweetness of the potato and the smoke of the eel adding some gustatory punctuation. The next layer of this dish was an intriguing study in textures, contrasting the crispy rice and sumac berries with the soft gelatinous feel of the sea cucumbers, while the pairing of prawn and tuna expressed the incredible delicacy of these products and the crunchy turnips and tender cod cheeks reiterated this dish's sensual terre et mer (earth and sea) theme.

Gagnaire works closely with his friend Hervé This, a molecular biologist whose specialty is the physiology of taste, and this collaboration explains his astonishing ability to tease, incite, and orchestrate such unique sensory experiences. In fact, every time I come here, I feel like an infant who's tasting everything for the very first time.

My main course, le veau de lait, forced me to think about what veal actually tastes like. Of course, I know what veal tastes like, but I'd probably never actually thought about what it tastes like—its sweetness, its milkiness, its herbaceousness. This dish was composed of a veal sweetbread grilled with coffee and cardamom with a puff pastry galette sprinkled with tiny chunks of praline, a miniature blanquette with carrot and ginger, and garnishes of baby cabbage, potato puree, and buffalo-milk mozzarella with bergamot (a small pear-shaped citrus fruit grown mostly in Italy). It was one of the most poignant dishes I've ever had, tender with nostalgia—blanquette de veau (veal in a lemony cream sauce) is a homey classic the French associate with their grandmothers and their childhoods—and the sweet fragility of youth that veal represents.

While waiting for my cheese course, I savored the almost monastic calm of the dining room—a few tables were clearly business lunches, but the majority were occupied by people who were embarked on the same quest I was: a short but intense journey to learn more about how we taste what we taste. This is very much the theme of the way that Gagnaire serves cheese, too. My aged Comté cheese came with thin languettes (little tongues) of white chocolate and a chutney of Moroccan peaches, and these garnishes worked to create an exquisite primal lesson in the taste of a single cheese. The chocolate drew out its sweetness, butteriness, and vaguely waxy quality, while the peaches played off of its graininess and gentle acidity.

Speaking about the métier of chef, Gagnaire, an amiable man who's a major Chet Baker fan, once told me, "We're very much like jazzmen in the way we work." I found myself reflecting on this comment over dessert, a remarkable caramel and angelica soufflé, which was an edible expression of jazz. The caramel soufflé was garnished with Pondicherry pepper and came with an angelica (a bittersweet herb)-flavored vacherin and a compote of preserved fruit and licorice ice cream, and was served with a glass of dry oloroso sherry that magnified the tastes of burnt sugar, winy fruit, and strong, masculine herbs. The combination was absolutely brilliant, a lyrical cameo that made me think of the plaintive melancholy notes of a jazzman's trumpet and also the comforting fugue of an old-fashioned English men's club. Interestingly, it was also an echo of Gagnaire's own favorite dish: warm oysters with fine shavings of ham and Xérès vinegar, which offers a similar riff on various tones of sweetness framed by the taste of maderized wine. More than any other chef in the world today, Gagnaire knows how to unlock the emotional content of taste, which is why a meal in his restaurant is a profoundly moving and completely unforgettable experience.

· ·

IN A WORD: Pierre Gagnaire is the most extreme chef in Paris, producing dishes that are remarkably intricate and as cerebral as they are sensual. Everything you eat here insists on your full attention and concentration as part of a stunning lesson in how we taste what we taste. Since Gagnaire is globally renowned, advance reservations, plus a willingness to spend a startling sum on a single meal, are imperative.

DON'T MISS: A reflection of his astonishing imagination, Gagnaire's menus change four times a year, but no one presents cheeses in a more imaginative way, and his "grand dessert," a tasting plate of desserts, is a grand experience indeed.

. . .

[61] 6 rue Balzac, 8th, 01.58.36.12.50. MÉTRO: **Charles-de-Gaulle-Étoile or George V.** OPEN **Monday, Tuesday, Thursday, and Friday for lunch and dinner. Wednesday and Sunday dinner only.** CLOSED **Saturday. www .pierre-gagnaire.com • $$$$**

Le Senderens and Le Passage

MY LAST LUNCH AT LUCAS-CARTON WHEN IT WAS STILL Lucas-Carton was with Susan, an attractive blond public relations executive from Yorkshire who has lived in Hong Kong for many years. We had an incredible meal, too, during which I told her about the first time I'd ever been to the restaurant.

One rainy afternoon in January just after I'd moved to Paris, I was waiting to cross the street in front of La Madeleine when a total stranger, a nice-looking Irishman in a well-cut suit, invited me to lunch at Lucas-Carton. At first I thought he was joking, but he quickly explained that he was in town for business and his professional contact had canceled at the last minute. He said he'd been looking forward to the meal for weeks but couldn't imagine eating alone. And before I could ask, he told me I'd been chosen because I was wearing a coat and tie and carrying a copy of E. M. Forster's *Where Angels Fear to Tread*, one of his favorite novels, which led him to guess I was both English-speaking and serviceably literate. I won't pretend I wasn't tempted, but because I also considered myself serviceably sane, I thanked him, said I couldn't afford it, and wouldn't be the guest of someone I didn't know. "Don't be silly. This may be the first and last time something so absurdly wonderful comes your way. It's on expenses anyway." I hesitated. "If you're worried I'm mad, I'll tell the waiter I can't be trusted with knives and have them cleared away. What do you say?"

Well, why not? A few minutes later, I was sipping Champagne compliments of the Irish Dairy Board, and what followed was a spectacular lunch, including Alain Senderens's astonishing lobster in vanilla sauce, an amazing preparation that turned the crustacean into a marine confectionery, and then the famous honey-and-spice-covered canard Apicius, based on a recipe that dates back at least two thousand years. The duck was sublime but totally overshadowed by the Côte Rôtie that Patrick had ordered: Three hours later, after profusely thanking Patrick, I stumbled back into the sleet, and a year later, I received a Christmas card from him with a picture of his three cute carrot-topped children.

"You'd have been a fool not to have taken him up on it, in the same way that you'd have been a fool not to join me today," said Susan, who was right on both counts, especially since six months after she and I dined together, Lucas-Carton ceased to exist when chef Alain Senderens remade it as Le Senderens, a sort of brasserie de luxe.

Senderens is a brilliant chef, but I could wring his neck for the ill-conceived makeover of what was one of the most beautiful dining rooms in Paris. Who needs metallic tub chairs, Corian tables, and a tented ceiling in an Art Nouveau dining room of such unique beauty that it's a listed national monument? Suddenly a setting in which I'd had several of the most enjoyable meals of my life had been vandalized, and though the interior design of a restaurant always plays second fiddle to what I find on my plate, I've found this transformation so disappointing that I can only hope that one day it'll all be ripped out and the room restored to its original beauty. The service suffered badly during this revision, too—Lucas-Carton had some of the best-drilled old-school service in Paris. Now it's hardly better than what you'd expect in an airport restaurant.

Happily, chef Senderens has been much more successful in the shrewd way he continually updates his cooking with savvy borrowings from various Asian kitchens and particular attention to creating contrasting textures in every dish. His food is visually beautiful, too, and his pioneering suggestion of a different wine or drink with every course remains as interesting and appealing as it was when he launched it many years ago.

My most recent meal at Le Senderens was excellent, too— warm house-smoked salmon with buttered cabbage and juniper berries, a sublime tartare of veal and langoustines with rice noodles and Parmesan shavings, and a brilliant dacquoise (a hazelnut meringue filled with buttercream) with Szechuan pepper, lemon marmalade, and ginger ice cream.

Le Passage, Senderen's casual restaurant on the second floor, is a real favorite of mine, since the brief menu includes many of the same dishes served in the now-discombobulated main dining room but in a more convivial bar setting at lower prices. In fact, many of the former regulars at Lucas-Carton have migrated to Le Passage, which has one of the most stylish crowds in Paris at lunch.

· ·

IN A WORD: Alain Senderens reconfigured his three-star Lucas-Carton into an eponymous brasserie de luxe a couple of years ago, and if the trendy modern furnishings and tented ceiling clash sadly with the original Art Nouveau setting, the kitchen remains outstanding.

DON'T MISS: House-smoked salmon with buttered cabbage and juniper berries; veal and langoustine tartare; zucchini flowers stuffed with crab; lamb filet with piquillo peppers and eggplant with grilled hazelnuts; duck foie gras poached in a Chinese bouillon; pigeon; dacquoise with Szechuan pepper; lemon marmalade and ginger ice cream; Tahitian vanilla millefeuille.

. . .

[58] 9 place de la Madeleine, 8th, 01.42.65.22.90. MÉTRO: Madeleine. OPEN daily for lunch and dinner. www.senderens.fr • $$$$

Taillevent

THE FRAGILE GOLDEN PASTRY CASE WAS SHAPED LIKE Venus's breast but incised with a fine swirling spiral that issued from a central nipple like a perfect architectural element. I cut it open, and inside was an impeccably cooked veal sweetbread wrapped in a mantle of wilted sorrel leaves, which had impregnated the pastry with a faint but sublimely sour perfume. I forked a slice, waved it through the green comma of sorrel sauce the waiter had spooned onto my plate from a silver sauceboat, and then tasted something so exquisite that it produced an instant primal groan of pleasure. The rich buttery pastry, the quiet muscle tension in the sweetbread, the galvanizing metallic taste of the sorrel sauce fused into a potent if evanescent moment of pleasure that left me elated. What I'd just tasted was a nearly transcendental expression of the way cooking can capture and convey human genius as surely as an oil painting or a sym-

phony. And if I'll never have the pleasure of living with one of Degas's magnificent paintings of ballet dancers, for example, this dish may have cost a thumping $100, but it was all mine and an experience of dumb animal bliss I'll never forget.

Just forty-five minutes earlier, I'd been sitting in the Métro picking at a tiny gravy spot on the sleeve of a blazer I'd been too busy to take to the dry cleaners and my thoughts were the usual filigree of anxieties that come from having too much to do and not enough time to do it in. Then I arrived at Taillevent, where you're admitted to a chic and very discreet club with the deference due a distinguished long-standing member, even if your membership begins only when you step through the front door and ends when the door closes behind you. After a little tinkering—the first table Bruno, a delightful Frenchman with one of the most sensitive and well-versed palates of anyone I know, and I were shown to flanked the busy service door, and since I knew my meal would be ruined by the distraction of waiters sorting silver and hurrying into and out of the kitchen, I summoned the courage to ask if we might be seated better. We were, very graciously, and over a flute of Champagne, the machine of daily life went still and we embarked on a three-hour cruise in another world, a privileged place of exquisite manners, courtly charm, and impeccable elegance.

The Japanese trio sitting next to us were, in fact, the most elegant people I'd seen in a long time, and studying them occasionally while we nibbled gougères, tiny puffy cheese pastries, and discussed the menu, I was reminded that elegance is the art of omission, something almost everyone else in the room appeared to understand, too. A handsome older southern woman in a simple but immaculately tailored black dress with a square neckline wore a simple choker of turquoise beads nearly the same color as her eyes, and her distinguished, rather leonine husband sat on the other side of Bruno, and a strikingly attractive English family—Mum in a vintage shantung suit that had probably been run up in Hong Kong, Dad in a blazer, and their three pretty, poised daughters in loose silk shifts—occupied the table in front of us. Together, our neighbors formed a quietly glamorous tableau that only heightened the implicit exclusivity of being seated in this cosseted dining room with caramel-colored wood paneling and polite modern art on the walls.

My first course of tiny tender ravioli stuffed with fresh goat cheese and fine ribbons of arugula and mousserons (wild mushrooms) no bigger than thumbtacks in a puddle of rich veal stock was a perfect example of chef Alain Solivérès's style. Solivérès, an intensely talented cook who came to Taillevent when Philippe Legendre moved to Le V at the Four Seasons George V, is a gifted, gutsy miniaturist who composes his dishes with an almost surgical precision that often belies his exceptionally lyrical culinary imagination. It was the finely sliced arugula, for example, that made this dish so good by adding texture and tiny vegetal dashes of punctuation to the earthy tones of the stock and mushrooms and the soothing lactic background of the goat cheese. Bruno's petit farcis, a riff on a traditional Niçois dish of stuffed baby vegetables, came as an edible still life that included a tiny eggplant, onion, tomato, and round zucchini, each of which had been perfectly cooked and contained a different stuffing. I could have sworn that tweezers had been needed to compose the mesclun (mixed baby salad leaves) that accompanied this dish, since some of the greens were so fine and feathery that they were almost invisible.

Similarly, the delicate scattering of freshly cracked peppercorns on the thick, exquisitely cooked slice of duckling that was

Bruno's main course was applied with such pharmaceutical artistry that it completely transformed the succulent fowl into something one was tasting for the first time. The garnish of sour cherries skewered on vanilla beans and a gossamer sauce of pan juices further rendered this one of the most remarkable dishes I've ever tasted. Since we wanted only one wine, I had initially planned on a red Meursault, but the delightful sommelier highly recommended a Givry, an excellent but less expensive red Burgundy, and although it would have benefited from being carafed, it was a brilliant choice. The wine list alone is a reason to come to Taillevent, since few restaurants in the world offer a more imaginative, approachable—the price range for a restaurant of this caliber is surprisingly friendly—and original carte.

Though many of the other customers that night seemed to have decided on one of the two tasting menus offered, I think food as ethereal as Solivérès's should be consumed homeopathically. I wouldn't have wanted both a fish and a meat course, and as magnificent as the cheese course may be, I was quite content with three courses.

Desserts are divided between those based on fruit and those based on chocolate, and wanting a conclusion that was more adagio than arpeggio, I ordered the croustillant d'abricots et roses de Damas. The tartness of the apricots met the residual sourness of the sorrel sauce on my sweetbreads perfectly, and perfumed notes of rose petal flattered the buttery richness of its caramelized tuile base. Bruno's baba au rhum, that most masculine of Gallic desserts, was the best one I've ever tasted, too, since the round sphere of fine sponge cake had imbibed just the right amount of syrup and smoky, ambered old rum, and a spoonful of ivory-colored vanilla-bean-flecked whipped cream referred back to the richness of his duckling.

As happens in the enclosed and pampered world of a luxury cruise ship, you become keenly observant of the smallest details, and some of them here were wanting. I can't understand why Taillevent doesn't serve better bread, and I shouldn't have had to ask for more of the luscious sorrel sauce for my sweetbreads. The wait for dessert also teetered on the brink of being uncomfortable. But I suspect that the late Jean-Claude Vrinat, who founded Taillevent in 1946 and who oversaw its ascent to becoming an international benchmark of gastronomic luxury, would have almost been flattered by these complaints, since they issue from subscribing to the context of perfection he so magnificently succeeded in creating at this restaurant, a place where hugely pleasurable and very personalized experiences are the coin of the realm. Oh, and just in case you were wondering about the occasion of this very special meal—knowing that I needed an infallible benchmark of gastronomic brilliance to pilot by, it was the first one I ate specifically to write this book.

· ✿ ·

IN A WORD: If you've ever looked at old photographs of the Duchess of Windsor or Maria Callas in fancy Paris restaurants and yearned to have an approximate experience of the taut postwar glamour they represent, you'll love Taillevent, which rather impressively manages to be the diva of dining in Paris without being remotely stuffy. Alain Solivérès is an extraordinarily talented chef, the restaurant has one of the world's top ten wine lists, and the service is superb.

DON'T MISS: Taillevent's menu follows the seasons, but dishes to look for include lobster boudin (lobster sausage); scallop rémoulade; ravioli aux mousserons (cheese-and-arugula-filled button-sized ravioli with mousseron mushrooms in veal stock); petits farcis (stuffed baby vegetables Niçois style); cream of watercress soup with Sevruga caviar; spelt risotto with bone marrow, black truffle, whipped cream, and Parmesan; caillette de porcelet aux épices et raisins de Malaga (a sublime dish of pork sausage wrapped in caul fat and tiny pork chops with carmelized cabbage and Puy lentils in a sauce studded with plump, juicy raisins); John Dory stuffed with olives; duckling roasted with cherries; chausson feuilleté de ris de veau (veal sweetbreads in pastry with sorrel sauce); chocolate ravioli; baba au rhum; croustillant d'abricots et roses de Damas (braised apricots on a caramelized crust with rose essence).

. . .

[62] 15 rue Lamennais, 8th, 01.44.95.15.01. MÉTRO: Charles-de-Gaulle-Étoile, George V, or Ternes. OPEN Monday to Friday for lunch and dinner. CLOSED Saturday and Sunday. www.taillevent.com ▪ $$$$

EATING THE UNSPEAKABLE

· ⁂ ·

IT MAY SURPRISE YOU, BUT I'LL CONFESS THAT I STU-
diously avoided the lobsters served by my grandmother at her
Rhode Island summerhouse for twenty years, or until I celebrated my twenty-first birthday by realizing what a fool I'd
been. Instead, as the others cracked and tugged and dug and
splattered, I sat quietly in my picnic-table corner eating a cheese-
burger. Why? I was a shy kid who hated messes and strong
tastes and smells; crimson, scalded lobsters were just too
"other" for me.

The fear of unknown victuals is often experienced as visceral, but during a couple of decades in Paris, I've learned that
such an aversion is almost always cultural. This is why a sub-
stantial appendix would be needed to list all of the famous
French delicacies I wouldn't have touched at gunpoint when I
arrived in Paris. Suffice it to say I wasn't wild about game,
found offal awful, and nothing could pry my shell open when it
came to oysters and mussels, to say nothing of bulots (sea snails,
or whelks). Most fish flopped, too.

So my first weeks in town were perilous. As the new correspondent for a fashion-mongering American press group, I was
invited to some of the grandest tables in town. The locals
wanted to size me up and make a good impression—and almost
to a one, their good intentions induced a gastro trauma or two.
How vividly I remember the first ambush. An elegant attaché de
presse with a particule before her surname—the telltale "de,"

"de la," or "du" that always indicates aristocratic aspirations if not a family tree that will stand up to rigorous genealogical investigation—organized a dinner with a set menu in a private dining room at Lucas-Carton, now Le Senderens but then one of the most opulent restaurants in the capital. As she rather heavy-handedly hinted, it would be my opportunity to meet a carefully selected group of very important Parisians. Yikes.

I can't say that I was much looking forward to the dinner, and I took an immediate dislike to the countess on my right with a face as taut as an expertly pitched tent when she confided that she found Americans amusing because we're mongrels. Right. The lady on my left kept correcting my French, making it nearly impossible for me to finish a single flawed sentence, and the very elderly man in front of me required shouting-level conversation due to an apparently faulty hearing aid. After I'd made some innocuous remark about the beauty of Paris at the top of my lungs, he said he preferred to speak in German or Russian. Mais, bien sûr (Yes, of course), I thought with some exasperation—after all, it's perfectly normal to expect an American to speak both of these languages.

When the first course was served, I was relieved to have a reason to withdraw from the conversation. On a large cobalt blue glass plate, a variety of the tiniest vegetables I'd ever seen surrounded a thatch of salad frilled with various herbs. I ate a dollhouse-sized carrot and a skinless cherry tomato and then prodded the pretty mound of leaves. For a few seconds, I couldn't believe my eyes. A tiny stiffened claw attached to the minute leg of something was nestled in the brush. God knows how this hideous little object had found its way onto my plate, but I didn't want to embarrass anyone, so I tucked it under a usefully large spinach leaf. And got busted. "Ah, la-la, Alexandre! You must try, it's so good, it's a grive," said the countess. She twiddled a little grive leg between thumb and index finger and started gnawing at the joint's pitiful quantity of dessicated meat. I twiddled, too, and then, with the lightning speed of an escaping convict, I landed the critter in my jacket pocket.

Then, just after the main course had been served, over the shoulder of the I-prefer-to-speak-German-and-Russian man, I caught a glimpse of someone in the mirror who looked amazingly like the main figure in the Edvard Munch painting *The Scream*. Moi. There was a dead bird—a pelican?—with a long beak on the plate in front of me. "Ah, quelle bonheur, une bécasse!" The countess was speaking to me, but I didn't look up. I was too busy starring in my own little version of *The Birds*. By the time this pterodactyl had invaded my porcelain, I was ravenous, so I picked up a knife and fork and went at it. The taste? Old wet dog and spoiled hamburger with a whiff of earthworms crushed on the road after a summer rain.

On the heels of this ornithological nightmare, I opted out of the beau monde circuit for a while, and, by following my basest instincts, I busted open a brave new world. Let me explain. If good manners (not wishing to offend), the fear of social disapprobation (being thought a rube), or plain old curiosity occasionally impel someone to try something he finds unspeakable, it's the possibility of love—and more specifically sex—that probably sees off more self-inflicted food taboos than any other motivation.

We were walking on a flat beach in Normandy next to an army green sea on a sunny September weekday after having spent a whole fugitive morning in bed. On any walk, one leads, the other follows, and on this day, I let myself be led. We didn't speak because we didn't need to, and I hoped this was the sign of a newborn complicity, so even when the walk started to get longer than I had in mind, I held my peace. Then, on the other side of a headland, there was a weathered wooden cabin just off the sand with striped umbrellas shading the handful of tables on a sandy terrace. "Oh, how charming—shall we have lunch?" Fine by me, or at least it was until we were seated and I realized we'd just dropped anchor at an oyster bar. Sipping Muscadet, I hastily plotted a dozen different ways of escaping the bivalves but couldn't coin anything credible ("I love you so much that all I want is a big ham sandwich, darling"—nope) before a big beaten-up aluminum tray filled with crushed ice was set on a stand and I found myself faced down by two dozen of 'em. Oh boy. "Tu aimes les huîtres?" "Oui, oui, oui, oui," I love oysters. Okay, here goes, and wow, I'm egg-beatered in the surf of love with a mouth full of seawater. And I love it. I really do. Punctuated by yellow butter grainy with sea salt and smeared on small pieces of rye bread, the oysters are almost as good as the sex that preceded them.

The relationship ended, but I licked my wounds in the possession of a real prize—a passion for oysters. And so it went. In the hope of pleasing a lover at the beginning of an affair or battening down the supply of good sex in one that had been well and truly launched, I ended up eating many of the foods I had once found repugnant—elvers, reindeer, Czech Christmas carp (really dreadful), the list is long. I didn't end up liking all of them, of course, but I became enough of a bona fide omnivore to happily travel thousands of miles to sample things spooky and unknown—fruit bat curry in the Seychelles, for example (bony, smoky, and gamey are all you need to know).

But why am I telling you all of this? It's because I used to be afraid to eat lobster, and if you recognize yourself in the timorous twit I once was, I want you to know you can change. To wit, why fly all the way to Paris to eat chicken breasts or steak? Push your limits instead. At worst, you'll have a gruesome gastro tale of your own to recount when you get home. More likely, you'll be amazed to discover that you actually *like* pig's feet, beef muzzle salad vinaigrette, and calf's brains. P.S. I'm still not wild about bécasse.

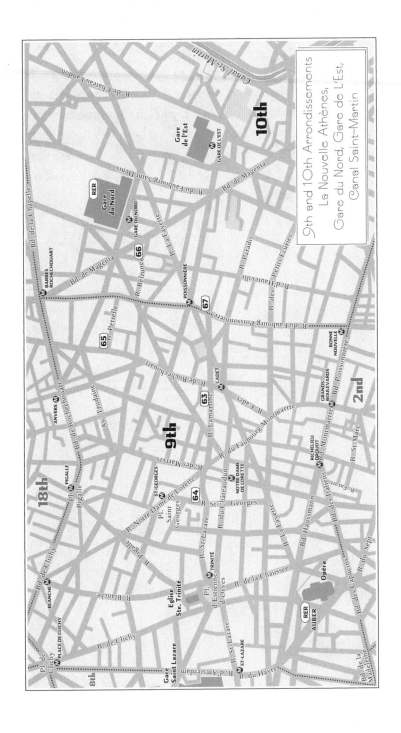

9th and 10th Arrondissements
La Nouvelle Athènes,
Gare du Nord, Gare de L'Est,
Canal Saint-Martin

9TH *and* 10TH
ARRONDISSEMENTS

•

LA NOUVELLE ATHÈNES,
GARE DU NORD,
GARE DE L'EST,
CANAL SAINT-MARTIN

Carte Blanche

AS THE REST OF THE WESTERN WORLD HAS LEARNED TO
eat well, kicking Paris, the once impregnable citadel of good
eating, in the shins has been nearly irresistible, which is why almost everyone has missed the big story. Okay, there are now
very good restaurants in cities like Minneapolis, Winnipeg,
Adelaide, and Auckland, but none of those places has the gastronomic underbrush of Paris. Within the last ten years, the
French capital has seen an extraordinary renewal of its gastronomic ballast, the neighborhood restaurant. Let me explain.

It was the friendly young woman at the charcuterie in the
rue des Martyrs where I buy the most delicious saucisson
(sausage) in the world who first told me about Carte Blanche in
the rue Lamartine. "C'est super bon! Et c'est pas cher" ("It's really good! And it's not expensive") she said, explaining that the

cook, Jean-François Renard, had previously worked at Beauvilliers when it was still the best restaurant in Montmartre.

Since I live within walking distance and am always looking for new locales, I booked for dinner that night with my friends Richard, from Cleveland, and Roberto, from Caracas, who also live nearby, and the three of us had an outstanding meal. I instantly liked the look of the place, too, with its zinc bar, exposed stone walls, and wooden tables set with votive candles. Sure, the service was a little too mannered and cool for a small neighborhood place—I wasn't surprised to learn later that the headwaiter had previously been maître d'hôtel at Pierre Gagnaire—but my scallop carpaccio with Granny Smith apples and mango cubes, Richard's luscious tartine, or open-faced sandwich, of foie gras and calf's foot, and Roberto's stuffed piquillo peppers and Basque charcuterie made this easy to overlook. Our main courses were excellent, too. Richard and I shared a tender roasted baby lamb shoulder, which came with a small cast-iron casserole of baby

vegetables, and Roberto loved his veal cheeks with cumin and cardamom. Desserts were outstanding, too, including a runny ginger-caramel cake served with madeleines and almond crème brûlée with sautéed Mirabelle plums. Walking home after dinner, I couldn't help thinking that food this good and affordable, served in a pleasant, casual setting, remains the realm in which Paris still uniquely excels. To wit, if you were to pluck Renard out of this sweet neighborhood setting and slot him into a large, glamorous dining room overseen by a high-powered PR person, he'd be a star. Happily, in Paris, the culture of good eating is still so nonchalant that a talent like Renard is content to earn his keep at an excellent neighborhood restaurant.

· ·

IN A WORD: Excellent, imaginative contemporary French food in a pleasant setting with well-drilled service makes this small restaurant in the heart of the city well worth seeking out.

DON'T MISS: As is true of many of the city's brightest talents, chef Jean-François Renard changes his menu regularly, but based on many meals here, I recommend the scallop carpaccio with Granny Smith apples and mango cubes; stuffed piquillo peppers with Basque charcuterie; tartine (open-faced sandwich) of foie gras and calf's foot; roast shoulder of baby lamb; veal cheeks with cumin and cardamom; pissaladière de thon (open-faced tuna tart); wild duck breast; runny ginger-caramel cake with madeleines; almond crème brûlée with sautéed Mirabelle plums.

. . .

[63] 6 rue Lamartine, 9th, 01.48.78.12.20. MÉTRO: **Cadet.** OPEN **Monday to Friday for lunch and dinner. Saturday dinner only.** CLOSED **Sunday.** ▪ **$$**

Casa Olympe

THE MURANO CHANDELIERS AND SCONCES ARE LOVELIER in this low-ceilinged dining room in the heart of Paris than they are in any Venetian palazzo, and I think it's because they perfectly channel the pedigreed nineteenth-century bohemian sensibility that makes the 9th Arrondissement one of the most delicious parts of the city these days. Casa Olympe is located on a sloping street running off of the Place Saint-Georges, a perfect pulse point of the changing tides of Parisian chic. If the area was fashionably louche as home to a funky, frolicsome arty crowd that included George Sand, Frédéric Chopin, and Hector Berlioz, along with more than its share of demimondaines and demimondains, when it was first built between 1800 and 1900, it skid into a long senescence after World War I, and this faded, slightly dreamy tone is still occasionally apparent even as the 9th has emerged as the next credible address for the Parisian bourgeoisie (who otherwise require the 6th, 7th, 8th, 16th, or 17th).

What's brought change to this dense, handsome, and profoundly Parisian quartier is the arrival of the Bobos, bourgeois double-income couples who have an arty sensibility and the means to indulge it. They love the herringbone parquet floors and wedding-cake moldings of the apartments in this area as a perfect expression of their own casual good taste and blowsy elegance, an aesthetic that's the quintessence of being a Parisian. No one makes a visible effort in this city, which is why even the most aggressively avant-garde foreign fashion designers are eventually not only tamed by the city's vividly stitched code of bourgeois pleasures but come to love these very same strictures.

At Olympe, Olympe Versini, a proud, powerful woman with a shiny black bob and a big temper, was formerly a figure of the Paris night, when she and an ex-husband ran Olympe, a see-and-be-seen party table popular with rock-and-roll and movie stars. Now she does passionate, personal cooking that expresses her own sinewy beliefs in the importance of eating and drinking well. Olympe opened this place, her own restaurant, eight years ago, after recovering from a bout of life changes, and since then she's created a delightful, intimate butterscotch-and-bordeaux dining room with an exquisite menu.

On a January night, following a performance of *Love Letters,* the A. R. Gurney play, translated into French and magnificently played by Philippe Noiret and Anouk Aimée, French friends from the north of France and I go for a late supper. And it's superb. All day, I've been looking forward to the chestnut-flour galette topped with a wobbly poached egg, a pinch of coarse gray sea salt and cracked black pepper, a drizzle of melted butter, and a sprig of chervil. This is the simple, soulful food Versini's ancestors—Corsicans who once lived on chestnut flour—brought to town and cooked defiantly and with love, and it's the type of cooking you think of when you're really hungry. Similarly, a casserole of winter vegetables braised with chunks of fatback from an organically raised pig is so full of flavor that we compete to mop up the sauce, much to the delight of the decorous but friendly middle-aged waitress who correctly takes such avidity as a compliment. "Mais, vous avez raison" ("But you're absolutely right") she says with the encouraging tones of a schoolteacher. Then a huge copper saucepan comes to the table, smoking with herbs from the maquis, the fragrant heath of thyme, rosemary, myrtle, and bay that covers much of Corsica. The exquisitely cooked lamb sits on a bed of crunchy golden brown diced potatoes, the better to soak up the juices of the meat. With two bottles of Côtes du Rhône, we eat all of it, and Jean-Marie, a wonderful older man with a snowy head of hair, ice blue eyes, and the most generous laugh I may have ever heard, says, "Alec, I've always remembered something you said to me, that enjoying a meal is as much about conviviality as it is about what's on your plate. Tonight, I think they're in balance."

He was absolutely right, too—Casa Olympe is one of those restaurants that induces a profound sense of well-being, and this is why I wasn't at all surprised to see the designer Jean-Paul Gaultier come in just before last orders and take a table by the window with some friends. His signature Jean Harlow–blond crew cut glowed almost white in the lamplight, and, as always, he was bright-eyed and smiling, a big, bashful, slightly needy boy who was looking for someone to mother him. He'd come to the right place. And so had I.

. ✿ .

IN A WORD: An intimate bistro with a Corsican accent that offers a snapshot of one of Paris's lesser-known and most delicious arrondissements, the 9th. Rapidly becoming a Right Bank annex to Saint-Germain, the area is popular with fashion types and the local bourgeoisie. Olympe is one of the best female cooks in Paris, and this is a place to go anytime you want a really good stick-to-your-ribs meal and a little bit of babying.

DON'T MISS: Black pudding; chestnut crêpe with fried egg and salt butter; ravioli stuffed with roast duck; tuna sautéed with bacon and baby onions; red mullet with baby onion flan; roasted lamb with Corsican herbs; red fruit salad with almond blancmange.

. . .

[64] 48 rue Saint-Georges, 9th, 01.42.85.26.02. MÉTRO: Saint-Georges. OPEN Monday to Friday for lunch and dinner. CLOSED Saturday and Sunday. ▪ $$

La Grille

THE DAY RESTAURANTS LIKE LA GRILLE NO LONGER EXIST, Paris will be a lesser place. Geneviève Cullerre and her chef husband, Yves, have been in the saddle here for forty years, but her welcome and his cooking remain as sincere as that of any wet-behind-the-ears young couple just starting out. Their hospitality is tempered by a wry but good-natured and utterly charming mien that tells you they've seen it all, and if some of it was lamentable, most of it—their customers, Parisian life, running a restaurant, their marriage, and you—was not only a lot of fun but often rather hilarious. On a rainy spring night, I called ahead to say we were running late—last orders are at 9:30 here—and when we came through the door with our dripping umbrellas and rain-streaked coats, Madame, dressed in a white polka-dotted short-sleeved rayonette dress with a matching short-sleeved jacket greeted us with a grin and whooped, "Nous avions peur de vous avoir perdus!" ("We were afraid we'd lost you!").

"I know this place! I've always loved it," said my friend Martine as we settled at a large banquette table in the back dining room, a curious Miss Havisham's bedroom sort of space with a well-worn Belle Époque stenciled terra-cotta tile floor, a decor of lace christening gowns, old hats, and helmets on a brass hat rack, and the odd dusty doll backdropped by the magnificent thickly painted but finely patterned wood-paneled walls. "I used to come here when I was working as a designer for a textile company in this neighborhood. I'd just moved back to Paris after my years as a Boston au pair, and it was my first job. I think this may have even been the first place I ever came for a real business meal," said Martine, adding, sotto voce, "Qu'est ce qu'elle est belle mais ça ne prends pas" ("She's very pretty, but it's not working out") and cocking her head toward the couple on a date at the table next to ours.

I glanced at them, a beautiful young woman with a long mane of thick chestnut hair, a knit vest, and a jacquard scarf intricately and elegantly tied at the base of her neck as only French women know how to do, and her date. His grown-out beard showed off porcelain skin, and his blue serge blazer was cut uncomfortably high in the armholes, so I didn't even need to see his gold signet ring to know he was a young French aristo.

From the brief purple mimeographed menu, we ordered marinated mackerel, salade frisée aux lardons, and a grilled turbot in sauce nantaise (beurre blanc with watercress) for two, plus a bottle of Martine's favorite red Sancerre, and then quickly returned to our conversation, much of which had to do with the new play of a mutual friend in New York and Martine's recent trip to Montevideo—she loves the Uruguayan capital so much that she's thinking of buying an apartment there. "Et alors! Ces pauvres bébés n'ont rien à boire. Il faut les aider!" ("What's going on here? These poor babies have nothing to drink—they must be helped!") said Madame to the waiter, while briefly kneading my shoulder.

Just as the first courses arrived, I found myself thinking that the worst thing to do in a restaurant is to go to dinner with someone who'll talk about the food. Anyone who really loves restaurants is always there because he's as much a voyeur as a gourmand, and all that's ever really needed during any successful meal is the occasional well-timed exchange of consensual remarks indicating that the food is really food. And at La Grille, it was. Sure, the salad had too much dressing, but Martine got a whole mackerel and did it proud, the bread was delicious, and we were silenced when the turbot was presented by the older waiter with the tight black service vest and dark blue eyes. On an oval steel serving tray fringed with watercress, the whole fish arrived—flat, thick, and perfectly grilled so that its skin had become a blistered golden robe—and was then whisked away to be boned. "Il est sauvage, et moi aussi" ("He's wild [as opposed to farm raised], and so am I") punned the waiter, and while he worked, Madame brought a sauceboat of Nantais sauce, a serving dish of steamed potatoes, and a sublime gateaux de pommes de terre, a sort of molded version of hash browns. Martine, never missing a cue, immediately protested that she couldn't eat that, and when I said "I can," I was rewarded with a kiss from Madame. "Je savais tout de suite que je l'adorerais" ("I instantly knew that I loved him"), she said, and I blushed.

By the time our oeufs à la neige (tufts of meringue floating on crème anglaise) and profiteroles came, I noticed that we were the only ones left in the dining room. A cigarette butt smoldered in an ashtray where the young couple had been, the squawking parrot upstairs had gone still, and the only sound was the lovely sound of cutlery on china from the other side of the partition, where the staff dinner was in full progress. The desserts were as good as the rest of the meal, a classic Gallic feed that's become a real luxury in a city that's changing as quickly as Paris, and when we walked up front after paying our bill, Madame didn't miss a beat. "J'espère qu'on a fait des conquêtes!" ("I hope we've made some conquests!"). She had indeed, but when we stepped outside to hail a taxi on the shiny wet sidewalk, I saw someone who hadn't, a solitary familiar figure in an army green moleskin coat with his arm raised, the aristo. He smiled when he saw us—"Si non çe soir, peut-être demain soir," he said with a shrug. "Au moins elle a aimé le resto." ("If not tonight, maybe tomorrow night—at least she loved the restaurant.") I did, too.

· ⸎ ·

IN A WORD: Beat tracks to this warm and wonderful old-fashioned bistro before the owners retire. It offers a solid dose of prewar Paris and a great feed, too.

DON'T MISS: Duck terrine with hazelnuts; mackerel in white wine; boeuf bourguignon; turbot au beurre blanc or sauce nantaise; oeufs à la neige; profiteroles.

. . .

[**67**] **80 rue du Faubourg-Poissonnière, 10th, 01.47.70.89.73.** MÉTRO: **Poissonnière.** OPEN **Monday to Friday for lunch and dinner.** CLOSED **Saturday and Sunday.** ▪ **$$**

Chez Michel

THIERRY BRETON IS A BRILLIANT CHEF. AMONG OTHER talents, he's one of the best fish cooks in Paris and an absolute master of the edible detail that lights up his consistently careful, caring, but ultimately lusty cooking, so it's always a pleasure to return to his funky and rather chaotic restaurant, one of Paris's

most deservedly popular contemporary French bistros. Breton is a Breton, and his menu, which has a chalkboard addendum that changes regularly, often features riffs of traditional dishes from Brittany and Breton foods rarely found in Paris, where the inaccurate perception of the cooking of France's westernmost province still runs to oysters and crêpes.

After training with Christian Constant when he was chef at Les Ambassadeurs, Breton struck out on his own by opening a good-value bistro in what was then a rather improbable setting, a 1939-vintage half-timbered building in a slightly scruffy neighborhood near the Gare du Nord. As his renown has grown, however, this tatty part of town has pulled up its socks, and Chez Michel has become a destination table, pulling Parisians of all stripes from all over the city.

I've eaten here many times and unfailingly come away delighted by the food but also hopeful that he might move to a more comfortable setting and spend a little more time training his staff. The trade-off for great eating here remains a certain discomfort—the tables are too tightly spaced—and a willingness to accept that expediency rather than polish is the priority of the waitresses. Ultimately, however, I'll gladly excuse these shortcomings for such exceptional food.

I especially love Breton's gift for simplicity and the way he jolts homey dishes like the sauté of veal with spring vegetables I had here the other night with haute cuisine levels of quality, refinement, and precision. Served in a copper-clad saucepan, the veal was tender and full of flavor, bathed in a cream sauce based on excellent veal stock, sprinkled with chives, and garnished with a delicious mixture of crunchy broad beans, string beans, baby carrots, and onions, which had obviously been cooked independently of the veal and added at the last minute.

I was dining with Suzy, a self-described "shopping goddess" and the author of the "Born to Shop" guidebooks who was in town for a night en route from her base in San Antonio, Texas, to her house in Provence, and, as is our custom, we freely foraged in each other's plates. Her starter of crabmeat in a creamy gelée made with shellfish stock had deep, ruddy marine notes but was vividly fresh and light, while my Corsican charcuterie, served on a cutting board with a small salad of purslane, a crunchy salad green, was outstanding. Corsica produces the best charcuterie in France, and a hunk of chestnut-wood-smoked mule sausage with a big hunk of some of the best bread in Paris—the restaurant bakes its own—spread with the country's best butter, from Jean-Yves Bordier in Saint-Malo, was an exquisite lesson in the virtues of simplicity. Bordier's bright yellow butter is so good that you eat it like a condiment, savoring its rich, vaguely herbaceous taste. Suzy's cabillaud (cod) also featured Bordier's handiwork, since it had a slight sauce of Bordier's hauntingly good seaweed-flecked butter, an ideal garnish for fish. She sulked briefly when I forked into her Paris-Brest, easily the best in Paris. Choux (puff) pastry filled with hazelnut buttercream and sprinkled with slivered almonds, it was created to commemorate a bicycle race between Paris and Brest in 1891 and is one of my favorite desserts. The shopping goddess was somewhat consoled by a slice of my kouign amann, a flat, layered, buttery Breton pastry served on a small cutting board, but that missing piece of Paris-Brest rankled enough that she booked a table for dinner on the night of her return trip through Paris, a meal I doubt we'll share.

· ⟨⟩ ·

IN A WORD: Chef Thierry Breton is one of the best young chefs in Paris, and the quality of his regionally inspired contemporary bistro cooking is consistently outstanding, especially given the relatively modest price of his prix fixe menu. Definitely worth traveling to no matter where you're staying in Paris, this place is also a superb choice for lunch if you're before or after the Eurostar train from London or trains to Brussels and Amsterdam, since the Gare du Nord is just around the corner. Reservations essential.

DON'T MISS: Sautéed ormeaux (abalone); scallops cooked in their own shells with salted butter and herbs; tuna steak with coriander; roasted John Dory with potato puree; kig ha farz (a Breton specialty of boiled buckwheat flour with pork and vegetables); roast veal with baby turnips; rabbit braised with rosemary and Swiss chard; Breton cheese tray with cider jelly; Paris-Brest; kouign amann.

. . .

[66] 10 rue de Belzunce, 10th, 01.44.53.06.20. MÉTRO: Gare du Nord. OPEN Tuesday to Friday for lunch and dinner. Monday dinner only. CLOSED Saturday and Sunday. • $$

Le Pétrelle

WITH ITS ENCHANTINGLY RAMSHACKLE PROUSTIAN DECOR, including a cat snoozing on a side table and a wonderful mix of nineteenth-century bric-a-brac that the owner, Jean-Luc André, has collected all over France, the oriental-carpeted dining room of this delightful bistro in the 9th has a slightly theatrical, authentically bohemian atmosphere. In fact, it feels more like a writer's study or even a psychiatrist's office than a restaurant. The space was originally the workshop of a picture frame maker who specialized in gilding, the minute application of small, fluttering squares of gold to elaborately carved woodwork. This palpable past adds to the blowsy, baroque charm of the place, and on a warm summer night, it was no surprise to spot the fashion designer Christian Lacroix—he's on record as saying that this is his favorite restaurant—dining with a friend. Le Pétrelle is, in fact, a new celebrity favorite in Paris, since Madonna showed up with her husband, Guy Ritchie, the following week.

What's pulling the famous faces are the delicious market menus that André, a self-taught chef, serves up and the wonderfully louche bohème redux atmosphere of the 9th Arrondissement, dubbed La Nouvelle Athènes, or New Athens, during the nineteenth century because it was home to a dense concentration of artists and eccentrics. Now, with the beau monde bailing out of Saint-Germain-des-Prés because it's become too expensive and touristy, the 9th is blossoming all over again, which explains this restaurant's intriguing clientele—here a rare-book dealer, there a costume historian, with only a sprinkling of young bankers.

Le Pétrelle is as diverting visually as it is gastronomically. A donkey's head made from straw hangs on the wall, there are two stunning wooden chandeliers plus crimson wall coverings that look as though they were originally ecclesiastical, and, at every table, miscellaneous flea market chairs, flowers from a country garden, and a little stack of books. On ours, *Les Années Pop* by

Pierre Le Tan, another regular, with charming pen-and-ink drawings of le tout Paris in those days when they were young and went to clubs every night—Valentino, Karl Lagerfeld, Gilles Dufour, Loulou de la Falaise, Yves Saint Laurent, the whole seventies gang whose aesthetic sensibility—a spontaneous mixture of flea market, ethnic, and modern—still informs Parisian life.

Within minutes of being seated, the gracious waiter served us a saucer of radishes with a ramekin of fleur de sel, the finest French sea salt, for dipping, and two thimble-sized goat cheeses sporting sprigs of thyme as an amuse-bouche, exactly the sort of stylish rustic hors d'oeuvre you'd expect at the table of a smart young hostess during a weekend in the country. On a still July night, two superb starters—a salad of poulet du Gers en gelée (cold jellied chicken, a dish it's easy to imagine Balzac eating) topped with summer truffles (more for their texture and perfume than their taste) and another one of rabbit terrine garnished with grilled eggplant slices, zucchini ribbons poached in lemon verbena broth, and a round zucchini roasted and stuffed with ratatouille immediately made indifferent appetites alert.

André's signature is a lavish but intelligent use of fresh herbs—long green whiskers of chive, aromatic sprigs of fresh tarragon and chervil, and other seasonal herbs from the Ile-de-France (the region in which Paris is located) instead of the Mediterranean trio—thyme, rosemary, and bay—that have come to dominate contemporary Parisian cooking. These neglected French herbs punctuate the originality of his disciplined and passionate market menus, too, highlighting the superbly fresh produce and the precision of his cooking and seasoning. They also give it a geographic marker—this is clearly the seasonal produce of the Ile-de-France—as did the garnishes of fork-mashed new potatoes and a mix of baby vegetables, including a crayon-sized carrot, a baby beet, a slender leek, and a roasted tomato that came with a tournedo of beef, and a succulent wild Scottish salmon steak served with pan juices deglazed with Xérès vinegar.

The black cherry clafoutis I had for dessert made me think of Colette. The ripe cherries bled sweet purple juice when I bit into them and were mounted in a perfect eggy custard; I think this dessert would have made her swoon, since she craved simple, sensual country cooking. Similarly, white peaches poached in lemon verbena syrup and accompanied by roasted apricots and a luscious iced vanilla meringue were something Sarah Bernhardt might have served to friends at a summer lunch in the garden at her country house on Belle-Ile, the magical island off the coast of Brittany. Then, just before the coffee, the waiter toured the dining room with a tray of warm, crumbly, buttery sablés (shortbread cookies), each one topped with a single raspberry, a final elegant flourish to a deeply satisfying meal.

· ·

IN A WORD: A dreamy, well-mannered, and very personal candlelit restaurant that offers some outstanding market-driven contemporary French cooking, along with a lot of romance in its eclectic decor. Très Parisien.

DON'T MISS: Sautéed white asparagus and morel mushrooms; artichauts en poivrade (marinated artichokes) with chervil root chips; scallops with truffles (in season); sea bass roasted with fleur de sel and crispy herbs; roast baby lamb with lemon thyme

and fava beans; moelleux au chocolat (runny chocolate cake);
rhubarb compote with strawberries.

. . .

[65] 34 rue Pétrelle, 9th, 01.42.82.11.02. MÉTRO: Anvers or Poissonnière.
Dinner only. CLOSED Sunday and Monday. • $$

THE FRENCH FOREIGN LEGION:
THE PARISIAN PASSION FOR
NORTH AFRICAN COOKING

· ·

THE FRENCH HAVE A COMPLICATED RELATIONSHIP WITH foreign food. When I first moved to Paris more than twenty years ago, foreign restaurants were still regarded as night-off standbys or places you'd go for quick, cheap, exotic eats instead of a serious meal. Today, even though most Parisians still insist on the primacy of French cooking, this attitude has changed enormously, the result of the deeper integration of Europe and also the travel that has broadened the gastronomic horizons of many Parisians.

Though Italian food is very popular in Paris, it's not what I'd generally recommend to anyone who wants something other than French cooking during a visit to the capital. Why? The French still prefer their pasta well cooked and their risotto mushy. Sidelining Italian food, then, the city's signature foreign cooking is North African, a result of France's long, intimate, and complex relationship with the Mahgreb—the North African countries of Algeria, Morocco, and Tunisia, all of which were once French colonies.

The French are in fact so besotted with North African cuisine that surveys of national eating habits regularly reveal that the country's second favorite dish—steak frites remains number one, *bien sûr*—is couscous, that most emblematic of North

African recipes: steamed semolina grains variously garnished with roasted lamb, spicy lamb sausage (merguez), chicken, fish, or vegetables and sauced with vegetables (carrots, zucchini, and turnips) cooked in bouillon.

This passion for couscous is very much a reflection of French history. France's colonial adventures on the other side of the Mediterranean began in 1830, when it took control of Algeria. During the century that followed, Algeria became so much of an appendage to France that it was a shock to the Gallic psyche when a bitter war for independence broke out at the end of the 1950s. This ugly struggle culminated with the independence of Algeria in 1962 and the repatriation of hundreds of thousands of French colonists, unkindly dubbed pieds noirs (dirty feet) by the mainland French. Similar exoduses followed the independence of Morocco and Tunisia in 1956, and there was also heavy immigration of North Africans to France to work in the country's factories, mines, and fields. Following the arrival of the ex-colonists and immigrants, restaurants opened to serve them the food they'd left behind, and as the French began vacationing in Morocco and Tunisia en masse, these expat tables slowly moved into the mainstream.

Today, Paris has the best selection of North African restaurants of any city in Europe. While most all of them offer a satisfying feed, the cooking of Morocco is perhaps the most refined and varied. In addition to couscous, other Moroccan specialties include tagines—meat or fish braised with prunes, olives, preserved lemons, figs, and other garnishes in a ceramic dish with a cone-shaped ceramic top—and pastilla, which is boned fowl, usually chicken, squab, or pigeon, cooked in layers of flaky pastry. The condiment that all North African kitchens share is harissa, a hot red pepper paste that also includes garlic, caraway seeds, cumin, tomato puree, salt, and olive oil. Traditionally, it's used to garnish couscous, with a spoonful or two being dissolved in a ladle of bouillon before being poured over the dish. Here's a list of my favorite North African tables in Paris.

L'ATLAS. This popular and long-running Left Bank Moroccan restaurant has an attractively decorated dining room and a reliably good kitchen. Try the salad of eggplant and artichokes, pigeon pastilla, and tagine of grouper with saffron. 10 boulevard Saint-Germain, 5th, 01.46.33.86.98. Métro: Maubert-Mutualité. Open Wednesday to Saturday for lunch and dinner. Tuesday dinner only. Closed Monday and Tuesday lunch.

LA BOULE ROUGE. Popular with showbiz personalities and fashion industry types, this lively Jewish-Tunisian restaurant serves up a variety of dishes not found elsewhere in Paris, including l'akoud (tripe cooked with tomatoes and cumin), minina (chicken soufflé with eggs), couscous bkaila (with spinach and beans), and couscous with dried apricots and pumpkin. It also serves delicious Tunisian-style grilled fish. 1 rue de la Boule-Rouge, 9th, 01.47.70.43.90. Métro: Grands Boulevards or Cadet. Open Monday to Saturday for lunch and dinner. Closed Sunday.

CHEZ OMAR. The Algerian restaurateur Omar Guerda got his start in Paris working as a waiter at La Coupole, and then took over this old-fashioned bistro when this now-trendy corner of the Marais was still a sleeping beauty. Through the years, he's turned Chez Omar into one of the liveliest and friendliest places to discover high-quality North African cooking. The star dish here is the couscous royale, grilled merguez sausages (spicy lamb links) and roast lamb served with fluffy semolina and a big bowl of vegetables in bouillon. Don't miss the Arabic pastries for dessert either, since they come from La Bague de Kenza, Paris's best oriental pâtisserie (pastry shop). 47 rue de Bretagne, 3rd, 01.42.72.36.26. Métro: Arts et Métiers or Temple. Open Monday to Saturday for lunch and dinner. Closed Sunday. No credit cards.

MANSOURIA. Fatema Hal is the most famous Moroccan cook in Paris, and her friendly, elegant restaurant is an ideal place to sample dishes like pigeon pastilla and lamb tagine cooked with twenty-seven spices or chicken tagine with figs stuffed with walnuts. 11 rue Faidherbe, 11th, 01.43.71.00.16. Métro: Faidherbe-Chaligny. Open Wednesday to Saturday for lunch and dinner. Monday and Tuesday dinner only. Closed Sunday.

WALLY LE SAHARIEN. Tucked away in the 9th, this attractive restaurant is decorated with kilim pillows, carved wooden armchairs, and rich fabrics. Formerly a camel driver in Algeria before he moved to Paris and became a restaurateur, owner Wally Chouaki serves his couscous Algerian style, or dry rather than with bouillon and vegetables, and it is excellent with mechoui (roast lamb). Other dishes not to miss include grilled sardines with a sauce of capers and basil, tchatkhouka (grilled eggplant, peppers, tomatoes, and garlic), and a delicious chicken pastilla. 36 rue Rodier, 9th, 01.42.85.51.90. Métro: Anvers or Notre-Dame-de-Lorette. Closed Sunday and Monday.

Astier

I CAN'T THINK OF BETTER PROOF OF THE RELIABILITY OF
my dictum that Paris restaurants with red-and-white jacquard
cotton tablecloths never serve bad food than the fifty-something-
year-old Astier, a tremendously popular bistro on a tree-lined
pedestrian street in the trendy Oberkampf district of the 11th
Arrondissement. Given the expedient popularity of bare-wood
tables in newer bistros (no laundry bill), these well-starched
and -ironed spreads—here also embellished with the restaurant's name—invariably signal a well-run restaurant with a serious kitchen, which is why unfurling one of Astier's heavy,
oversized red-and-white jacquard napkins is always a happy
occasion.

I also treasure the debatable taste of the drop lamps made
from panels of lemon-lollipop-like tropical seashell, the fifties-
vintage corduroy-style wooden paneling, and the plum velvet
curtains of this busy dining room, since they send the message

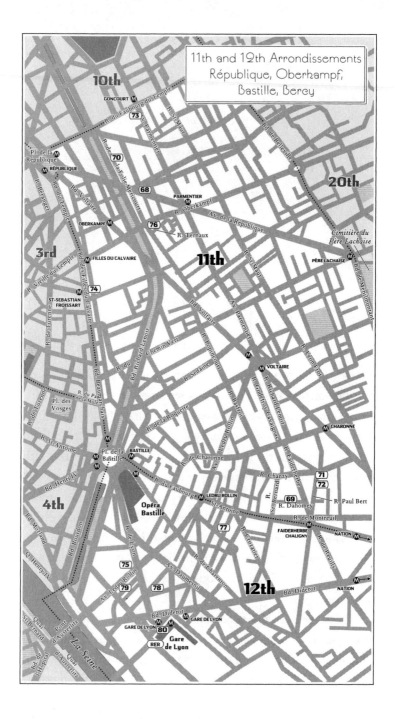

that what really counts is what you find on your plate. Happily, Frédéric Hubig-Schall, the shrewd, hardworking, affable young restaurateur who bought Astier two years ago, innately understood that the regulars would be heartbroken if anything changed, so instead he hired Bernard Henry, one of the smarter and more charming young sommeliers in Paris, to bone up the wine list, and Benjamin Bajolle, a talented young chef who trained at the Hôtel Meurice, to delicately tinker with the menu. And as dinner on a warm July evening proved, their efforts have been a roaring success.

I hadn't been to Astier for a while, but the front door still stuck the way that it did when I first ate here twenty years ago, and inside the dining room was packed, mostly with Parisians but also with foreigners who'd heard of its famous holy cow, the serve-yourself cheese tray that's part of the prix fixe menu. Studying the menu over a nice cool glass of white Sancerre, I was impressed by the way it had been discreetly reset to the twenty-first century without any overt changes that might ruffle the feathers of die-hard traditionalists. House classics like the marinated herring with warm potato salad and fricassee of rabbit in mustard sauce were still available, but a variety of other more stealthily modern dishes tempted.

Curious, I ordered the oeufs cuits durs et coeur de sucrine aux deux mayonnaises as a first course, and it turned out to be a delicious and witty take on one of my favorite French starters, the deceptively homely bistro classic of hard-boiled eggs served with mayonnaise. In reality, this simple-as-water dish has a quiet genius, because it offers a brilliant miniature of the art of cooking by contrasting the nude perfection of nature, a boiled egg, with a sauce that stars the same ingredient transformed by human ingenuity. In Astier's new version, the four halves of egg came with two different mayonnaise-based sauces, one green with herbs, the other given a red tint and a roguish edge by the addition of some sauce vigneronne, red wine and shallot sauce. The tweaked sauces were delicious, as was the addition of a centerpiece of hearts of gem lettuce, which weren't just a feint at healthy eating but a nice contrast of texture and taste—when they're this small, sucrine has almost the same bewitching crunch of something deep-fried, with a tauntingly sweet taste. Bruno's starter, a salade de racines (salad of roots), turned out to be a pleasant summer salad of carrots and beets with mixed greens, including some baby beet greens, in a light mayonnaise with a risqué tint created with beet juice.

My onglet de veau (veal hanger steak), a thick, juicy cut of meat packed with flavor, came with potatoes sautéed in duck fat to give them a savory richness, while Bruno's main course of plump grilled shrimp with fine strips of Niçois lemon and tapenade (a southern French condiment of finely chopped black olives and anchovies) was a delicious seasonal nod at Mediterranean cooking on a summer night. It took a while for the famous cheese tray to reach our table—no one's ever in a hurry to see this lovely array spirited away—but, buoyed by the infectiously jovial atmosphere of this place, we were in no rush.

The owner, Hubig-Schall, buys the cheese himself at the nearby Aligre market and also sources directly from the main Paris food market in suburban Rungis, and his assortment is so perfectly composed, beginning with a gentle chèvre or two, running through a variety of cow's milk cheeses, and concluding with a blue or another strong cheese, that it's a superb opportunity to deepen one's knowledge of French cheeses. The cheese tray is also a very generous gesture as part of a menu that's one of the best buys in Paris.

In recognition of the fact that most diners will have sated themselves with cheese, desserts tend to be light, including refreshing watermelon soup (small chunks of melon in its own juice) with vanilla-scented fromage blanc ice cream that Bruno chose, and my own airy fresh apricot yogurt, which was topped with luscious lemon verbena cream.

At a time when many young French chefs have taken a detour down the road of a mannerist creativity inspired by the intriguingly Dalí-esque cooking of the Spanish chef Ferran Adria, this very good meal was deeply reassuring, proving as it did that contemporary French cooking succeeds through subtle and refined evolution rather than rather than revolution.

· ☁ ·

IN A WORD: Following a change of owners, this boisterously popular fifty-year-old bistro in a once quiet, now-trendy corner of the 11th Arrondissement has recently been given a clever new lease on life by the talented restaurateur Frédéric Hubig-Schall. The appealing menu of traditional French classics and a few contemporary dishes changes regularly, but the legendary cheese course survives as part of a prix fixe menu that's one of the best buys in Paris.

DON'T MISS: Marinated herring with warm potato salad; cream of lentil soup with smoked duck breast; foie gras terrine; fricassee of rabbit in mustard sauce; entrecôte with frites; turbot with béarnaise sauce; the cheese tray; crème caramel; prune tart with ice cream; pear and apricot crumble.

· · ·

[**68**] **44 rue Jean-Pierre Timbaud, 11th, 01.43.57.16.35** MÉTRO: **Parmentier.** OPEN **daily for lunch and dinner. www.restaurant-astier.com** ▪ **$$**

Auberge Pyrénées-Cévennes

BOOMING THUNDER ON A NIGHT IN EARLY MAY MADE IT A relief to slip through the front door of this epic bistro in an old working-class neighborhood behind the place de la République just before the downpour. Aside from serving up a truly gargantuan and generally very good feed, this cozy old slipper of a place with a decor of copper pans, antlers, alarmingly long

sausages hanging from pegs, and a rare and very fine example of the intriguingly ugly wallpaper once commonly found in French hotels and restaurants (flowers and gourds in red, spearmint, and pumpkin) offers a revealing sociological snapshot of how Paris is changing.

The husky voice of the pretty blond hostess is muffled by the halting but charming efforts of some English tourists who've dusted off their university-vintage French. More locally, her old-fashioned French diction—unself-conscious, a little loud, and often resorting to snorts of laughter, stands out against the perfectly denatured version of Molière's tongue spoken by the Bobos (bohemian bourgeois types, as they're somewhat derisively known in Paris), young, affluent, educated professionals with a taste for the accoutrements if not the reality of a bohemian lifestyle, who flock here to satisfy a craving for the same authentic Old Paris they're so swiftly and unwittingly destroying.

A good meal is always in the details, and for me the most important one is often the welcome. Greeted with smiles when I arrived, I was set up with a glass of cold white Macon wine and a complimentary saucer of delicious saucisson (sausage) within a minute or two of being seated. While waiting for my friends, I started chatting with Françoise Constantin and learned that she's a Lyonnaise who went to work at that city's famous Café des Fédérations when she was seventeen. She waited tables there for thirteen years, met her husband, Daniel, and they moved to Paris and eventually bought this bawdy old trooper of a bistro. Daniel later explained that business is good because the "young kids moving into the neighborhood have a yearning for the food their grandmothers made. A lot of their mothers might have been liberated working women who spent as little time in the kitchen as possible, but these kids know and love good food."

The British tourists flinched with every thump of thunder, and Françoise attempted to reassure them that disaster wasn't imminent. "Au moins il n'y a pas de neige ce soir" ("At least it's not snowing tonight"), she said, which left them mystified. At last, Judy, Bob, and Lynn arrived, and our practiced quartet à table was hungry. We ordered frisée au lardons, caviar du Puy, and terrine de maison. The frisée (curly endive) salads came with perfectly coddled eggs, hunks of salty, chunky bacon, and a grinding of black pepper, and they were delicious. The "caviar," as the Auvergnats, who founded many of Paris's most venerable bistros when they migrated to the capital en masse from their south-central region at the beginning of the twentieth century, puckishly named the earthy lentils that grow out of the stony soil of their home turf, was nicely seasoned with good olive oil, chunks of carrot, and sprigs of thyme, and the earthy garlicky country terrine brightened when eaten with a few cornichons (gherkins pickled in vinegar) fished out of a salt gray crock with a pair of wooden tweezers.

If there was anything flawed about the meal, it was the daunting abundance of the main courses. Judy's quenelles (pike perch dumplings) came as a pair and overwhelmed her, while Lynn barely touched the copper-clad saucepan of sliced sautéed new potatoes that accompanied her ris de veau (veal sweetbreads) in port sauce. Bob and I weren't able to make a dent in the massive servings of the cassoulet that is the kitchen's pride, and all of us felt a little wilted, because we hate to waste.

Even after this avalanche of white beans, sausage, and preserved duck, however, I couldn't pass up a Saint-Marcellin from La Mère Richard, a spark plug of a woman who's built a whole life on aging these small, puffy raw cow's milk cheeses from the Dauphiné region to perfection and who has a stand in the main market of Lyon. Judy never eats dessert, but Bob ordered a Colonel—lemon sorbet with a shot of vodka—and Lynn was delighted by fresh raspberries with a dainty sprig of mint that held out a promise of refreshment after this fine, ample feed, a meal that came as much from the hearts of this passionate young couple as it did from the shiny copper-clad saucepans in Daniel's kitchen.

· ⸙ ·

IN A WORD: This is a bistro that defines the genre—rustic, friendly, generous, and with a menu of well-prepared regional French classics. Come with a big appetite and a desire for a relaxed, friendly meal in a sepia-toned setting.

DON'T MISS: Foie gras; frisée au lardons (curly endive salad with coddled egg and chunks of bacon); harengs pommes à l'huile (marinated herring with boiled potatoes); brandade de morue (shepherd's pie made with salt cod and garlic); cassoulet (casserole of white beans, sausage, and preserved duck); ris de veau au Porto (veal sweetbreads in port sauce); Saint-Marcellin cheese.

. . .

[70] 106 rue de la Folie-Méricourt, 11th, 01.43.57.33.78. MÉTRO: République. OPEN Monday to Friday for lunch and dinner. Saturday dinner only. CLOSED Sunday. • $$

Le Bistrot Paul Bert

SOME PARIS RESTAURANTS ARE INSCRUTABLY SEXY. THIS mysterious frisson never comes from exposed skin, or too much of it anyway, to say nothing of a waiter or a waitress wearing

bunny ears and a cotton ball on their tail. No, in Paris eroticism is usually implied, which is why there are few better vehicles for expressing it than food. There's no surefire way to explain it, but some Paris restaurants find their erotic groove when the holy trinity comes together—a good-looking staff serving great food generates a receptive crowd that gets off on their vibe and, in doing so, puts a hot spin on a place. It's this deceptively low-ball formula that explains why this bistro on a short, quiet street in the 11th Arrondissement has become almost irresistible. Ask any Parisian food writer where to eat in Paris right now, and Le Paul Bert always figures.

The problem with this accelerating celebrity is that by the time it reaches your ears, the hype has generated impossible expectations. So let's set the record straight. Le Paul Bert is a very good restaurant, but if most of the meals I've had here have been excellent, a couple have been clunkers. In the end, beyond the buzz, it's nothing more than a well-intentioned neighborhood bistro with an able kitchen working with good produce, a happy calculus that's accentuated by pleasant service, a charming dining room, and an excellent wine list, period.

This being said, no one I've ever brought here has been disappointed. For starters, there are the sassy young waiters in low-slung jeans and the great human salad of bohemians and bourgeois types, the latter being explained by the fact that this place is sort of the home away from home for many French winemakers when they come to the capital, hence the fantastic wine list. Then there's the nonchalantly retro and decidedly Parisian decor, including vintage cheese box covers, enameled advertising panels, and winsomely amateur still lifes picked up at the flea market. This scene creates a laid-back Gallic groove, and the punters at the old-fashioned wooden tables with scuffed-up legs get off on eyeballing one another, especially since the good food, great wine, and heterogeneous fauna make for fine flirting fodder.

The chalkboard menu changes regularly but ensures an unfailingly toothsome run of well-prepared seasonal comfort food at reasonable prices. On a cool late spring night, I loved my eggs sunny-side up in a ramekin with first-of-season morels and a morel-flavored cream sauce, a rich and thoroughly satisfying starter for someone who'd been able only to graze through the course of a busy day. Bruno, my partner, went for the salad of ris de veau (veal sweetbreads), nicely browned pieces of veal sweetbread on a bed of haricots verts and spring vegetables napped with a suave Xérès-vinegar-spiked vinaigrette, and then had an entrecôte dotted with pearly buttons of moelle (marrow) and accompanied by a mound of crispy golden homemade frites. My cod steak was thick and flaked apart into nice firm white petals of fish that were a pleasure to eat when seasoned with a drizzle of olive oil, some of the gray (unprocessed) sea salt placed on the table in a little jar, and a little fresh lemon juice; flanking the fish was a fan of roasted white asparagus and baby carrots no thicker than a pencil. Justified by the first-rate produce that makes up its ingredients, the cooking at Le Paul Bert tends to be simple, even plain, which is why it is such a welcome table for anyone craving a good, convivial feed without a lot of bells and whistles. Desserts are superb, including a locally famous île flottante (floating island), a big cloud of fresh meringue floating on a pool of yellow custard sauce (crème anglaise) and garnished with a scattering of crushed pralines, and a massive Paris-Brest, a round choux (puff) pastry filled with hazelnut and mocha cream. And for my money, the Cairanne Domaine de l'Oratoire Saint-Martin, a fruity red with good bones, is easier, and much more fun, to drink than water.

. . .

IN A WORD: A very popular, stylish, and convivial bistro with a great crowd and atmosphere. It has a terrific wine list at very fair prices, and the kitchen sends out wonderful French comfort food and bistro standards.

DON'T MISS: Eggs with morels; salade de ris de veau (salad with sweetbreads); head cheese with pickled girolles mushrooms; cod steak with olive oil; tuna with baby vegetables; entrecôte with bone marrow and frites; ris de veau; terrine de campagne; tarte fine aux pommes et glace rhubarbe (apple tart with rhubarb ice cream); Paris-Brest; île flottante.

. . .

[72] 18 rue Paul Bert, 11th, 01.43.72.24.01. MÉTRO: Faidherbe-Chaligny. OPEN Tuesday to Thursday for lunch and dinner. Friday and Saturday dinner only. CLOSED Sunday and Monday. • $$

Le Chateaubriand

INAKI AIZPITARTE HAS A LONG, GENTLE, AND SLIGHTLY vacant face, sort of like that of a medieval monk, or maybe a shepherd, who has gone for a very long time without seeing or speaking to another person. Originally from the French Basque country, he's a self-taught chef who washed dishes in Tel Aviv and bounced around Latin America before becoming interested in food and moving to Paris. Since he couldn't afford to go to cooking school, he learned by working instead, making his way through a variety of Paris kitchens before he found his way to Montmartre and a job as chef at La Famille. This long, narrow restaurant furnished with fifties- and sixties-vintage flea market finds was where Inaki was discovered, and five years later, the experience still seems to have left him slightly stunned and privately puzzled. He'd be a deer caught in the headlights, but he's not so much afraid of the media as much as he is bewildered by it.

Now settled at Le Chateaubriand, an atmospheric old bistro created from an old-fashioned grocer's, he seems to have found both a quiet perch from which to continue developing what he describes as his "cuisine de vagabond" and a highly appreciative audience. This formerly working-class neighborhood in the 11th Arrondissement has been flooded by stylish young couples in search of that rarest of urban prey—a charming apartment made affordable by its need for major renovation—and it's the energy of these smart young things that gives this place the feel of a come-one, come-all party night after night (the restaurant

is much quieter at noon, when it serves a short, simple menu to people who work locally). Frédéric Peneau, formerly the proprietor of the Café Burq in Montmartre, hosts the crowd from behind the long bar just inside the front door with smiles, guffaws, and backslapping, while Aizpitarte makes only an occasional rare appearance, which is slightly frustrating, since it's only natural to be curious about the man behind the stunning contemporary food served here.

Aizpitarte is a brilliant miniaturist, composing original, origami-like compositions of taste that are often potent and pretty. In fact, if he weren't a chef he could easily be a brilliant jeweler, so striking is his talent for the minutae of aesthetics and taste. His starter of raw fresh peas, diced daikon (Japanese radish), and a raw egg yolk, all sprinkled with rice vinegar and hidden in a pale green foam flavored with nori, the Japanese seaweed, was hauntingly good as a set of tastes and textures never before encountered or even imagined. Similarly, a recent creation of raw foie gras enclosed in transparent slices of daikon and dotted with magenta buttons of beet was a remarkable dish, almost aesthetically pure but stunningly sensual at the same time.

The bawdy atmosphere of this restaurant, with its suspended globe lamps, bare wooden tables, and bluff waiters, creates an odd foil to what comes to the table, too, since the basic experience of Aizpitarte's food is to taste everything like a newborn baby, or with a suddenly virgin palate.

The menu changes constantly—Aizpitarte serves a single menu nightly, but everything is clean, assertive, and delicate, which makes a meal here a source of real meditation. Weeks after trying his coarsely chopped tartare of beef with ground peanuts, I wondered why no one had ever thought of it before, and his saddle of lamb with smoked eel and pork breast with grated celery root and réglisse (a licorice-flavored root) stopped conversation. Two weeks later, friends visiting from San Francisco were stunned by the lamb "retour de Maroc" (just back from Morocco) with its emulsion of green tea and a scattering of coriander flowers.

One of Aizpitarte's recipes from his stint at La Famille, peach gazpacho, a superbly balanced and refreshing pureed soup that I often make when white peaches and tomatoes coincide in the market, perfectly sums up the winsome naiveté in his cooking. If the peach and the tomato meet in perfect balance, the sweetness of the former surprises by tempering the acidity of the latter. This recipe is as simple but perfect as a grade school math lesson, one plus one equals two, but now the two are one.

· ▲ ·

IN A WORD: Inaki Aizpitarte is one of the most interesting and original young chefs working in Paris today. Not everyone will like the noise and crowding at this place, but Aizpitarte's food is more than worth a little discomfort.

DON'T MISS: The menu changes constantly here, but some dishes make repeat appearances. If you spot them, don't pass up: julienned cucumbers with smoked fish; blanquette de veau à l'orange; mackerel ceviche with Tabasco; veal mignon sautéed with potatoes; tuna with asparagus and chorizo; black chocolate cream with emulsified red pepper.

. . .

[73] **129 avenue Parmentier, 11th, 01.43.57.45.95.** MÉTRO: **Goncourt.**
OPEN **Monday to Friday for lunch and dinner. Saturday dinner only.**
CLOSED **Sunday.** ▪ **$$**

Le Duc de Richelieu

THE FOOD ON FRENCH TRAINS—WHICH ARE SO EFFICIENT and so fast—is absolutely dismal, running to industrial sandwiches and microwaved pasta in Styrofoam cups. Unfortunately, just when it is needed more than ever, the Parisian tradition of good eating around train stations is on the wane as fast-food places muscle out the bistros and brasseries that once offered travelers a good, solid meal before they boarded the rails. I retain a soft spot for the serviceable Terminus Nord across the street from the Gare du Nord, but there's no place to celebrate an arrival or prepare a departure within an easy walk of the Gares Montparnasse (Brittany and southwestern France), de l'Est (eastern France), or Austerlitz (southwestern France and Spain).

This is one of the reasons I like Le Duc de Richelieu so much. It's an easy five-minute walk from the Gare de Lyon and so the perfect address for a solid, happy feed before heading to Lyon, Avignon, or points farther south. The simple food is so good, however, that I come here even when I'm not catching a train. Founded in 2004 by Paul Georget, one of the proudest and most generous bistro keepers in Paris—he formerly ran Le Gavroche near the old Bourse (stock exchange)—this place has the famously jocular, slightly bawdy, and completely unique atmosphere generated when Gauls eat great grub.

Le Duc de Richelieu is a happy, no-nonsense sort of place with a forgettable decor of raspberry-colored walls, wooden tables, and bright wall sconces. But all's right with the world when an order of jambon persillé arrives—the pale aspic is dense with chopped parsley and richly flavored shredded ham. Oeufs mayonnaise, another prewar bistro stalwart, are excellent, too—the hard-boiled eggs are free-range and the ivory color of the mayonnaise says "homemade"—and the céleri rémoulade (grated celery in a mayonnaise sauce) is firm and flavorful, a far cry from the food-service product that sadly prevails elsewhere.

As befits its unself-conscious the-way-we-were personality—moderation has no place at this table, and any mention of a gastronomic inconvenience like cholesterol causes eyes to roll skyward—Le Duc's specialty is meat, including some of the best steaks in town. The pavé de boeuf (a thick, square steak) comes with superb homemade frites, the lamb chops are succulent, and the côte de boeuf (rib steak) for two is a Cro Magnon's feast. Other old-fashioned dishes like blanquette de veau—veal in lemon-spiked cream sauce—are nicely made, too, and desserts like baba au rhum will make sure you sleep most of the way to Nice. Among the various house Beaujolais, the Morgon is the best bet. If Paul Georget and his son-in-law Stéphane Derre opened branches of Le Duc near the city's other main stations, they'd be doing Paris a profound public service.

· ·

IN A WORD: A place to make carnivores roar with pleasure—a lively, friendly, slap-on-the-back type of bistro with solidly good cooking and great atmosphere. Keep it in mind if you're traveling through the Gare de Lyon, especially since it serves late.

DON'T MISS: The beef and the Beaujolais (Morgon, Chiroubles, or Saint-Amour), an unbeatable combination.

. . .

[78] **5 rue Parrot, 12th, 01.43.43.05.64.** MÉTRO: **Gare de Lyon.** OPEN **Monday to Saturday for lunch and dinner.** CLOSED **Sunday.** • **$$**

L'Écailler du Bistrot

AS FAR AS I'M CONCERNED, PARIS IS THE BEST SEAFOOD
city in the Northern Hemisphere. Why? Supply and demand.
Parisians love fish and insist on top quality, which, happily,
doesn't always cost an arm and a leg here either. Then, too,
France has one of the largest fleets of artisanal fishermen in the
world. These small boats land fish by line instead of using the
long nets of industrial trawlers, a practice that avoids damaging
the catch, and they put into port regularly to rush what they've
landed to market.

The fish served at this charming wood-paneled dining room
come from Le Guilvinec in Brittany, one of France's premier
ports, and the oysters from one of the country's best producers,
Cadoret in Riec-sur-Belon, also in Brittany. So to discover just
how good the local catch of the day can be, this is an ideal ad-

dress. The sister restaurant of its next-door neighbor, Le Paul Bert, one of my favorite bistros, this place has a terrific chalkboard menu that changes daily, a guarantee of impeccable quality and great eating. My most recent meal began with the excellent house-smoked salmon and a dozen fines de claire oysters, served room temperature instead of chilled so that you can really taste them, followed by a thick pollack steak sautéed in salt butter and served with baby spinach and an outstandingly meaty turbot with cèpes mushrooms, a lovely terre et mer (land and sea) combination. The caramel apple dessert—a baked apple lashed with salted caramel sauce—is a homey treat, and the white Saumur Champigny, a nice dry Loire Valley pour that's ideal with seafood, not only is delicious but keeps the bill down.

IN A WORD: An excellent fish house with moderate prices and friendly service.

DON'T MISS: Tuna tartare; house-smoked salmon; oysters; turbot with cèpes mushrooms; the assorted shellfish platter; fresh crab with avocado; roasted sea bass; lobster.

. . .

[71] **22 rue Paul Bert, 11th, 01.43.72.76.77.** MÉTRO: **Faidherbe-Chaligny.** OPEN **Tuesday to Saturday for lunch and dinner.** CLOSED **Sunday and Monday.** ▪ **$$**

La Gazzetta

UZÈS IN THE GARD IS ONE OF MY FAVORITE TOWNS IN THE south of France, a handsome, unspoiled place in the sun that

you still won't find in Peter Mayle. I have a wonderful friend
there, too, Calista, a retired English novelist with a Burne-Jones
face who taught me a course in Victorian literature when I was
a student in London a long time ago. Among her many good
qualities is the fact that she loves to eat, and so a summer or two
ago, when she called for a chat, I was intrigued by her enthusi-
asm for a new local chef, a Swede named Petter Nilsson. "His
food is just lovely, he's a real Nordic angel," she said, and as it
turned out she was absolutely right. The next time I was in
Uzès, we went to dinner at Les Trois Salons, and I was astonished by his sugared and salted cod with pumpkin water and juniper berries in a sauce of sweet Cévennes onions, and Lozère
lamb with a walnut-breadcrumb crust and a sauce of pan juice,
lamb sweetbreads, and dates.

Next I heard, Nilsson was cooking in Paris at La Gazzetta,
an appealingly laid-back place in the 12th Arrondissement behind the Bastille. This part of the city had an urban edge fifteen

years ago, but, rather like SoHo in New York, it has calmed down now that the original pioneers have had children and stopped clubbing. They like their food, though, and since New York is their favorite shadow city, or the foreign city they understand best, the loftlike downtown atmosphere at La Gazzetta won them over right away.

Since the arrival of Petter Nilsson, La Gazzetta has been all good news, too. He does a simple menu at lunch, and then in the evening he serves up a short carte that puts his talent on show. His dinner offer changes regularly, but dishes like a starter of caramelized endive with dill, horseradish, lemon, and almond puree, and grilled cod with a mash of Brussels sprouts, tarragon, and capers, show off his gift for creating subtle but fascinating juxtapositions of flavors and his love of contrasting textures. If it's on the menu, don't miss his superb dessert of ricotta ice cream with shavings of Corsican brebis (sheep's cheese) and unusual but exciting garnishes of hazelnuts and olives. Since he's arrived in Paris and found a larger audience for his winsome but audacious and very personal cooking, Nilsson just gets better and better, so go now to catch a rising star.

· · ·

IN A WORD: The loftlike dining room with low lighting and friendly service provides a perfect setting for Petter Nilsson, a very talented young chef who cooks in a pure, clean, contemporary bistro idiom that's unique in Paris. This is an ideal choice when you want really interesting food in the context of a reasonably priced, low-key meal.

DON'T MISS: Nilsson's chalkboard menu changes all the time, but dishes that'll tip you off to his style include caramelized endive with dill, horseradish, lemon, and almond puree; cod with

a mash of Brussels sprouts, tarragon, and capers; pizza with daikon and wild watercress; veal with bulgur, cauliflower, and broccoli; ricotta ice cream with Corsican brebis, hazelnuts, and olives.

· · ·

[77] 29 rue de Cotte, 12th, 01.43.47.47.05. MÉTRO: Faidherbe-Chaligny. OPEN Tuesday to Saturday for lunch and dinner. CLOSED Sunday and Monday. http://lagazzetta.fr · $$

Le Quincy

SUDDENLY IT'S 1972 ALL OVER AGAIN. EVERY TIME I VISIT this small, cozy bistro near the Gare de Lyon, I have the pleasure of confirming the pith of truth at the core of my memories of my first visit to Paris. This is how the city smelled—a whiff of coal,

beef bouillon, honest sweat, damp wool, sour tobacco smoke—
and this is how those long-ago meals unfolded, and still unfold
here, with a waiter in a black vest pouring a glass of white wine
as an apéritif and then cutting a thick slab of dried sausage onto
your serving plate to nibble as you study the menu. Then *le pa-
tron*, a sturdy gray-haired man with thick blue-framed glasses
and an indigo cotton serving jacket arrives, offers the menu—
"Un peu de lecture?" ("A little reading material?"), sizes you
up, and launches into his commentary, teasing you toward certain choices, making sly but harmless jokes about your American accent, asking where in the States you're from, and then
plunging back into the menu. "Just because it's almost Easter is
no reason not to have the rabbit, the foie gras is made here, the
caillette d'Ardèche are meat patties made with Swiss chard and
wrapped in caul fat, served with salad and really delicious, the
oxtail's been cooking for ten hours, tonight's not a good night
for fish. Do you need a little more time? Of course you do,
there's no hurry, don't worry, we don't want to upset your digestion."

On the second pass, things become more serious. There's
more consultation, punctuated by a joke or two about how
young people have become lazy and don't know the meaning of
work. His sharp pencil is poised on his pad. We order the house
terrine with a cabbage salad dressed with garlic cream, the caillette d'Ardèche, the rabbit in shallot and white wine sauce and
the poularde en sauce vin jaune (fattened chicken sautéed with a
sauce of vin jaune, the maderized wine from France's eastern
Jura region), and a bottle of Saint-Joseph, an amiable Rhône
valley red.

Now there's time to savor this vest-pocket restaurant
fronted by a small terrace, with red checked curtains in the win-

dows, faux wood varnished walls, and the main dining room with its gray and white Belle Époque tiled floor, tables dressed with pink and red jacquard tablecloths that include the restaurant's name, and a pleasant clutter of the bric-a-brac accumulated over the course of one man's life as a restaurant owner. In this case, the attractive detritus—a mounted stag's head, a series of framed pay stubs showing how the taxes and social security charges imposed on the French workingman and -woman have grown continuously over the course of thirty years, and a faience plate that says "The best clock is your stomach"—all tell the story of owner Michel Bosshard's career, and it's a tale that's as jovial, opinionated, and joyously French as he is.

If the terrine's a little fatty, its accompanying cabbage salad, a nice mix of white cabbage and Savoy finely grated and dressed in a delicious garlic cream, saves it, while the caillette, a patty in neat slices on top of a bowl of perfectly dressed mixed salad leaves, is succulent and perfectly seasoned. So is the rabbit, a whole rack of it, meaty and moist, served on a plate in a shallow bath of rich shallot-scented sauce with a side dish of noodles and croutons. The poularde is a succulent bird that comes in a copper saucepan, and its mushroom-rich sauce has a lovely dry edge of vin jaune. A complimentary tasting portion of another house specialty, brandade de morue, salt cod flaked into garlicky potatoes, arrives, and the meal turns into a feast. After such a meaty meal, dessert seems improbable, but no one who has had the chocolate mousse here will be able to pass it up. Because he's had some fun with us, Bobosse, as Bosshard is known, swings by again at the end of the meal to offer us complimentary glasses of plum eau-de-vie, which he flames inside big snifters to release its ambered perfume of fruit, leather, and tobacco. We take a sip, and Bobosse stands by, grinning. "Vous ne pourriez pas me dire que la vie n'est pas belle, non!" ("You can't tell me life isn't beautiful, right?"). Right indeed.

· ⟨⟩ ·

IN A WORD: The jovial Michel Bosshard is an old-school restaurateur who's made this cozy bistro one of the best and longest-running tables in town. Go for his sly sense of humor, the way-we-were atmosphere, and the menu of beautifully prepared traditional bistro dishes.

DON'T MISS: Terrine de campagne with cabbage salad; foie gras; caillette d'Ardèche (a patty of pork and Swiss chard); stuffed cabbage; rabbit and shallots braised in white wine; chicken in vin jaune sauce; brandade de morue (baked salt cod, garlic, and mashed potatoes); veal chop with morel mushrooms; chocolate mousse.

. . .

[79] **28 avenue Ledru-Rollin, 12th, 01.46.28.46.76.** MÉTRO: **Gare de Lyon.**
OPEN **Tuesday to Friday for lunch and dinner.** CLOSED **Saturday, Sunday,**
and Monday. No credit cards. ▪ **$$$**

Le Repaire de Cartouche

DINNER TONIGHT WITH JUDY, A CHARMING NEW ORLEANS—
born journalist who has lived in Paris for thirty years and is one
of my most regular dining companions, at this long-running hit
of a bistro between the Place de la République and the Place de
la Bastille, left me stumped. Why? In spite of chef Rodolphe
Paquin's impressive track record, there was one serious misfire
during the meal—Judy's otherwise lovely miniature cast-iron
casserole of succulent guinea hen with spring vegetables had
been dosed with truffle oil, which is the culinary equivalent of
spraying insect repellent on wholesome, fresh food.

In the Métro on the way home I chewed on this one for a
while. To wit, I'm lucky, I live in Paris, and I know what a good
cook Rodolphe Paquin is, but what about you? What if you de-
cided to have a meal here on my recommendation and it ran
aground on one of the saddest cheats in contemporary cooking
("truffle" oil, which is nothing more than olive oil spiked with
synthetic flavor)?

This is the quandary that lurks between the lines of all books
about food, although I've never seen anyone take it by the horns
before. There's nothing more subjective than taste, especially
where food's concerned, since it is grounded in the most indis-
putable biological righteousness: everyone knows what tastes

good because they eat only things they like. But what if I say it's delicious and you say it's not, or vice versa? Who's right? Both of us, which is why it is important to admit that any of the cooks I praise can have an off night and any of the restaurants might not cast the same spell for you that they have for me. On the other hand, I've been to all of the places I recommend many times, and so these chefs have won my confidence despite those occasions when I've ordered badly or the kitchen was having a bad day, which is why I decided to include Le Repaire de Cartouche in this book.

When Paquin gets it right, which he usually does, he's a brilliant chef. Consider my starter of pork pâté with foie gras enclosed in a pastry crust. A layer of luscious chestnut-colored gelée, the natural juices of cooking meat, had set inside the baroque curls of the pastry cap on this beautifully made concoction, which was deliciously seasoned and obviously prepared with real passion and skill. My tuna steak with grilled eggplant and a light sauce of tomatoes, black olive slivers, and olive oil was delicious, too, and if Judy's main course misfired, her starter terrine of grilled eggplant layered with red pepper mousse was rich, earthy, and very satisfying. In season, Paquin is also one of the best game cooks in Paris, and he has a winning way with desserts, including a sublime cranberry and chocolate chip clafoutis (baked custard pudding with chocolate chips) cooked to order.

The white stucco decor of the main dining room is a bit drab, but a very good wine list, including one of the best all-purpose reds around, Domaine Gramenon Côtes du Rhône "Poignée de Raisins," and Paquin's generous, hearty cooking make this easy to overlook. Overall, Le Repaire de Cartouche remains one of the better bistros in Paris—just give that truffle-oil-drizzled guinea hen a wide berth.

· ⛩ ·

IN A WORD: This popular bistro between the Place de la République and the Bastille pulls a hearty, happy crowd who come to feast on chef Rodolphe Paquin's generally excellent and very imaginative cooking.

DON'T MISS: Pâté de porc au foie gras en croûte (pork and foie gras pâté in a pastry crust); cold pea soup with ham; terrine of eggplant and red pepper; timbale of potatoes and sea snails; pan-fried foie gras; roast suckling lamb with white beans; grouse cooked in cabbage; tuna steak with grilled eggplant; pigeon roasted with baby vegetables; chocolate mousse with ginger; cranberry and chocolate chip clafoutis; chestnut mousse millefeuille.

· · ·

[74] 8 boulevard des Filles-du-Calvaire, 11th, 01.47.00.25.86. MÉTRO: Saint-Sébastien Froissart or Filles du Calvaire. OPEN Tuesday to Saturday for lunch and dinner. CLOSED Sunday and Monday. ▪ $$

A la Biche au Bois

AFTER A POLITE EXCHANGE OF BUSINESS CARDS AT A NOVEMBER gallery opening in Saint-Germain-des-Prés, I was surprised the following day by a phone call from Mr. X, who suggested lunch at A la Biche au Bois. I accepted instantly because he was handsome and smart and told fascinating stories about his abbreviated childhood in Tunis. Originally from Burgundy, his family owned a department store in the Tunisian capital, and his

earliest memories were of jasmine-scented nursemaids, street-car rides to Mediterranean beaches, and favorite foods, including couscous and un poisson complet (grilled fish with various garnishes) in the style of La Goulette, a popular seaside suburb.

So we met for lunch, and in retrospect, he knew what he was doing. While I was silently panicking before a menu that was mostly gibier (game)—in season, this is one of the best addresses in town for a wild feast—he cornered me right off the bat. "You're not one of those idiot Americans who don't eat game, are you?" So with quiet trepidation on my part, we shared thick pink meaty slices of roebuck paté and then lièvre à la royale, or hare stuffed with foie gras and truffles and served with an unctuous glossy mahogany-colored sauce of its gizzards. The latter may just be the ultimate expression of Gallic culinary genius, too, since a dozen different flavors are melded into one that's so rich and nuanced it produces a strong jolt of primal pleasure.

If I never go to A la Biche au Bois without thinking of that long-ago lunch when a stupor of good food and wine found me dumbly nodding in agreement with the declaration that it's only natural to have more than one lover at a time, I've had many decidedly delicious if considerably more innocent meals here through the years, most recently in the fine company of John and Sue, an erudite and good-humored couple from Baltimore.

On an Indian summer day at noon when this snug old-fashioned place was packed with hungry businessmen, John had game terrine and a gorgeously juicy venison steak, I loved my oeufs en cocotte with cream and tarragon and then dove into a casserole of stunningly good coq au vin, and Sue contented herself with a nicely cooked salmon steak. The three of us shared a platter of perfect golden frites and a bowl of potato and celery bulb purée that came as sides. An excellent cheese course was included in the 25.90 Euro lunch menu, one of the best buys in Paris, and I finished up with a pleasantly eggy crème caramel. A complimentary pour of Armagnac was the final punctuation of this feast, and we went off into the afternoon with renewed affection for this honest, generous, old-fashioned bistro, which is just the kind of place that makes people fall so hard for Paris.

IN A WORD: Though the décor of brown vinyl seats and antlers hung on the walls won't win prizes, this friendly bistro has a seriously good kitchen, and is one of the best buys in Paris, especially when game is in season.

DON'T MISS: Terrine de chevreuil (roebuck); céleri rémoulade; foie gras; coq au vin; wild duck in black currant sauce; partridge with green cabbage; venison with prunes.

. . .

[75] A la Biche au Bois, 45 avenue Ledru-Rollin, 12th, 01.43.43.34.38.
MÉTRO: **Gare de Lyon.** OPEN **Monday to Friday for lunch and dinner.**
CLOSED **Saturday and Sunday. ▪ $$**

Le Train Bleu

IT WASN'T UNTIL I ARRIVED IN PARIS THAT I REALIZED I was starving for grandeur. It's not that there wasn't any in New York City, the hub of the tentacular metropolis in which I grew up—Grand Central Station remains one of my favorite buildings in the world, and the quiet exultation associated with crossing its vaulted limestone concourse is one of my earliest memories—but it wasn't until I got to Paris that I learned what grandeur was really all about.

On a frosty January evening in 1975, I lugged my much loathed tweed-sided American Tourister suitcase up the staircase leading to Le Train Bleu after reading in *Let's Go Europe* that it overlooked the main hall of the station and was one of the most beautiful restaurants in the world. I couldn't afford to eat there, but the guidebook tipped me off that I could at least afford a coffee.

Coming through the doors, I was stunned by a vision of the nineteenth-century opulence that had made Paris the envy of the world. Waiters in black tie and fitted black waistcoats, most of them with mustaches, raced through the room bearing trays overhead, a few shiny potted palms offered a hopeful suggestion of imminent southern luxuriance, and the vaulted ceiling with balmy pastel scenes alluded to the cities you could ex-

change Parisian grit and gray for—Antibes, Marseilles, Nice, and Menton, among others. Rock crystal bud lamps punctuated lavish gilt floral moldings, the herringbone oak parquet stretched for what seemed to be at least a mile, and the various quadrants of the dining room were demarcated by massive oak-framed banquettes.

Taking it all in, I forgot my rain-dampened ski jacket and my fear that the $300 in my wallet might not be enough to travel comfortably from Paris to Athens and back over the course of a month. My coffee came, and when I noticed a tiny chocolate wrapped in gold foil on the edge of the saucer, my heart melted. So this was Paris, a place where a pauper could become a prince for a few francs. The mingling smells of tobacco smoke, roast lamb, perfume, sweat, wine, an odd and ancient whiff of coal smoke, vinegar, and drawn butter made me wildly happy, and when I dug into my pocket for a cigarette, I was startled by sulfur and looked up to find that the bartender with the pencil mustache and finely oiled streaks of hair stretched over his bald dome was waiting to light my smoke. "C'est magnifique, Le Train Bleu, n'est ce pas?" he said with a grin.

Almost twenty-five years later, on a warm April Sunday night, something bit me and I invited Bruno to dinner here. En route, I qualified the excursion: it was unlikely that the food would be very good, and the place was likely to feel wilted on a Sunday night—it might even be almost empty—but a stiff shot of grandeur would do us both good before the onslaught of a busy week.

So we arrived and were met with a jolly welcome and shown several possible tables before deciding to sit at the head of the busy dining room near a window overlooking the station's main concourse. Flanked by a Russian family on one side and two

Dutch businessmen on the other, we sipped Champagne and were mutually surprised by the restaurant's gracious and solid service.

Bruno subsequently spotted the husband of his psychiatrist, a well-known French actor dressed in a crumpled black velvet jacket, being fawned over by the waiters, and we wondered where his shrink, "Le docteur de ma tête" (his head doctor), might be, perhaps in their country house in Provence on this long weekend.

We ordered smoked salmon, saucisson de Lyon (pork sausage studded with pistachios) with warm potato salad, steak tartare, and, with some reluctance—the actor's roast lamb served in thrilling rare slices tableside from a silver-domed gueridon was very tempting—guinea hen with buttered Savoy cabbage and a garnish of Morteau sausage, plus a nice bottle of Delas Saint-Joseph, a reliably suave red Côtes du Rhône.

In the meantime, we were both impressed by the handsome cheese tray purveyed to the Dutchmen, who made more than the most of it, and it was fun to watch the waiter pouring hot chocolate sauce from a silver-plated teapot with a side-mounted spout over two plump ice-cream-stuffed profiteroles for the Russian ladies and explaining to their men that the bottle of Saint James rum brought to table with the baba au rhum wasn't for drinking but for sprinkling on their sponge cakes, which were flanked with fat vanilla-bean-flecked rosettes of whipped cream. I said nothing to Bruno but cautiously decided that we might actually eat well.

And I was right. My saucisson—five thick slabs of sausage covering a full dish of parsley-and-oil-dressed baby potatoes— was delicious, as was Bruno's thick slice of smoked salmon with a side of lentils, mixed salad greens, and whipped cream, which, we agreed, would have been improved by a bit of horseradish. The next surprise was that Bruno's steak tartare was prepared tableside—the waiter splashed olive oil and an egg yolk into a deep glass bowl, added capers, parsley, and chopped onion, plus dainty dashes of Tabasco and Worcestershire sauce—Bruno had ordered it doux, or not too hot—and then folded in the coarsely ground beef, kneading it all together and then transferring it to a plate, where he formed a tidy pattie. Decent fries and a side of salad accompanied the meat. My guinea hen was moist, nicely crusted, and flavorful, and even if someone had been a little heavy-handed with the white peppercorns in the cabbage, it was a very satisfying dish. The profiteroles were surprisingly good, too, and coffee came with a tiny meringue and a miniature chocolate bar that reassured me that even if the computerized female voice announcing TGV departures below was woefully current, this grand monument to everything that ever made France such an irresistible destination had barely changed at all.

Mind you, this is not a gourmet destination but rather a place to wallow in timeless Gallic grandeur and have a decent feed while doing so. And as I observed during this meal, the magnificence of this restaurant, a place unique in the world, continues to leave children, pensioners, and everyone in between absolutely awestruck.

IN A WORD: Even if you're not about to board a train, the nineteenth-century splendor of this magnificent restaurant at the Gare de Lyon is worth seeking out for its surprisingly good cooking and spellbinding decor.

DON'T MISS: Saucisson de Lyon with warm potato salad; smoked salmon; pied de cochon (breaded pig's foot); veal chop with wild mushroom lasagne; steak tartare; roast leg of lamb; baba au rhum; vacherin; profiteroles with hot chocolate sauce.

. . .

[80] Gare de Lyon, place Louis-Armand, 12th, 01.43.43.09.06. OPEN daily for lunch and dinner. www.le-train-bleu.com • $$$

Au Vieux Chêne

"I DON'T SEE ANYTHING WRONG WITH HAVING SLEPT WITH both sisters. In fact, it's rather amazing how different they are in bed," chuffed the man, apparently an architect on the basis of his mane of curly red hair and elaborate titanium-framed eyeglasses. Marie-Odile and I exchanged raised eyebrows. "Mais bien sûr" ("But of course") Marie-Odile said, and the woman sitting on the other side of us, who'd also overheard the architect's declaration to a bunch of colleagues, laughed out loud at Marie-Odile's sardonic verbal dart. "That crew really needs to go back to the drawing board," Marie-Odile whispered to me, nodding her head at the architects. And then, "When did everyone find out about this place? I've never seen Hermès scarves in here before."

Food as good as chef Stéphane Chevassus's never remains a secret for long, so this dark horse of a bistro in a residential corner of the outlying 11th Arrondissement has become a word-of-mouth address among the creative tribes of Paris—filmmakers, producers, photographers, artists, writers, architects, and designers. The menu makes a few alluring promises right up front, since chef Chevassus, ex–Michel Rostang and Guy Savoy, states that he uses only the freshest seasonal produce from the most ecologically correct farmers. There's nothing precious about this mani-

festo, either, since his goal is food that's as naturally delicious as possible, right down to the last petit lardon (little bacon bit). What these good intentions don't convey, however, is the unself-conscious sincerity of the cooking. Quite simply, Chevassus and his crew know and love food and wine and earnestly want you to have a great meal. But as the sign on the wall that says "A day without wine is a day without sunshine" gives away, this is a happy, easygoing place with a homey decor created by antique enameled advertising signs, soft lighting, a big zinc bar inside the front door, and stenciled nineteenth-century floor tiles.

I loved my simple starter, a terra-cotta ramekin filled with a coddled egg, a few strips of smoky piquillo pepper, and some frizzled slices of country ham, and Marie-Odile's langoustine tails rolled in crispy browned angel's hair pasta and garnished with fresh mango slices were superb, too. Though Chevassus's elegant pigeon sautéed with Chinese cabbage and garnished with galangal-spiked mushrooms is a favorite, I chose a snowy filet of cod with chive-dressed potatoes as my main course, and it was perfectly garnished with olive oil and brined lemons, the latter being one of the best and most popular French borrowings from the North African kitchen, since pickling concentrates and mellows the fruit. Marie-Odile's monkfish with lentils in a creamy shellfish sauce was outstanding, too, but both of us looked on longingly as our neighbors were served two whole, deliciously crusted legs of baby lamb, which came to the table sliced on wooden chopping boards with sides of salad and pommes dauphinoise.

"It was a great experience. I had lots of sex and saved a lot of money, plus the food's wonderful, but after three years in Sydney you miss the rest of the world," said a woman at the architects' table. "Maybe I should try Sydney, then," quipped Marie-Odile, just as her dessert and my cheese course from Alléosse, one of the city's best cheesemongers, was served. She loved her rhubarb and strawberries with almond milk, and my Loire Valley chèvre, Saint-Félicien, and Roquefort were superb. "Australia does sound like it has its advantages, but I could never give up these cheeses," I replied. "And I'm not going anywhere until I've been back here to try that lamb," said Marie-Odile. You shouldn't either.

· ⌢ ·

IN A WORD: Located in the rapidly gentrifying 11th Arrondissement, this is a stylish bistro serving excellent contemporary French cooking. A welcoming atmosphere and intelligent,

friendly service in a pleasant old-fashioned dining room with a certain funky charm make this place well worth going out of the way for.

DON'T MISS: The menu here changes regularly, but outstanding recent dishes include coddled egg with roasted piquillo peppers and grilled country ham; langoustines wrapped in angel hair with fresh mango; quail with green asparagus and oven-dried tomatoes; monkfish with lentils and shellfish sauce; cod garnished with olive oil and preserved lemons; roast agneau de lait (baby lamb) with salad and pommes dauphinoise; lamb shoulder in date juice on a bed of braised spinach; pigeon sautéed with Chinese cabbage with a side of galangal-seasoned mushrooms; strawberries and rhubarb with almond milk.

. . .

[69] 7 rue du Dahomey, 11th, 01.43.71.67.69. MÉTRO: Faidherbe-Chaligny. OPEN Monday to Friday for lunch and dinner. Saturday dinner only. CLOSED Sunday. • $$

Le Villaret

IN THE CONSTANT CHURN OF THE NEW, SOME EXCELLENT Paris restaurants fall between the cracks. As I was reminded by a superb dinner at a sidewalk table on a balmy May night, Le Villaret is one of them. Though it doesn't generate much buzz, it's quite simply one of the city's best bistros.

Le Villaret's been around for a while and in fact was one of the first tables to take a serious contemporary approach to bistro cooking. To wit, the talented chef, Olivier Gaslain, serves bistro dishes that are cooked with the same care, precision, and imagination as anything you'll find in a haute cuisine restaurant, and the service is friendlier and more engaged to boot.

As the funky old working-class Oberkampf (the name is that of a French industrialist of German descent best known for creating toile de Jouy, one of the most famous French textile prints) neighborhood of the 11th has grown younger and trendier, Le Villaret has become something of an anomaly, a serious table in a part of town where the most popular restaurants serve pennywise spins on ethnic eats—Latino, Brazilian, North African—and sound tracks are de rigueur. Still, even though we were early, this place filled up completely on a Wednesday night, and many of its well-dressed customers, quite obviously from other parts of Paris, arrived by cab, a sure sign of an address with seriously good word of mouth.

Some came from even further afield, including the deeply tanned mother and father from Philadelphia and Miami who were dining with their Paris-based son. His brother from New York was also on hand, which led me to guess that they were in Paris for an important family occasion. "Okay, sweetheart,

she's very nice, but would she ever be willing to live in the U.S.?
You can't stay over here forever, you know, and the kids, when
they come, they should learn English," said Mom, and an im-
pending wedding became clear. The groom-to-be continued to
dutifully translate the menu for his parents and brother before
he answered her question. "She wants to live in Israel," he said
while leafing through the wine list. "Israel? What's wrong with
Philadelphia? Or Miami? And what are joues de lotte again?"
"Monkfish cheeks." "Who knew fish have cheeks? Do they
smile, too? And so tell me, what's wrong with Philadelphia? Or
Miami?"

Elsewhere in the half-timbered dining room, a solitary
French woman executive read a neatly folded copy of *Le Monde*
between courses, there were several besotted young couples on
dates, and everyone else seemed to be wearing neatly pressed
linen on the occasion of the year's first really warm night.

Since I've become enough of a Parisian that people watching
is one of my favorite pastimes, I love sidewalk dining, and for
this, Le Villaret is ideal, since the rue Terneaux has little car
traffic but a constant motley stream of Parisians on foot. Just as
Hugh and I were served our first courses, the concierge of the
building in which the restaurant is located trundled by with the
big, recently emptied green plastic garbage bins that are one of
the city's less acknowledged emblems. A stout older woman
with salt-and-pepper hair in a pine-tree-print rayon housedress,
she paused and looked at our plates. "Bon appétit, Messieurs. Il
est très bien, ce cuisinier" ("He's good, that cook").

My tangle of seared girolles mushrooms and finely sliced
baby squid served in a shallow white bowl and flecked with tiny
bits of parsley and garlic was superb, and when Hugh finally
stopped ranting about his boss at UNESCO, he tucked into his
homemade terrine de tête (pig's head cheese, also known as

brawn, and made from meat recovered from the animal's head after boiling) with wild asparagus and girolles and rolled his eyes. "This is just so good, which is why I always bring friends from Brisbane when they come to town. Everyone in Australia's always going on about how great our cooking is. And it is, but you'd be hard put to find anything this wonderfully funky and old-fashioned even in Sydney or Melbourne."

My firm, fleshy monkfish cheeks—these fish do have cheeks, and they're prized meaty morsels—had been pan-seared before being posed in a pool of smoky bacon-flavored bouillon with first-of-season peas, and the contrast between the smoke, the sweetness of the peas, and the light crusting on the fish was delectable. Hugh's boneless jarret de veau (veal shank) came with tender sliced baby carrots and artichokes in a lemon-brightened, stock-dashed sauce of Isigny cream (Isigny in Normandy is reputed for the quality of its cream and is also the ancestral seat of a famous American with French origins, Walt Disney).

My cheese course was a stunner, presented in a wooden case with four shelves filled with chèvres, Coulommiers, Camembert, and a deliciously nutty Comté. Hugh's first-of-season cherries were sautéed in salt butter and brown sugar and served with a huge dumpling of buttery mascarpone cream, a truly sublime dessert, and as we were dawdling over coffee, I heard the woman from Philadelphia and Miami over my shoulder. "You know what, dear, this food's just too good to be ruined by your wedding. Let's talk about it again tomorrow," said Mom, a wise lady with the right priorities.

· ·

IN A WORD: Hidden away in the trendy Oberkampf district, this friendly, well-run contemporary French bistro serves outstandingly good food and is a real dark horse on the Paris restaurant scene.

DON'T MISS: Winter vegetables in chicken stock with foie gras; asparagus and artichokes in bouillon with a poached egg; terrine de tête with wild asparagus and girolles mushrooms; lotte (monkfish) cheeks with baby peas in bouillon; roast chicken with cabbage in Arbois wine sauce; roast shoulder of lamb with white beans and potatoes; strawberry and raspberry soup with a salt-butter sablé (shortbread biscuit); sautéed cherries with mascarpone cream; pear clafoutis.

. . .

[76] **13 rue Ternaux, 11th, 01.43.57.89.76.** MÉTRO: **Parmentier.** OPEN **Monday to Friday for lunch and dinner. Saturday dinner only.** CLOSED **Sunday. $$**

THE RISE AND FALL OF
THE PARISIAN BRASSERIE

· ❧ ·

THE AFFAIR MAY BE WANING, BUT THIS DOESN'T DIMINISH my pleasure in remembering that in 1986 it was love at first bite. Returning from three exhausting weeks of work in Italy to Paris and an apartment in the Latin Quarter where I'd spent

only one night—I'd left for Milan the day after I moved in—I gazed disconsolately at the contents of my refrigerator: a bottle of duty-free aquavit, the Danish spirit distilled from caraway seeds—a houseguest gift I'd yet to open—a flat half bottle of white wine, and a jar of anchovies from the previous tenant.

No possible recipe came to mind using these ingredients, so I looked up a pizza delivery place. When I called to order, I was told, "We're not delivering tonight. Il neige." It's snowing. I'd slept all afternoon that Sunday after getting home and so was surprised when I went to the window and saw that the city was covered with deep snow, with more falling so fast and furiously that I could barely see the Sorbonne across the street.

I had three choices. I could drink a large glass of aquavit and nibble an anchovy or two; I could bundle up and set out in search of an open restaurant in a neighborhood I didn't know; or I could toss in the towel and jump back into bed. I sat by the window and watched the snow coming down on a fast diagonal into the pretty amber penumbra of a streetlight and pondered. Though tempted by the last option, it seemed sort of lame to duck a first chance to learn something about my new neighborhood. So I had a fortifying shot of aquavit and went out to see what I could find.

Under its white mantle, the city was still, stately, and stunningly beautiful. I walked to the corner without passing another soul and turned left toward the busy boulevard Saint-Michel. A few more steps and I stopped to peer through the lace curtains and streaky patches of condensation in the windows of a well-lit restaurant. It wasn't very busy, but it was open and the small dining room was attractive. I'd only gone around the corner from my apartment, which didn't seem very adventurous, but I liked the looks of the place and there'd be other occasions to go further afield.

As I'd lived in Paris for only a few months, my French was wobbly and I wasn't yet comfortable eating alone in restaurants, so I rather dreaded going inside. Happily, my apprehension was misplaced. When I asked the owlish maître d'hôtel in a black spencer jacket by the door if they had a table for one, he smiled and said, "Mais bien sûr!" ("But of course!"). Settled on the saggy red leatherette banquette of a table for two, I sipped a kir (white wine with crème de cassis) and studied the menu, quietly pleased with myself for not having settled for an anchovy supper. "Quel sale temps!" ("What awful weather!") said the older waiter in a snug white apron when he came to take my order— a gratinée (onion soup), filet of beef with béarnaise sauce, frites and sautéed spinach, and a half bottle of the house Bordeaux.

Just a table down from mine, a pretty older woman with a spray of glossy red plaster cherries pinned to her gray dress and some soft white curls peeking out from under her gray angora cloche hat caught my eye and smiled. "Bonsoir, Monsieur!" she said, and I felt completely at home in this small dining room with a cantilevered mirror running the length of one wall just below the ceiling and a tarte Tatin sitting on the bar next to stairs that led to the téléphone et toilettes in the basement. The older man sitting across the table from her appeared to be reading a book, but then I realized that he was reading to her and craned to see if I could read the title of his volume—Baudelaire, the great romantic French poet. With the possible exception of one rainy afternoon in a coffeehouse in Cambridge, Massachusetts, I'd never seen anyone reading poetry to his dinner companion before, and it struck me as desperately romantic. I'd folded open next to my fork one of the two rolled-up New Yorker magazines I'd brought with me, but it was more fun looking around. There was still a crust of snow melting on top of the big fur hat of the beautiful young woman across the aisle. Her boyfriend, who wore a heavy black cabled turtleneck and a peacoat, ate his salad without taking his eyes off her, pausing between bites to draw hard on his cigarette. I watched as she was served what I later learned is choucroute garnie, sauerkraut garnished with sausages and other cuts of pork. She nibbled a shaggy forkful of shredded cabbage, then speared a brick-colored sausage with her fork and held it out to her boyfriend. He bit it in half, she laughed, and I looked away.

My soup came and was piping hot under a cap of molten, blistered cheese, which released a puff of potent steam redolent of beef and onions when I pierced it with my spoon. My Bordeaux was good, too, maybe even a little too good, since I had only a glass left by the time my steak arrived. After the nice old lady and her husband a table down bade me good night, I noticed they'd barely touched their bottle of excellent Médoc and was thinking about how good it would be with my meat. "Est-ce-que vous avez jamais vu une bouteille du vin volante?" asked the waiter who'd just served me. It took a minute to register what he'd said— "Have you ever seen a flying bottle of wine before?" "Non," I said, thinking I must have misunderstood him. He looked left and right like someone pantomiming a burglar, then quickly picked up the bottle of Médoc and planted it on my table. "Et maintenant vous l'avez vu!" ("And now you have!") he said with a wink.

I'm sure I blushed, surprised by his solicitude and also dumbstruck by my luck in finding this place. Dessert—a big slice of tarte Tatin with a spoonful of crème fraîche that was udderly (*sic*) fresh and rich—was superb, too, and after I paid my bill, I thanked the maître d'hôtel effusively for a lovely meal. He shrugged. "Mais c'était mon plaisir de vous recevoir, et bien sûr, Monsieur, il n'y rien au monde qui est mieux que les brasseries de Paris" ("But it was my pleasure to have you here tonight, and of course there's nothing better in the world than the brasseries of Paris"). I asked for a card, and during my brief walk home in the snow, I gloated in anticipation of revealing my find the next day at the offices of the style-driven publishing company where I was the newest editor.

Every Monday we had a meeting to discuss the weekly churn of assignments and suggest new story ideas. I let everyone else go first, waiting to show them that the new boy in town had a card up his sleeve. When my turn came, I announced I'd discovered a remarkable restaurant in the Latin Quarter, a discreetly stylish, convivial place with great food, a fascinating crowd, and wry, complicit service. "Sounds fantastic—what's it called?" asked the bureau chief. I fished the card out of my pocket. "Brasserie Balzar." "Oh, please!" they groaned almost in unison, with someone adding, "Alec, it's one of the best-known restaurants on the Left Bank."

I was crestfallen for a few minutes, but later, in the quiet of my office with the door closed, I retrieved my initial elation, knowing that this solitary meal on a snowy night in Paris was something I'd treasure for many years to come.

So I learned that the Balzar is one of the great brasseries of Paris and eventually what a brasserie is, something I couldn't have told you that day either. All I knew after my dinner at the Balzar was that it channeled everything I love about Paris, its spellbinding chic and animation, a certain metropolitan glamour at once winsome and wistful, and most of all the nonchalant but reflexive sensuality that quietly exhilarates daily life in the French capital. Looking at Monet's paintings of Parisian streetscapes, I'd often wondered where and what the throngs on those damp gray boulevards ate or exactly what sort of room you'd have stepped into if you were hungry after shopping and caught in a rain shower at the end of the nineteenth century. So now I knew, later understanding that the brasserie is a quintessentially Parisian institution, usually a large and lavishly decorated place where waiters in long white aprons worn over fitted black jackets dash around delivering big aluminum trays studded with freshly shucked oysters bedded on mounds of crushed ice, along with steaks, grilled fish, and choucroute garnie.

Invented during the second half of the nineteenth century to feed the hungry crowds generated by the growing affluence of industrializing France, the birth of tourism, and a boom in rail travel, brasseries, along with their cozy, homey cousin, the bistro, are the culinary incarnation of Paris. Swift-paced but friendly, anonymous but communal, they offer up a vivid palette of intriguing vignettes of urban life and its endless possibilities along with a gastronomic refrain of how culinary pleasure can be casually democratic in one of the world's greatest cities—for a long time, brasseries weren't expensive.

The first Parisian brasserie was founded by Frédéric Bofinger in 1864. Bofinger's innovation was to serve draft beer with plates of charcuterie (sausage and cold meats), and after his simple place became popular, he remodeled and dressed it up, feeding a new rage for this format of restaurant.

Many of the most famous Parisian brasseries were founded by Alsatians who sought refuge in the capital following the disastrous Franco-Prussian War (1870–1871), when a big slice of eastern France came under the rule of the German kaiser. In Alsace, brasseries, or breweries in French, served their suds in taverns adjacent to their brew halls with plates of charcuterie and hearty local specialties like choucroute garnie, juniper-berry-scented sauerkraut garnished with sausage and various cuts of pork, including kassler (pork loin), bacon, and occasionally a jarret (pork knuckle). Choucroute garnie became the Parisian brasserie's signature dish, but brasserie menus evolved to suit Parisian tastes. Since Parisians love oysters, many brasseries added bancs à huîtres—sidewalk oyster stands where écaillers, or oyster shuckers, in blue cotton smocks and rubber boots prepare lavish trays of fresh oysters and other fresh shellfish, including langoustines, shrimp, mussels, cockles, and clams.

From 1890 to 1930, dozens of brasseries opened in Paris. Since they served similar menus, their owners competed by commissioning jaw-dropping decors, initially in the same resplendent, sinuously floral Art Nouveau style used by the Paris Métro and, after World War I, in the sleek Art Deco style that epitomized the Roaring Twenties.

Perhaps the apotheosis of the brasserie occurred on December 20, 1927, when a festive crowd of some 2,500 Parisians thronged the boulevard Montparnasse on the Left Bank in the 14th Arrondissement to celebrate the opening of La Coupole, the sprawling brasserie that became one of the epicenters of Parisian life during Les Années Folles, or the Roaring Twenties. The merrymakers got through some 1,200 bottles of Mumm Champagne that night, and the sleek new Art Deco–style brasserie's reputation was instantly made as the Parisian press reported their bibulousness, the mountain of oyster shells produced by the opening-night feast, and the naughty shenanigans of the arty crowd that then made Montparnasse its home.

During my first years in Paris, I was a regular at many of the city's storied brasseries. I loved their liveliness, they served late and on weekends, and they were perfect for dining with a gaggle of friends and blowing off the blues on a Sunday night over a plateau de fruits de mer. Everyone I knew had their favorites. Christa liked La Coupole and Julien, while Christophe was keen on Le Vaudeville, Jutta had a soft spot for Brasserie Flo, and I loyally championed the Brasserie Balzar. I also liked Saturday lunch at Brasserie Lipp and Au Pied de Cochon for onion soup after hours—this brasserie serves round the clock, twenty-four hours a day—and Chez Jenny for its good choucroute on a wintry day.

Though I never went to any brasserie with lofty gastronomic expectations—they were more about good times, people watching, and simple, tasty food—I couldn't help but notice when their quality started slipping at the beginning of the 1990s, by which time most of them had been bought up by two restaurant groups, Groupe Flo and Frères Blanc. After founder Jean-Paul Bucher bought Brasserie Flo in 1968, Groupe Flo became a brand name that gobbled up one grande old dame after another, including La Coupole, Bofinger, Julien, Le Boeuf sur la Toit, Le Vaudeville, Terminus Nord, and Brasserie Balzar, while the rival Frerès Blanc's stable ran to Au Pied de Cochon, Charlot, La Lorraine, Chez Jenny, Le Procope, and l'Alsace, among others.

Eventually, however, the mediocrity of the brasseries' food became so flagrant that I reluctantly concluded that most of them had become unfrequentable. The problem was that behind the scenes, it was accountants, not cooks, who edited the menus and order sheets and who eliminated expensive kitchen staff by enthusiastically embracing almost every industrial shortcut devised by France's booming food service industry, notably mass-produced sauces, soups, salads, frites, and desserts. Every year, it seemed, there was less real cooking going on behind the swinging doors, maybe just a bit of grilling, frying, and reheating.

Today, there are only a handful of brasseries left that warrant a meal by a traveler to Paris, and the luster of the city has been slightly dimmed by their decline. Still, I suspect it's only a matter of time before a new generation of inspired restaurateurs recognizes that this profoundly Parisian institution is as valid today as it was a century ago and the brasserie is reborn. I certainly hope so.

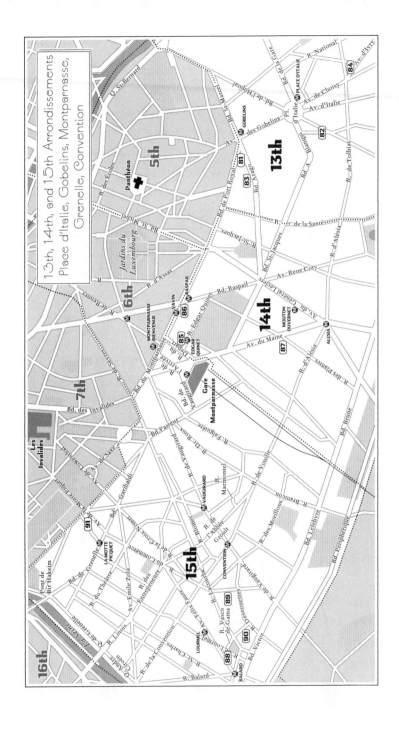

13th, 14th, and 15th Arrondissements
Place d'Italie, Gobelins, Montparnasse,
Grenelle, Convention

PLACE D'ITALIE, GOBELINS, MONTPARNASSE, GRENELLE, CONVENTION

L'Avant Goût

THOUGH IT ENJOYED A BRIEF BLAZE OF COUNTERCULTURE glory in the sixties as a popular address for soixante-huitard types (what the French called the student protesters who tore up

the Latin Quarter in May 1968), the pretty La Butte aux Cailles (Hill of the Quails) neighborhood in the 13th Arrondissement has been quiet ever since these rebels settled down as academics, researchers, artists, and writers and decided they'd rather own stones than throw them. In fact, one of the newsiest things to have happened in this quartier lately was the opening of L'Avant Goût a few years ago. Suddenly, rave word of mouth about chef Christophe Beaufront's cooking meant this off-the-beaten-track part of town had a restaurant that was pulling Parisians from other parts of the city. Beaufront, who trained with Guy Savoy and Michel Guérard, converted an old café into a great-value modern bistro where his husky-voiced wife ran the dining room and the menu ran to edgy dishes like his signature pork pot-au-feu with fried ginger chips. The place quickly became a roaring success—in fact, it was often so noisy you had to shout at your tablemates, a problem since rectified with an acoustically tiled ceiling, and it became tough to snag a table.

I hadn't been for a while but joined South African friends, winemakers from Paarl, who'd come to town with the nearly impossible task of peddling their wares to the French, most of whom still refuse to take any wine but their own seriously, for dinner on a Saturday night. Wedged in between a large table of Franco-Cambodians celebrating a birthday and an elegant older Parisian couple dining with the son of an English colleague and his wife, we ate very well indeed, but not every dish was a success. Ravioli filled with fresh cod in a foamy sauce of shiitake mushrooms were delicious, with an intriguing contrast of textures, but a ball of herbed goat cheese surrounded by radishes, Nyons olives, and broccoli florets in a shallow jar came off like one of those "I hate to cook" recipes you see in women's magazines, and shrimp wrapped in kadif, crunchy Lebanese pastry threads, were bland enough to make eavesdropping on the next table more tempting. It turned out that the natty older gent was a nuclear scientist recruited to teach at Columbia in 1940, just before the Nazis invaded France, and he went to great lengths to point out that the Americans liked Philippe Pétain before the Germans invaded and he became the leader of Vichy France, the Nazi puppet state.

Happily, the main courses showed why Beaufront remains a talent to be reckoned with. A snowy filet of cod had been marinated in herbed crème fraîche before cooking, which made it wonderfully moist, and it was served on a bed of perfectly cooked lentils. Duck breast with date chutney was succulent and perfectly seasoned, and the South Africans loved their pot-au-feu—various cuts of pork, sweet potato, fennel bulb, ginger chips, and a glass of the spicy bouillon in which it had been cooked. Desserts were excellent, too, including melon sprinkled with anisette and garnished with a ball of tarragon ice and a candied sweet potato with pineapple compote. L'Avant Goût may no longer be avant-garde, but it's a very good restaurant that's well worth the trouble of booking the requisite week or two in advance.

· 🐖 ·

IN A WORD: Chef Christophe Beaufront's popular bistro isn't as cutting edge as it once was but it still offers an excellent feed for a very reasonable price. With his creativity anchored by classical training, Beaufront's contemporary French cooking remains extremely appealing.

DON'T MISS: The menu changes regularly here but usually includes Beaufront's signature dish of pot-au-feu de cochon aux épices, braised cuts of pork in a spicy bouillon with sweet potatoes, fennel, and a garnish of fried ginger. Other good dishes include ravioli with fresh cod in shiitake mushroom sauce;

piquillo peppers stuffed with smoked haddock rillettes; cod marinated with crème fraîche and herbs with lentils.

. . .

[**82**] **26 rue Bobillot, 13th, 01.43.80.24.00.** MÉTRO: **Place d'Italie.** OPEN **Tuesday to Friday for lunch and dinner. Saturday dinner only.** CLOSED **Sunday and Monday.** ▪ **$$**

Le Bambou

FOR DAYS AFTER MY FIRST MEAL AT LE BAMBOU, I WAS desperate to return to this crowded, chaotic restaurant in an inconvenient corner of the 13th Arrondissement, Paris's most Asian neighborhood. I'd been invited by my friend Nancy, a Vietnamese-American woman living in Washington, D.C., with the caveat that you go there only to eat, since they don't let you linger at the table or take reservations and the decor and lighting are awful. She was correct on both points. Still, the chance to see her and meet her Paris relatives was too good to pass up, and so I found myself in this superb Saigon hash house in excellent and truly charming company.

What Nancy didn't prepare me for was some of the best Vietnamese home cooking I've ever had outside Vietnam, a country I've visited a half-dozen times. As the only non-Vietnamese at the table, I was shy about ordering but plunged in with a gluttonous request for Vietnamese ravioli, green papaya salad with shrimp, and a big bowl of pho topped with sliced nems (deep-fried spring rolls). Everything I ordered was exceptional, sending me back to the tiny Saigon restaurants where I'd squatted on knee-high fluorescent plastic stools and stuffed myself with some of the best food I've ever eaten. The dishes her family ordered were spectacular, too, including Saigon-style omelettes brimming with bean sprouts, squid and shrimp, and duck in a caramelized sauce with fresh pepper. Our meal occurred in a blur, as almost every meal here does, but as someone who passionately loves Vietnamese food, I'm more than willing to put up with the noise and so would suggest that you come early or very late, and in as large a number as possible to sample some of the best Vietnamese home cooking in the French capital.

· ·

IN A WORD: Though it's as crowded, noisy, and uncomfortable as a rush-hour subway car, this clamorous Vietnamese in Paris's modern "Chinatown" serves some of the best Vietnamese food in town. Just remember that you're going on a tasting mission rather than in search of a cosseted dining experience.

DON'T MISS: Vietnamese ravioli; green papaya salad with shrimp; bo bun (nems and pho, or beef noodle soup); Saigonese omelette.

. . .

[**84**] **70 rue Baudricourt, 13th, 01.45.70.91.75.** MÉTRO: **Tolbiac.** OPEN **Tuesday to Sunday for lunch and dinner.** CLOSED **Monday.** ▪ **$**

Jadis

TO MY SATISFACTION, THE SAME SCRIPT PLAYS OUT THE same way every time I meet friends for a meal at Jadis, a storefront place with a simple décor of dove-gray and white walls with Bordeaux-red trim in a quiet residential neighborhood on the outskirts of the 15th Arrondissement. Invariably, they arrive late and exasperated, muttering about the godforsaken location and grumbling that the food had better be good, and then a couple of hours later, I see them off into the night cooing with pleasure over chef Guillaume Delage's superb cooking and the pleasure they feel at having "discovered" such an offbeat destination.

Delage is one of the hardest-working and most intensely focused young chefs in Paris today. His dual-speed menu lets you choose between bistro classics or a smaller range of dishes that are the fruit of his experience and imagination. If I've eaten superbly well when opting for Delage's own creations, I have a weakness for his traditional dishes for the simple reason that they're so brilliantly executed.

Jadis is a place I often take visiting food professionals, and my most recent meal was with a delightful couple of chefs who live in Providence, Rhode Island, and who have a Paris pied-à-terre and very demanding palates. There were four of us at the table: two had the delicately acidulated oyster velouté (creamy

soup) with shavings of Cantal cheese that accentuated the milk-iness of the bivalve and the other pair a very original salad of Puy lentils with bulots (sea snails) and chunks of smoked bacon. I loved the unexpected but brilliant detail of pairing cheese with oysters to fully express the milky nuances of their taste, and also the way Delage had created a bridge of vegetal richness be-tween the earthy lentils and iodine-bright snails by cooking them in the same rich court bouillon. Next, a spectacularly good roast shoulder of lamb served in a copper casserole on a bed of fat white Mogette beans with black olives and sun-dried toma-toes and ocean perch in a rather timid but pleasant wasabi sauce with a delicious side of fluffy sweet-potato purée, and then the grand finale, Delage's sublime warm bittersweet chocolate soufflé for dessert.

· ⬩ ·

IN A WORD: In an out-of-the-way location in the 15th Arron-dissement, a talented young chef has created an outstanding bistro that offers a changing roster of contemporary French and traditional bistro dishes.

DON'T MISS: The menu changes regularly, but dishes not to miss include pâté en croute, lamb's feet and button mushrooms in lemon sauce, terrine of artichokes and foie gras, oyster velouté, shrimp with black rice, roast shoulder of lamb, île flot-tante à la pistache, and dark chocolate soufflé.

. . .

[89] Jadis, 208 rue de la Croix-Nivert, 15th, 01.45.57.73.20. MÉTRO: Porte de Versailles. OPEN for lunch and dinner Monday to Friday. CLOSED Satur-day and Sunday. • $$

Le Beurre Noisette

DURING THE LAST TWENTY YEARS, THE QUIET, LEAFY, residential 15th, Paris's largest arrondissement, has become terra nova for young chefs looking to hang out their own shingles. Why? Rents are lower than in the single-digit arrondissements, this prosperous part of town provides an instant clientele, and Parisians from other neighborhoods have gotten used to traveling to offbeat corners of the city in search of great eating at good prices, all of which means that Le Beurre Noisette, the talented chef Thierry Blanqui's amiable modern bistro, is booked solid at lunch and dinner.

It's an address that's very much worth the trek, too, since Blanqui, who trained at La Tour d'Argent and with Christian Le Squer at Ledoyen, easily awed the palates of my friends Bert and Noël from Los Angeles. They have two of the world's most experienced and discerning palates, but on a hot summer night, none of us thought we were very hungry until our first courses arrived. "This is terrific," said Noël after tasting her fresh pea soup with mint and crumbled bacon. My sautéed supions, or baby squid, were spectacular, too—lightly crusted by perfect grilling and seasoned with fresh herbs, shallots, lemon, tomato cubes, and sesame seeds. Burt loved them, too, and Bruno's pressé de jarret de porc et foie gras, terrine of boned pork shank with duck foie gras, was brightened by a small salad of mixed baby lettuce leaves and fresh herbs, and the contrast between the unctuous foie gras and chewy meat was sexy and elegant.

Our waiter clearly enjoyed Bert's impeccable French and punning sense of humor, and the small, pretty dining room buzzed with the pleasure of people having a good meal. Main courses were excellent, too. Two of us had the John Dory, which was served whole, a welcome change from the lamentable Parisian trend to fish filets, with a medley of vegetables à la Greque, or poached in vinaigrette, and drizzled with a vividly herbal pesto sauce, and roasted cumin-dusted lamb shoulder was garnished with Moroccan-style preserved lemons, a lovely foil for the rich meat. Noël, one of the lustiest eaters I know, reveled in her assorted pork plate, which included a juicy chop, a length of grilled Auvergnat sausage, a slice of grilled smoked filet and crispy bacon topping a mound of mashed potatoes. While we were eating our chocolate quenelles with crispy carmelized tuiles, or cookies, and soup of summer fruit, we heard a woman at the next table tell the waiter, "Vous êtes au bout du monde ici, mais la cuisine vaut vraiment la peine de venir" ("You're at the end of the earth, but the cooking's really worth the effort of getting here"), and we agreed wholeheartedly.

· ☙ ·

IN A WORD: Though it's a chore to get here, chef Thierry Blanqui's bright, fresh contemporary French bistro cooking is worth it. Moderate prices, friendly service, a nice selection of wines, and a few sidewalk tables during the summer add to the pleasure of a meal here.

DON'T MISS: The menu changes regularly, but dishes to look for include sautéed rolled tête de veau (calf's head) with salad; sautéed supions (baby squid) with tomatoes; shallots, herbs, and sesame; cold pea soup with bacon; calf's liver with Parmesan polenta; pressé de jarret de porc et foie gras terrine (pork and foie gras terrine); John Dory with légumes à la Grecque (marinated vegetables) and pesto; grilled pork plate; roasted lamb shoulder with cumin and preserved lemons; quenelle de chocolat (scoops of chocolate-and-cream mousse); summer fruit soup.

. . .

[90] 68 rue Vasco de Gama, 15th, 01.48.56.82.49. MÉTRO: Lourmel. OPEN Tuesday to Saturday for lunch and dinner. CLOSED Sunday and Monday. ▪ $$

La Cave de l'Os à Moëlle

CHEF THIERRY FAUCHER IS PART OF THE CONSTANT GANG, the band of chefs who trained at Les Ambassadeurs at the Hôtel Crillon when Christian Constant was chef there. He was also one of the earliest, and nerviest, to strike out on his own with a bistro in a remote corner of the 15th Arrondissement that served a single five-course meal at each sitting.

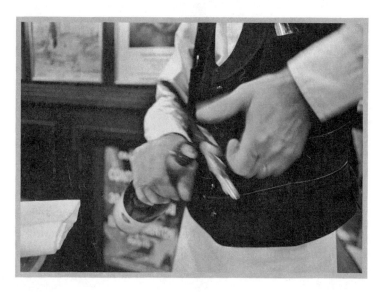

In the beginning, L'Os à Moëlle, Faucher's cozy, lace-curtain restaurant, had a lot of buzz, and even though I didn't particularly like the idea of the one-size-fits-all menu—it serves a single prix fixe menu daily—it was a lot of fun and you generally ate well. Over the years, however, the price has crept up to a level where I'd rather choose my meal than have it imposed, and the formerly relaxed and giddy atmosphere has been steam-rollered by multiple services and its international success. The last time I was here, I came with a couple of cookbook writers from New Zealand, and since it was their choice, they were muted in their disappointment. It wasn't that we didn't eat well—the food's still very good—but rather that this restaurant has gone the way of airline travel, becoming an experience that's changed from something exhilarating and very special into one that's workaday.

This is why I prefer La Cave de l'Os à Moëlle, Faucher's hugely popular and very Parisian wine bar nearby. As long as you come in a group—tables of two might feel lost here, especially if you don't speak French—the table d'hôtes formula (you're seated at tables with other customers) is usually a lot of fun, and the food, served on a buffet, runs to excellent home-style French cooking. Bread, salad, and wine are served by waitresses, but soup, starters, main courses, dessert, and cheese are all help yourself on side tables.

My last meal here was on a chilly night within a week of Christmas, which meant that Laurent, Carole, Bruno, and I were in need of babying, which is exactly what we found here. Ravenous, I could barely stay away from the terrines on the buffet—a first-rate terrine de campagne (made with coarsely ground pork), pâté de boudin noir (made with blood pudding), pâté de poulet (chicken), and a pot of earthy and delicious pork rillettes (shredded pork cooked in its own fat). There was also a big bowl of freshly chopped vegetables and pot of aïoli (garlic mayonnaise) next to it. It would have been easy to make a meal out of this spread, but after shamelessly gorging ourselves on these starters, we moved on to the steaming tureen of delicious cream of celery soup warming on the range at the end of the room.

The beef and mushroom ragout served as our main course was excellent, too, although I'd had my fingers crossed for the roast chicken on a bed of spinach and chopped kidneys that I'd had the last time I was there. We finished off the fresh chèvres on the cheese tray and then savaged the desserts, which included apple crumble, rice pudding, crème caramel, tarte Tatin, prunes stewed with chunks of lemon, and pears simmered with stick cinnamon. "I could happily eat here every night," said Carole. For me, La Cave really fits the bill when I want a hearty, generous, rustic French meal served in a relaxed, convivial setting.

· · ·

IN A WORD: Chef Thierry Faucher's popular wine bar puts on a superb spread of delicious, home-style Gallic grub and captures the hip, friendly buzz now gone from his much too popular original restaurant L'Os à Moëlle.

· · ·

[88] 181 rue Lourmel, 15th, 01.45.57.28.28. MÉTRO: Lourmel. OPEN Tuesday to Sunday for lunch and dinner. CLOSED Monday. ▪ $

La Cerisaie

AMONG THE REGIONAL KITCHENS THAT ARE THE GLORIOUS bedrock of French cooking, the food of southwestern France is

the brawny macho towel snapper. This is why French presidents feel compelled to demonstrate their love of such emblematic dishes as cassoulet (preserved duck, sausage, pork, and white beans) and the region's more arcane dishes, including roasted ortolans, or tiny birds, that the late François Mitterrand gobbled down under legally dubious circumstances on his last New Year's Eve.

The gastronomic posturing of politicians to one side, Parisians love this rich, hearty cooking, too, which may seem surprising in view of recent trends to healthier, lighter eating. When it comes to good food, though, they have a contrarian weakness for such atavistic pleasures, which is what explains the popularity of La Cerisaie.

To be blunt, this broom closet of a restaurant in Montparnasse isn't for everyone. There's no decor to speak of (a forgivable sin in my book when the food's this good) and the tiny room gets as crowded as a rush-hour Métro car at both lunch and dinner. But if overpacked dining rooms don't put you off, you're in for a treat, since the young chef Cyril Lalanne's take on the southwest is tender, sincere, and absolutely delicious, and his wife, Maryse, who runs the dining room, is a charming, good-humored hostess.

I'm still savoring the foie gras raviolo in pot-au-feu bouillon I had the last time I had dinner here. The single tender pasta pillow contained a stunningly good piece of foie gras, and the bouillon was rich, deeply flavored, and ancestral, just the sort of simple, consoling pleasure you might be served at a farmhouse supper in the heart of la France profonde. My friend Nanette's white asparagus from Les Landes was brilliantly bathed in a parsley-infused oil that amplified its natural bittersweet taste, and her spiced goose breast with roasted peaches was sublime, too. I loved my tuna with piperade (the Basque garnish of sautéed peppers, onions, and tomatoes), and my baba à l'Armagnac was a clever regional riff on the classic sponge cake in rum syrup and came under an alluring cloud of whipped cream. Nanette claimed that her chocolate tart with coffee ice cream was worth the price of her airplane ticket from New York and booked for dinner again two nights later after we paid our bill. "If I ate like this every day, I'd be shopping at Lane Bryant [the plus-size clothing shop] before I knew it. But hey, summer's still a few months away and I've always said I want a man who loves me for my mind," she said over after-dinner coffee at Le Select, a café just a few streets away in the heart of Montparnasse.

· · ·

IN A WORD: Though this minuscule restaurant in Montparnasse isn't a good place to share secrets, it's worth putting up with the elbow-to-elbow seating for chef Cyril Lalanne's excellent southwestern French cooking.

DON'T MISS: The menu changes constantly here, but dishes I've enjoyed include squash soup; velouté de châtaigne et foie gras (chestnut and foie gras soup); terrine de confit de canard (preserved duck terrine); sautéed foie gras with polenta; tuna steak with piperade (Basque garnish of tomatoes, onions, and peppers); sautéed goose breast with roasted peaches; Noir de Bigorre (a race of southwestern French pigs) pork chop; baba à l'Armagnac; chocolate tart with coffee ice cream.

. . .

[85] 70 boulevard Edgar-Quinet, 14th, 01.43.20.98.98. MÉTRO: Montparnasse. OPEN Monday to Friday for lunch and dinner. CLOSED Saturday and Sunday. ▪ $$

Le Dôme

AH, LA VIE EN ROSE: IT'S THE METROPOLITAN LURE OF THE French capital, a spontaneous mixture of chic, frivolity, and sensuality that fills Paris-bound jets from cities around the world daily, and amazingly enough it's still around if you know where to find it. Long after the flame has guttered out in Montparnasse, where the cafés and restaurants of legend are now the province of tourists and clock-watching out-of-towners (the last train or Métro is the virtual hourglass on many of their tables) who still cast themselves as hopeful voyeurs at a now much

diminished bohemian scene, this grand and stunningly extravagant seafood restaurant keeps the magic alive.

It's shocking, really, to pay such prices for fish, but then it
would be foolish not to. Here, the price of admission is not only
a really good meal but a brief passage on a grand old barge that
remains one of the best addresses in town for anyone who wants
to eat from Neptune's spear.

Assiduous students of Paris history will quickly tell you that
the Dôme wasn't always this way, a place where most of the
blazers tossed over chair backs are cashmere and the janitor
finds a Christian Dior scarf or two under the tables as he brooms
the room before heading for the night bus. No, the Dôme was
once a smoky workaday café where people like Trotsky jotted
down their oddball and sometimes dangerous ambitions on
paper napkins while nursing a coffee for hours as a way of escaping the cold reality of cheap lodgings.

This high-minded seditiousness is long gone, but a whiff of
bohème still hovers over the cultivated Parisians—politicians,
artists, and editors—who come here to change the world for at

least the time it takes to devour a big tray of some of the best oysters in the city or tuck into a perfect sole meunière line-caught off the Ile d'Yeu on France's Atlantic coast. This is why I knew it would be perfect for dinner with my friend Catherine, a book editor from New York. She also loves fish, and I think Paris is the best city in Europe for anyone who loves seafood, which is explained by the fact that France makes a fetish of freshness and has two coastlines, Atlantic and Mediterranean, both of which yield up different delicacies, as well as a proud, hardworking fleet of traditional fishermen who catch fish by line rather than in nets, which damage them.

Catherine instantly took to the glittery crowd and festive atmosphere created by the busy dance of serious waiters in aprons and the wonderful burble, my favorite metropolitan noise, of people eating well. We ate delicious tiny, sweet pink shrimp from Brittany with flutes of Champagne, and then, knowing I could filch one or two, I left the meaty Gillardeau oysters to Catherine and ordered ormeaux (abalone) as my first course. Fished off the Channel Islands, they rarely appear on Paris menus because they're quite rare and not easy to cook, since too much heat makes their succulent flesh rubbery. Here they were exquisite, cut into fine strips and gently sautéed in salted butter with a bit of garlic and parsley. Catherine's sole was "sublime," and my freshly salted cod with aïoli (garlic mayonnaise) was gorgeous. To oblige our waistlines, we split a slice of the very good fresh raspberry tart for dessert and enjoyed the wake of a truly excellent meal over coffee.

· ·

IN A WORD: Few restaurants in Paris offer a better take on classical French seafood cooking than this soignée grande dame in Montparnasse. Its catch of the day is just that, and it's impeccably cooked and served in a simple but festive setting that thrums with a worldly crowd having a good time. You'll also net a big bill here, but it's worth it.

DON'T MISS: Breton shrimp; oysters; smoked salmon; ormeaux (abalone); sole meunière; grilled sea bass; roast turbot with hollandaise sauce; raspberry tart.

. . .

[86] **108 boulevard du Montparnasse, 14th, 01.43.35.25.81.** MÉTRO: **Vavin.** OPEN **daily for lunch and dinner, except during July and August, when it's closed on Sunday and Monday. •** **$$$**

L'Ourcine

EVEN BEFORE YOUR FIRST COURSE ARRIVES, L'OURCINE, in a funky corner of the 13th Arrondissement that reminds me of New York's West Village, is a very easy place to like. The

staff is smart and friendly, and the rustic dining room with generously spaced wooden tables, a small bar inside the front door, and a tomettes (clay tile) floor cue you that chef Sylvain Danière has an auberge state of mind. What you wouldn't know unless you'd been here before, of course, is just how wonderful the food is going to be. Danière trained with the bistro wizard Yves Camdeborde, the chef whose La Régalade, now under new management, daringly renewed the idiom of Paris's most beloved restaurant category, but if he remains one of Camdeborde's most loyal lieutenants, chef Danière is starting to spin his own style, with very exciting results.

The chalkboard menu changes regularly, but Danière's precise, passionate cooking doesn't miss a beat, whatever you choose. On a balmy May night, my meal led off with a complimentary shot glass of scallop mousse topped with tiny fried croutons (these tasty little bread cubes are a signature of the Camdeborde school if ever there was one), and the way the mousse concentrated the flavor of the mollusk was more exciting than anything I'd eaten in a haute cuisine restaurant for a long time. The cute young couple from Houston next to us ordered exactly the same first courses as we did—the terrine of fennel bulb and foie gras for me and the young Texan woman and a pressé of pig's head (meat from the pig's head pressed into a loaf) for my friend Arnaud and the young woman's husband—and all of us loved these fully flavored but delicately composed dishes. The fennel bulb and foie gras terrine was real art, with fresh chervil separating each layer of perfectly cooked liver and vegetable, and an accompanying crouton-topped salad of slivered beet root, mizuna, and other herbs brightening the dish. Arnaud, a professor of physics who, given my knowledge of his field, is, happily, very interested in food, insisted that I try his pig's head terrine, which was crunchy, earthy, and exact.

Our main courses were exquisite, too—brandade de cabillaud, Danière's riff on the famous garlicky potato dish of whipped potato and salt cod from the southern city of Nîmes, and a juicy breast of duckling on a très vieille France (old-fashioned France) bed of baby peas and wilted lettuce. I found it interesting that a young Turk like Danière was doing a dish as classically French as the duckling breast, and when I mentioned it to the waiter, he said, "Mais c'est ça que les gens veulent manger aujourd'hui" ("But this is what people want to eat these days"). While chatting with the young Texans, edgy types with a lot of curiosity about the world, the birthday cake of a Bolivian politician visiting France and his table of seven was served, and after the whole room had applauded, everyone was offered a glass of Champagne. L'Ourcine is that kind of place, profoundly Parisian, charmingly low key, generous, and dedicated to good times and great food.

IN A WORD: An outstanding contemporary bistro with relaxed, friendly service, an appealingly rustic atmosphere, and chef Sylvain Danière's remarkable market-inspired cooking.

DON'T MISS: Danière's menu evolves constantly, but dishes to pounce on if they're available include fennel bulb and foie gras terrine; spider crab ravioli with endives; seafood bisque; yellow pollack roasted in olive oil; stuffed chicken breast with Chinese cabbage; brandade de cabillaud; duck breast with baby peas and lettuce; filet mignon of pork with whole garlic cloves and baby potatoes; chocolate quenelles with saffroned crème anglaise.

. . .

[83] **92 rue Broca, 13th, 01.47.07.13.65.** MÉTRO: **Les Gobelins or Glacière.**
OPEN **Tuesday to Saturday for lunch and dinner.** CLOSED **Sunday and Monday.** ▪ **$**

Le Père Claude

THOUGH THE DECOR'S MORE REMINISCENT OF AN AIRLINE
office than a Paris bistro—think a bland modernity with no real
character—it's hard not to love Claude Perraudin's place,

which explains why it's one of the most popular restaurants on the Left Bank. Perraudin, a contemporary of the better-known Guy Savoy, the late Bernard Loiseau, and Jean Ramet, learned his trade with some of France's greatest chefs, including Jean and Pierre Troisgros, Michel Guérard, and Paul Bocuse, but instead of reaching for the stars, he contented himself with firing up a gas rotisserie in this tranquil corner of the Left Bank and serving generous portions of the sort of rustic country comfort food city dwellers crave.

Thirty years later, this place is still packed with a mix of silk-stocking locals and politicos. Both the conservative former president Jacques Chirac and the socialist former prime minister Lionel Jospin are fans, evidence that carnivores' credentials are still essential to the credibility of French politicians and that perfect roast chicken crosses party lines. Sport stars like Zinédine Zidane, smart tourists, and UNESCO staff fill out the crowd, which has become noticeably younger since Perraudin put his son-in-law in charge. Interestingly, the plancha (flat metal grill) is now as busy as the rotisserie, a sign of the popularity of fish in Paris.

The menu is tweaked seasonally, which meant a terrific sauté of first-of-season cèpes (porcini mushrooms) as a starter on an early September night. Girolles mushrooms with Iberian ham were another excellent starter, but go with a first course only if you're really hungry, since portions are huge. The meat—beef, rack of lamb, and one of the best veal chops in town—comes to the table with perfect mashed potatoes, while tuna steak rides in on a mound of nicely seasoned salad greens.

The pot-de-crème au chocolat, velvety chocolate custard, is the favorite dessert, and service is brisk. The wine list is uninteresting, but the house Bordeaux is easy drinking with this food. Reservations are essential. It's hard to think of a better choice for a Sunday night or a relaxed meal during the week when you're suffering from a surfeit of gastronomy and crave just meat and potatoes.

· ·

IN A WORD: Great Gallic comfort food is the draw at this rotisserie-oriented bistro with a stylish clientele that often includes a famous face or two.

DON'T MISS: Escargots; terrine maison; frogs' legs sautéed with garlic and fresh herbs; entrecôte with mashed potatoes; veal chop, assiette du Père Claude (rotisseried beef, lamb, veal, chicken, and blood sausage); clafoutis aux pommes (baked custard with apples); crème brûlée.

. . .

[91] **51 avenue de la Motte-Picquet, 15th, 01.47.34.03.05.** MÉTRO: **La Motte-Picquet.** OPEN **daily for lunch and dinner.** ▪ **$$**

Au Petit Marguery

LOOKING FOR A QUIET PLACE TO STUDY FOR A FRENCH test at Long Lots Junior High School in 1970 on a warm Indian summer day, I slipped outside and headed for the field of tall grass behind the school. Just before I reached my favorite spot, I was startled to see none other than Madame Barrow, my French teacher, sitting on a blanket with a picnic spread out next to her. "Bonjour, Alexandre," she said with a smile. "Bonjour, Madame," I replied. "I was looking for a quiet place to study." "Quelle bonne idée. Would you like some help?" Actually, I didn't—the last thing in the world I wanted was a one-on-one with her, but there was no polite way to escape, so I sat down next to her blanket, glancing at her picnic—something that looked like meat loaf, a long thin piece of bread, some cheese,

and a few peaches. We went over the dialogue I was supposed to have memorized, which began with the phrase "Dis donc, où est la bibliothèque?" ("Hey, where's the library?"), and when we'd finished, I felt a certain adolescent anguish at finding myself in the gray zone of an ill-defined social situation with a teacher. "What a beautiful day," she said. I nodded. "Autumn always makes me think of my hometown." I nodded again. I knew she was French but didn't know where she was from. "I'm from a small town called Épinal in eastern France. It's famous for its printing works." She was a handsome redheaded woman in her late forties, and that day she wore a pleated skirt and a pea green chiffon scarf deftly knotted at the base of her neck. "I met my husband, who's American of course, in Paris after the war. Are you hungry? Please try some of this pâté—it's almost real French pâté, since I made it myself." I looked at her meat loaf with dread, wondering what strange things it might contain— she'd already titillated us in class by talking about the weird things the French ate—tripe and kidneys and duck's livers— but I was too polite to refuse the wedge she cut and presented to me on a small piece of bread. There were strange-looking little green things in it. "Those are green peppercorns," said Madame Barrow, following my eyes. So I ate it, and in the space of two seconds, a bolt of the wildest taste I'd ever had in my mouth sent my head spinning. She must have known what she was doing, since she chuckled. "It's venison pâté, made from the meat of a deer. I got the recipe from the chef at one of my favorite restaurants in Paris, Au Petit Marguery." She was still chuckling as I helped her fold up the blanket on which she'd been sitting, bringing to an end our secret picnic.

I told Mariana, a friend from New York, this story over dinner at Au Petit Marguery the other night. "Tsk, tsk, a lonely war

French bride making off with a bit of your boyhood innocence. I just love it!" At the time, of course, it would never have occurred to me that Madame Barrow was lonely, although she did tell funny stories about her first few years in America. What she'd had in mind was Manhattan, and what she got was a corn farm in the Midwest. Fortunately, fate had intervened when Mr. Barrow's brother inherited the farm and her husband took a job with a big chemical company that eventually sent them east, which is how she'd ended up as a French teacher in Connecticut. All of these years later, I remain grateful to her, however, for making the French language interesting to me, for that bullet of taste that I found so fascinating, and for the address of Au Petit Marguery, which remains one of my favorite restaurants in Paris.

In business for more than eighty years, it is a sweet, comfortably frumpy, and very welcoming place in a quiet corner of the quiet 13th Arrondissement, and I recommend it to people like Mariana, who loves traditional French food and prewar Parisian atmosphere. "I can get all of the trendiness I want in New York.

When I come to Paris, I want real Paris, tulip lamps, white lace curtains, old tile floors, all of this," she said, gesturing at the room as our first courses were served by a gracious waiter in a long black apron. Encased in a thin lemon yellow ribbon of fat, my foie gras de canard was unctuous, earthy, and delicious. Mariana had the lobster and artichoke salad, a dubious choice in my opinion, since this is the sort of dish I'm always suspicious of in restaurants, fearing that the lobster will be either frozen or picked from claws that other patrons were too lazy to crack. But no—this was beautifully cooked Breton lobster riding firm fresh artichoke hearts and gorgeously dressed in walnut oil and a good Xérès vinegar. Sticking with our respective themes— foie gras and lobster—she had a perfectly grilled lobster with herb butter and I went for the piece de boeuf, cooked rare as ordered, in a luscious sauce of cèpes and foie gras. Both were superb, and over the sugar-dusted Grand Marnier soufflé that we shared for dessert, I taunted her with an account of my last meal here, an autumnal feast I had celebrated here in lieu of a Thanksgiving turkey six months earlier.

As Madame Barrow knew, Au Petit Marguery is one of the best places in Paris to go wild, since few places take game more seriously when it comes into season. Gathered with a bunch of American friends, I'd tucked into a terrine de canard sauvage, a dense loaf of coarsely chopped wild duck with a bright punchy woodsy taste, followed by lièvre à la royale, hare in a rich dark velvety sauce made from its own blood and innards. It's one of the great dishes of the French kitchen, and it was superb. "Stop, stop! You're torturing me. The only time of the year I can get to Paris is during the summer," said Mariana, who'd done a rant of her own on the good summer fruit she'd just spent two weeks eating while renting an apartment near Saint-Paul-de-Vence in the south of France.

We could have stayed at the table trading food stories and talking politics until the cows came home, and indeed we were the last customers in the restaurant that night, but still we got a big grin and a warm "Bonsoir, bon retour!" as we stepped out into the warm summer night.

· 🙵 ·

IN A WORD: This gentle old-timer is not only one of the best places in town to eat game in season (October to January, depending on when the hunting season opens) but a great choice for the sort of carefully prepared, high-quality traditional French dishes that inspired Julia Child's career. Warm, professional service makes any meal here an occasion.

DON'T MISS: Fromage de tête (head cheese); grouse puree; hure de sanglier (wild boar head cheese); lobster and artichoke salad; terrine de foie gras; bourride de Saint-Jacques au fenouil;

grilled lobster with herb butter; lièvre à la royale; roast partridge on canapés; wild duck in buttered cabbage; rosette de
biche (venison) à la romaine; veal sweetbreads in port sauce
with spinach.

. . .

[81] 9 boulevard de Port-Royal, 13th, 01.43.31.58.59. MÉTRO: Gobelins.
OPEN Tuesday to Saturday for lunch and dinner. CLOSED Sunday and
Monday. www.petitmarguery.com ▪ $$

Le Severo

THOUGH THERE ARE STILL A COUPLE OF GOOD STEAK
houses at La Villette, once the site of Paris's abattoirs, there's no
need to trek to that remote part of town for some really good
meat when you can head for this charmer with a jaunty red-
painted facade in Montparnasse.

Owner William Bernet once worked at the famous Niver-
naises butcher shop in the 8th Arrondissement, and he really
knows his viande, which is why this place is packed to the rafters
daily with a very stylish Left Bank crowd. As I discovered the
last time I went, it's also the perfect place to ponder the deli-
cious contradictions that compose a perfect Parisienne.

Two tables down from us I spotted Loulou de la Falaise, who
was once Yves Saint Laurent's muse. With her caramel-colored
hair, lapis lazuli blue eyes, and Roman nose, the delicate de la
Falaise is a character out of a Colette novel, which is why it
didn't really surprise me to see her tucking into a thick, juicy
steak with a big side of mashed potatoes. At a time when many
women seem to subsist on bowls of wispy greens, it was almost

erotic to watch her happily wielding her knife on a gorgeous piece of beef and seemingly oblivious to all of the tediously clinical tenets of "healthy" eating.

"I'm hoping there's a message here," said my TV producer friend Alison from Los Angeles. "If she can eat like that and look so good, maybe I can, too?" My favorite meals are those with no limits of any kind, so I was delighted when Alison threw caution to the winds and we shared a big platter of mixed charcuterie to start—andouillette (sausage made from the pig's colon and intestines), rosette (dried pork sausage), and sublime homemade pork rillettes (pork preserved in its own fat). "This place has a great buzz," said Alison as she smeared a slice of baguette with rillette. "And it's pretty, too." Next, I indulged my inner caveman with a superb mound of impeccably seasoned steak tartare topped with chopped shallots and capers and accompanied by a massive heap of hot, crisp, freshly made frites. Getting into the scheme of things, Alison plumped for the boudin noir, a blood pudding sausage. "This is incredible. I haven't eaten like this since I used to visit my grandmother in Pennsylvania," she confessed. "You know, in L.A., it's all about the fear of gaining weight, and then there's the bizarre relationship to food that so many entertainment industry people have. Every other person in my office brings their lunch—sprouts, tofu, and fruit—which is just fine, but all of this fabulous lustiness goes missing. Do you know what I mean?" I do indeed, which is why I unpacked my suitcase twenty-two years ago and never went home. I doubt you'll be surprised to hear that we both ordered chocolate mousse for dessert and that it was superb. "Oh, well, I've been thinking about breaking up with my boyfriend anyway," said Alison as she tucked into the airy wave of cream and dark chocolate.

IN A WORD: This very popular bistro in Montparnasse is carnivore central—it serves some of the very best meat in Paris. It's also a terrific address for wine lovers, since more than two hundred bottles are listed on the chalkboard wine lists that line the walls of the pretty tiled-floor dining room with its glossy wooden tables set with crisp linen napkins.

DON'T MISS: Salade de chèvre (goat cheese on a salad of mixed baby greens); terrine de pot-au-feu; charcuterie plate; côte de boeuf; steak tartare; foie de veau (calf's liver); boned pig's foot; boudin noir (blood sausage); crème caramel; chocolate mousse.

. . .

[**87**] **8 rue des Plantes, 14th, 01.45.40.40.91.** MÉTRO: **Alésia or Mouton-Duvernet.** OPEN **Monday to Friday for lunch and dinner.** CLOSED **Saturday and Sunday. ▪ $$**

FASHION PLATES:
A BRIEF HISTORY OF
STYLISH DINING IN PARIS

· ❦ ·

ARIS WAS THE CITY THAT MADE EATING FASHIONABLE and perfected not only the art of public preening but two of the most popular metropolitan settings for participating in this urban rite, the café and the restaurant. Le Procope, the city's first café, opened in 1685, and the popularity of its convivial atmosphere quickly inspired dozens of similar establishments. Within a century, idling over a coffee or other refreshment and watching the world go by had become a quintessential part of stylish Parisian life.

Paris was also the birthplace of the modern restaurant. In 1765, a soup maker named Boulanger opened a shop near the Louvre where he sold bouillons restaurants, meat-based consommés intended to restaurer, or restore, a person's health. Given the heartening motto over the door of his restaurant, "Come unto me, all ye that labor in the stomach, and I will restore you," it's not surprising that Boulanger's place was a hit.

The first restaurant, in the modern sense of a place where people sit at tables during fixed serving hours and order from a multichoice menu, was La Grande Taverne de Londres, opened by Antoine Beauvilliers in 1782. According to the great French gastronome Jean-Anthelme Brillat-Savarin, the reason it became a roaring success was that it was "the first (restaurant) to combine the four essentials of an elegant room, smart waiters, a choice cellar, and superior cooking." Fed by growing affluence and leisure time, the Paris restaurant scene blossomed during the nineteenth century, with certain tables becoming de rigueur places for fashionable types to see and be seen.

The Café de Paris on the boulevard des Italiens and Restaurant Durand at the corner of the Place de la Madeleine and the Rue Royale pulled a glittering crowd of artists, politicians, and writers, including the novelists Anatole France and Émile Zola, but the most celebrated restaurant of nineteenth-century Paris was the Café Anglais on the boulevard des Italiens. Its crowning moment was the Three Emperors Dinner, served on June 7, 1867, to the Russian tsar Alexander II, his son the tsarevich (later Tsar Alexander III), and King William of Prussia, the first emperor of Germany, when they were in Paris to attend the Universal Exposition of 1867. The Paris press breathlessly reported every aspect of their meal, including the menu the trio dined on—soufflés with creamed chicken, filet of sole, scalloped turbot, chicken à la Portugaise (with tomatoes, onions, and garlic), lobster à la Parisienne (medallions of decorated, gelatin-glazed lobster), duckling á la Rouennaise (boned slices of its breast, its grilled legs, and liver in a red-wine and liver sauce), and ortolans (tiny songbirds known as buntings that are roasted and eaten whole), all washed down with eight different wines. Needless to say, on the heels of this feast the renown of this restaurant spread to every corner of the globe, and it became an essential reservation for not only modish Parisians but elegant foreigners visiting the capital.

When the Ritz Hotel opened in 1898, it set a new standard for both luxurious accommodations and refined dining. Chef Georges-Auguste Escoffier's superb cooking delighted every-

one from the crowned heads of Europe to the writer Marcel
Proust, who dined here almost nightly after his beloved mother
died in 1905. The beau monde's other favorite address during
La Belle Époque (1890–1914) was Maxim's, which almost more
than any other single Paris address codified the modern idea of
the fashion restaurant, or a place that people went to see and be
seen as much as they did to eat and drink.

After World War I, the burgeoning popularity of movies and
the rise of celebrity journalism turned a handful of Parisian
restaurants, including Fouquet's, Lapérouse, and La Coupole, all
of which are still in business today, into household names as the
haunts of the rich and famous. Television further fueled the public interest in restaurants patronized by celebrities, as did the
heady nightlife and fashion scene in Paris during the 1970s, when
fashion designers started to become as famous as the clients they
dressed. By the 1980s when I moved to Paris, the complicit code-
pendency between the international fashion tribe—models, journalists, designers, hairdressers, photographers, and stylists—and
the aristocrats, socialites, and movie stars whose patronage could
make or break them meant that restaurants you went to because
they were fashionable were thriving as never before. Everyone
wanted to be in the same big room, and restaurant owners understood the game, too, since a well-circulated photograph of, say,
the designer Yves Saint Laurent and his muse Loulou de la Falaise
dining at a place brought a cachet that was almost as precious as a
Michelin star. At that time, there were two main types of see-and-
be-seen tables—old-school places like Le Voltaire, an excellent
Left Bank bistro, and funky, individual, off-the-beaten-track
places such as Anahi, an Argentinean steakhouse with excellent
meat in the appropriate setting of an old butcher shop in the
Marais. Aside from the buzz in the room, what all of these places

had in common was that they served good food—this was Paris, after all.

Little did I know at the time that this fundamental truth— that even the most fashion-conscious Parisians wouldn't go anywhere where the food wasn't good—was about to be up-ended by Gilbert and Jean-Louis Costes, a shrewd pair of brothers from the south-central region of the Auvergne, who'd recently opened a very trendy café in Les Halles, the neighbor-hood surrounding the old main food market of Paris.

The first time I went to the Café Costes, I loved it. In the late eighties, it was boldly, bracingly different from the usual drab, smoky French café, and though I'd never heard of Philippe Starck, now one of the world's best-known interior designers, I loved his decor for this place. Apparently inspired by a Bu-dapest train station, it had creamy walls with dark-varnished wooden tub chairs at round caramel-colored tables, a dramatic mezzanine, and polished aluminum furniture on the terrace out front. Oh, and the food? Forgettable sandwiches, salads, and omelettes, but somehow it didn't matter. The Café Costes was cool, and it was always packed.

By the time it closed in 1994, this café had made the reputa-tions of both Starck and the Costes brothers. On its heels, the Costes launched an eponymous hotel in 1996 that completely recoined the idiom of stylish lodgings. Instead of liveried door-men, there were men in black, and the usual tall oak front desk was replaced by a leather-topped desk softly lit by a lamp with a pleated raspberry-colored silk shade. When I checked in to write it up for a travel magazine, I fell instantly for interior de-signer Jacques Garcia's lush, Napoléon-III-cum-New-Orleans-bordello decor, but I had a rude shock when I went downstairs for dinner. A beautiful but snake-eyed hostess told me the

restaurant was *complet*, full. I protested that I was staying in the
hotel, but she just shrugged and walked away. I was dumb-
founded. The restaurant wasn't a famous Michelin-starred
table, and no one had told me a reservation would be necessary
when I checked in, so I assumed I could just show up and be
seated. Wrong.

Eventually I managed to get a table by sidestepping the offi-
cious hostess and appealing to her male colleague, and this only
confirmed my worst suspicions. The social currency of this
place was in-your-face New York–style attitude, period, the
end. My high dudgeon aside, the dining room offered some
first-rate people watching, but my meal—maybe an arugula
salad with Parmesan shavings and perhaps some Thai-style
grilled chicken?—was forgettable. Observing the scene that
night, it dawned on me, however, that something socially seis-
mic was shifting in Paris. Despite the snooty service and dull
food, the room was packed, and from my perch, I watched the
hostess raise the blood pressure of hopeful diner after hopeful
diner. All she seemed to know how to say was "Non, complet,"
but then this was the point. With nightlife out of fashion in Paris
since the beginning of the 1980s, the Costes brothers had co-
opted the New York, and to a lesser degree Parisian, formula of
velvet-rope discotheque disdain and applied it to the restaurant.

As someone who passionately loves the conviviality of good
food and the weird and wonderful randomness of any roomful
of strangers eating together, I found this newly minted and zealously enforced formula depressing. What it said was that appearances matter and food doesn't—what is most important is
making the scene, or just being there.

Unfortunately, my consternation seems to have made me
part of an unfashionable minority, since today the Costes
run several dozen thriving Parisian hotels and restaurants—

Georges, atop the Centre Pompidou; Café Marly at the Louvre; L'Avenue on the swanky Avenue Montaigne; and L'Esplanade across the street from Les Invalides among them, and they've all succeeded by baiting the same social hook with an arbitrary and ersatz exclusivity and hiding it in sleek and sexy settings with great lighting by name-brand interior designers. Their success has inspired a whole subgenre of Costes knockoffs, too. These places have become so common that even though I still love arugula, there are days when I suspect you could roof every building in Paris with the amount of the stuff that the Costes's tables run through in a week. I also wonder if the ubiquity of out-of-focus Asian cooking and upmarket fast food like saumon tartare will be the death knell of real French cooking. Why? The first generation of French who haven't had stay-at-home mothers and grandmothers to tutor them in their country's culinary heritage have come of age in a state of gastronomic oblivion and indifference, and the Costes and other restaurateurs who peddle style over substance have appropriated them as happy and perplexingly loyal customers to the detriment of real restaurants, places where the food still comes first and there are real old-fashioned cooks in the kitchen.

The huge success of the Costes empire, along with the proliferation of other superdecorated restaurant-bars where food plays a minor supporting role to decor and atmosphere, has made the fashion restaurant the most visible and successful category of restaurant in many central Paris neighborhoods, too, most notably in and around the Champs-Élysées in the 8th Arrondissement. But the phenomenon has spread to the city's outlying neighborhoods, too. Now, almost every other corner café that closes for a revamp reemerges with a lounge-bar look featuring velvet-upholstered banquettes and low lighting, a disc jockey compilation soundtrack, and a deracinated international menu running to sliced tomatoes with mozzarella—a pretty sad choice in the middle of winter, when the tomatoes come from Belgian or Dutch greenhouses; hamburgers; a few vaguely Asian dishes; and inevitably something with, you guessed it, arugula.

There's some hope on the horizon, however. Fashion thrives on impermanence and the ruthless repudiation of what was only recently coveted. By embracing this process of creative destruction, and even mocking it, the Hôtel Amour, a laid-back but very hip hotel-restaurant in the 9th, has become tremendously popular. It helps, too, that the Amour is a relaxed and reasonably friendly place, and if the menu served in the lobby cum restaurant is simple, it is also pretty good. Interestingly enough, Thierry Costes, a son of Gilbert Costes, is one of the three main partners in this venture, so maybe the twenty-year disconnect between food and fashion in Paris will be repaired; maybe it'll even become fashionable to insist on eating really good food again.

· ·

L'Astrance

CHEF PASCALE BARBOT AND MAÎTRE D'HÔTEL CHRISTOPHE
Rohat of L'Astrance, the most exciting modern French restaurant in Paris, will forever associate me with bread crumbs. Let me explain.

Some ten years ago, I went to dinner one night with no expectations. A London newspaper had asked me to write about Lapérouse, an old warhorse of a restaurant overlooking the Seine on the Left Bank—it was doing historic Paris restaurants, and this one's been around forever. I politely suggested that there might be better candidates, because as far as I knew, this place was still a slumbering tourist table flogging its past: it has several charming tiny private dining rooms with badly scratched mirrors—as the legend goes, these cuts were made by ladies testing the veracity of newly offered diamonds (real diamonds cut glass). The editor was unyielding, so off I went. The stale-smelling dining room was mostly empty on a winter night, and though the young maître

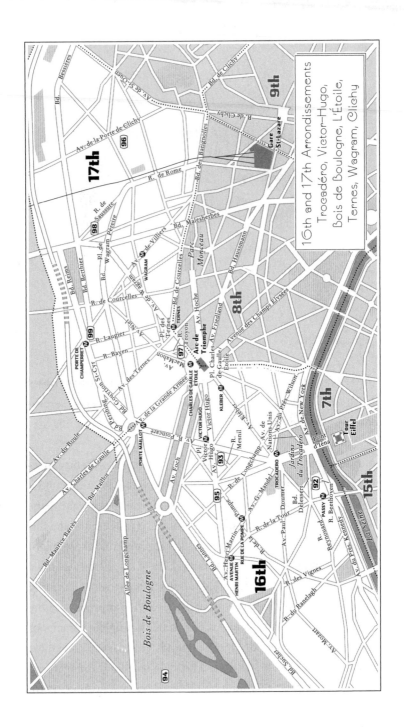

16th and 17th Arrondissements
Trocadéro, Victor-Hugo,
Bois de Boulogne, L'Étoile,
Ternes, Wagram, Clichy

d'hôtel was unexpectedly charming and gracious, I was more interested by my friend Anne's gossipy account of a recent visit to Los Angeles than I was by the menu.

Then we were served an amuse-bouche, or complimentary starter, which the maître d'hôtel described rather unpromisingly as "milk soup." The small shot glass was warm to the touch, and there was something black and brown, fine and grainy floating on the frothy surface of the soup. I tasted it and instantly knew what it was—toast crumbs. The chef had scrapped toast crumbs into his soup, and I was galvanized by this garnish for being so ingenuous, homely, and oddly delicious. When the maître d'hôtel came to clear away our shots, he asked if we'd enjoyed the soup. I said I liked it very much, especially the toast crumbs, and he did a double-take. "Yes," he stumbled—the only time I've ever known him to—"yes, they are toast crumbs," and at the end of the meal, which was superb, the chef, a slight, elfin man with a wry but gentle smile stopped

by our table. We chatted, and he told me that he and his colleague had previously worked at Arpège, chef Alain Passard's
thumpingly expensive place in the rue de Varenne, and had just
moved over here. A few weeks later, however, eager to repeat
the experience and discover more about them, I booked at
Lapérouse again, and my hopes were dashed by exactly the type
of polite, ordinary, expensive meal I'd originally been expecting. They were gone.

A few months later, though, I had a postcard from them (I'd
left my card). Chef Pascal Barbot and maître d'hôtel Christophe
Rohat were opening a little restaurant in the rue de Beethoven in
the 16th Arrondissement. I was there the first week their new
place, L'Astrance—named for a wildflower in Barbot's native
Auvergne—was open and had one of the best meals I've ever
eaten. I also had a much longer conversation with Barbot, who
once cooked for the admiral of the French Pacific Fleet and lived
in Sydney for a while, experiences that had changed him. "While
I was in Australia and the Pacific, I became much more interested
in fruit and vegetables. The classic ingredients of French cooking, especially cream and butter, didn't taste good in these settings, so I started experimenting. Working at Arpège, I was also
exposed to Alain Passard's love of vegetables, and all of these
things had a big impact on me," said Barbot.

Since every meal I've ever eaten here has been better than
the last, I always look forward to L'Astrance, although the dif-
ficulty of snaring one of this small dining room's twenty-six
places and the rising prices have made it an infrequent pleasure.
Still, at the cusp of late spring, which is one of the loveliest times
of the year in Paris, and to celebrate the arrival of some of my
oldest friends in town from San Francisco, I tackled the reservation process the necessary month ahead of time and secured a

table for dinner on a night in late May, peony time, when Paris is floral and flirtatious.

We arrived at this discreet duplex dining room with silvered walls and apricot banquettes and embarked on a wonderful voyage. Christophe Rohat, who has a voice like dark gray velvet, an instrument that perfectly matches his dignified and elegant serving style, suggested a tasting menu with individual wines for each course, and its first note was an amuse-bouche that was spring in a shot glass—warm goat's milk, lemon, fresh peas, and scissored herbs, a vivid, refreshing concoction that foreshadowed the pleasures to come.

Barbot's contemporary haute cuisine is a whimsically customized experience. He changes his menu daily, and it varies from table to table according to what Rohat and the kitchen decide you should try. Next up for us was a miniature brioche painted with rosemary butter and accompanied by a tiny ramekin of Parmesan cream, a stunning but potent miniature that brilliantly demonstrates the difference between France's culinary avant-garde and that of Spain. France, thank goodness, is not Spain, where dry ice and exploding bonbons have become the norm. No, even at the most creative outer limits of a new, widely traveled generation of chefs, French cooking remains guided by a rigor and refinement that profoundly respects the palate, and instead of chemistry-set antics, Pascal Barbot astonishes with his winsome love of flowers, berries, herbs, and seeds.

A plump oyster sitting on a slice of roasted beet on a bed of shredded oxtail in a pool of Camembert foam offered a tiny universe of taste so harmonious and sensual I thought of *The Ripening Seed*, Colette's novel of quickening adolescent sexuality set on the beaches of Brittany. All of these flavors were naive but together they formed a composition that was racing with desire. Another dish, tuna belly cooked sous-vide (individually vacuum-packed in plastic at a very low temperature) and served with fresh peas, nasturtium flowers, and blazes of a sauce made with ground dark orange Espelette pepper and Chorizo sausage drippings—Barbot sweats the sausage to recover its rich, paprika-flavored fat—was vivid and smoldering like a flamenco dance, while turbot cooked with an oxalis (red clover) condiment and garnished with crunchy green cabbage and a lemon-ginger sauce had an almost geisha-like allure.

As these cameos of color, taste, and texture succeeded one another, my San Franciscan friends were astonished. "What I find most amazing about this food is that even when it's knowingly sensuous, it remains innocent and sincere," one of them said, and as if to prove the point, we were served quenelles of fromage blanc drizzled with pomegranate syrup, a product Barbot discovered in Beirut, in small pools of perfect crème anglaise, a dessert that was the equivalent of watching a belly dancer from the window of a room in a convent.

Luxuriating in the glow of a brilliant meal, we were eating fresh fruit—Barbot doesn't like the traditional onslaught of mignardaises, or sweets and pastries, that follow most of the highest-altitude French meals because he finds them superfluous and unhealthy—when he stopped by. He said he'd recently been inspired by travels to India and was experimenting with techniques, foods, and spices he'd found there, and when I questioned him about his move toward a small-plate format, or meals composed of many small tasting portions, he became momentarily pensive. "I can't express myself on a big plate," he said. "I look for the extreme in terms of flavors. My favorite elements to compose with are l'iodée [the brininess of the sea and all of its minerals], le lacté [the sour edge of dairy products], la terre [the earth, or produce that conveys the primal taste of the soil], and la chair [flesh, in the meatiest sense of the word]. This is my little universe." I can't imagine better contemporary culinary compass points either, which is why every meal here leaves me longing for the next one.

·　·

IN A WORD: Chef Pascal Barbot is the most consistently creative young chef in Paris, with an extraordinary culinary imagination and a mastery of technique that has made him one of the great chefs of his generation. Using almost no added fat in his cooking and starring vegetables and fruit on his menus, he proves that healthy eating can be pleasurable and, by doing so, is one of the most influential French chefs in terms of creating a cuisine for the twenty-first century. Stunningly good service by maître d'hôtel Christophe Rohat succeeds by freeing some of France's best cooking from a pompous nineteenth-century straitjacket. Reservations at least a month in advance are imperative.

DON'T MISS: Barbot changes his menu so regularly that you're unlikely to come upon any of the dishes that I've enjoyed here, but dishes that explain his style include his signature avocado ravioli stuffed with crabmeat and glossed with almond oil; mushroom and foie gras galette; turbot with oxalis (a cloverlike herb) condiment; green cabbage and lemon ginger sauce; tuna belly with chorizo drippings; sautéed pigeon with baby potatoes; fromage blanc quenelles with pomegranate syrup and crème anglaise; chocolate biscuit with milk sorbet.

. . .

[92] **4 rue Beethoven, 16th, 01.40.50.84.40.** MÉTRO: **Passy.** OPEN **Tuesday to Friday for lunch and dinner.** CLOSED **Saturday, Sunday, and Monday.** ▪ **$$$$**

La Bigarrade

COOKING AS PERFORMANCE ART MAY BE WELL ESTABLISHED
in Paris by now—the open kitchens of L'Atelier de Joël Robuchon and more recently Yam'Tcha are good examples of the
local trend toward cooking for an audience—but no one puts on
a more intense or intriguing show than the one pulled off twice
daily from Tuesday to Friday by Christophe Pelé at La Bigarrade, his tiny place in the tranquil Batignolles neighborhood of
the 17th Arrondissement.

Since Pelé went out on his own (he was previously at the Parc Monceau), he and his sous-chef have begun their remarkable performance anew each day, side by side behind a short stainless steel counter up a step from the small gray, white, and lime green shop-front dining room with just twenty covers. Though many well-run kitchens have a certain balletic quality, the way Pelé and his second work together evokes the private concentration of watchmakers and the speed and grace of a pair of figure skaters.

As long as you're willing to accept Pelé's carte blanche approach to running a restaurant—there's no menu at La Bigarrade but rather two set no-choice menus that change almost daily, the eight-course Gourmet (45 Euros) and the Gourmand (65 Euros), with an additional meat course, the results of their gastronomic marathon are superb, often even dazzling.

Though I'm frequently exasperated by the coyness of blind tastings and unannounced menus—at La Bigarrade, you'll have to bully the waiter to find out what you'll be eating, which is necessary if you prefer to drink a single well-chosen wine— every meal I've had at La Bigarrade has been a suite of astonishingly original tasting dishes that are Fabergé in their intricacy, taste, and beauty but without being precious. I also admire a chef who so reliably rises to the self-imposed challenge of devising a new menu daily according to what he finds in the market. The constant style of Pelé's cooking might best be described as Franco Zen, with an emphasis on texture and brilliantly elaborated spectrums of taste.

The opening tease of a recent dinner was a typical example of the chef's gastronomic precision and creativity—a fat Gillardeau oyster, sliced and garnished with sorrel purée, cubed fennel bulb, and herring caviar, all of which declined the natural taste of the oyster. Next, a perfectly grilled rouget in red-pepper juice with leeks and poutargue (pressed tuna roe), and then a meaty cepe mushroom topped with a fine slice of lardo di Colonnata (Italian fatback) and lemony ficoide glaciale (ice lettuce), another brilliant little dish. Main courses were disarming in their potent, almost monastic purity: steamed cod came with caillé de brebis (fresh ewe's milk cheese) and a purée of preserved lemon and asparagus, while a filet of rare-cooked Spanish free-range pork was brightened by a slaw of carrot, daikon, and réglisse root. Mocha cardamom cream with nougat marcapone and a crispy wand of pain d'épices (spice bread) and a last little fruit salad of fennel bulb, carrots, and pears in passion fruit soup showed that Pelé's a terrific dessert chef as well.

The only fly in the soup? Stuffy waiters. The service they mete out is irreproachable, however, and nothing can dent the wonderful ambience created by an intimate quorum delightedly discovering Christophe Pelé's cooking.

· ·

IN A WORD: Chef Christophe Pelé creates a different tasting menu daily at this simple storefront restaurant in the Batignolles neighborhood of the 17th Arrondissement. An impeccable culinary craftsman in the best French tradition, he finds inspiration in the cooking of India, Japan, Thailand, Morocco, and the Mediterranean countries.

DON'T MISS: Pelé's menus rarely repeat themselves, so every meal here offers a fresh discovery of his brilliant cosmopolitan cooking.

. . .

[96] **La Bigarrade, 106 rue Nollet, 17th 01.42.26.01.02.** MÉTRO: **Brochant.** OPEN **Monday for dinner, Tuesday to Friday for lunch and dinner.** CLOSED **Saturday and Sunday • $$$**

L'Entredgeu

TUCKED AWAY IN AN OUTLYING CORNER OF THE 17TH AR-
rondissement, this charming little bistro would be a perfect set
for a scene from a 1950s Simenon detective novel because it is,
as the French would say, still very much *dans son jus,* or in its
juice, which means an old object or place that hasn't been restored. During my last lunch here I kept expecting the late
French actress Simone Signoret to come through the door, since

this is exactly the kind of place I always pictured her in—a happy, busy bistro with lace curtains, a checkerboard floor, wooden sconces, a jaunty decor of yellow walls and plum-painted woodwork, an old sign indicating the Lavabo and a bar just inside the front door where a waiter joked with the regulars while drying glasses.

If the mise en scène is deliciously vieux Paris, chef Philippe Tredgeu's edgy cooking offers a delicious, fresh, modern riff on traditional French regional dishes and bistro favorites. Tredgeu previously cooked at chef Thierry Breton's Chez Michel and Chez Casimir, and this background shows up in his outstanding fish cooking. The chalkboard menu changes regularly, but consistently offers a variety of wonderfully earthy choices, like my starter of charred piquillo peppers stuffed with a tender, flavorful beef ragout. Lovely blond Maryse, whom I've known for many years, ordered the daily special of langoustine tails in a bright herbal bouillon and then gorgeously grilled slices of rolled lamb roast served on a bed of mixed spring vegetables including tiny peas, swiss chard, and broad beans. My John Dory filets were superb. Known as Saint-Pierre in French, this firm white fish is one of my favorites, and it had been perfectly cooked and was served with a delicious compote of chopped tomato, sliced fennel bulb, and fava beans.

Neither of us had been here for a while for the same reason. This place has become so popular, it's always crowded, especially in the evening, when it does two services (book the second one for a more relaxed meal). On this balmy afternoon we had plenty of room for a change, and the service was swift and disarmingly sincere, the atmosphere warm and relaxed.

Just as our desserts were served—an excellent baba au rhum (sponge cake soaked in rum-spiked syrup) intriguingly served with prunes and fantastic stout ice cream for me, and compote de fraise et rhubarb for Maryse—the two nice insurance execs (they were both wearing little AXA lapel pins) at the table next to us asked if we wanted to help them finish a celebratory bottle of Monbazillac, a lovely dessert wine from the Dordogne. I'd never refuse such a friendly offer, and during the conversation that followed, we quickly discovered a thick cross-hatching of common interests and tastes—both Maryse and Jean-Marc were originally from Normandy, while Armand had just discovered one of my favorite places for lunch in New York during a business trip there—Mary's Fish Camp—but the main thing we agreed on was that L'Entredgeu is, in Armand's words, "vachement bon!" or damned good.

IN A WORD: Despite its remote location in the 17th Arrondissement, chef Philippe Tredgeu's charming bistro with a decor worthy of a Doisneau photograph is one of the hottest word-of-mouth addresses in Paris. You'll understand why after you've tasted his superb contemporary bistro cooking. Note, too, that this place is one of the city's best buys.

DON'T MISS: The chalkboard menu is revised daily, but dishes I've loved here include piquillo peppers stuffed with beef ragout; langoustine tails in herb bouillon; oyster tempura with a sauce gribiche; fish soup; stuffed squid in a vinaigrette made with their own ink; roast cod; roast lamb with spring vegetables; carmelized pork belly; lièvre à la royale (wild hare in a sauce of its blood and gizzards) with macaroni gratin; colvert (wild duck) with roasted fruit; baba au rhum with prunes and stout ice cream; brioche perdue with carmelized apples; strawberry and rhubarb compote.

. . .

[99] 83 rue Laugier, 17th, 01.40.54.97.24. MÉTRO: **Porte de Champerret.** OPEN **Tuesday to Saturday for lunch and dinner.** CLOSED **Sunday and Monday.** ▪ **$**

Guy Savoy

CHEF GUY SAVOY'S PARIS RESTAURANT OFFERS AN EXPERIence of gastronomic luxury that's as solidly engineered as a Mercedes and as consensually tasteful as a string of good pearls. This is why it's filled noon and night with a well-dressed and necessarily well-heeled—this place is bloodcurdlingly expensive—international crowd who keep their perplexed reactions to the designer Jean-Michel Wilmotte's somber, masculine dining rooms to themselves and instead concentrate rather self-consciously on enjoying some of the best-drilled service in the

world. Of course the food's very nice, too, but this isn't a place you come if you're craving culinary adventure. Instead, you choose this restaurant when you want a safe, stylish, and unfailingly gracious experience of modern French cuisine, a formula that slyly appeals to people for whom a meal here is usually just one special occasion in lives that are filled with them.

So does it cut the mustard for anyone like me whose nerves are rattled by spending almost $1,000 on dinner for two (mine consisted of two flutes of Champagne, a medium-priced bottle of Condrieu, and two glasses of sublime Jurançon dessert wine in addition to two starters, two main courses, and a shared dessert)? I'm not ducking, but it depends on what you're looking for. The last time I dined at Savoy, the two of us had a delightful time and a very good meal, but as impeccable as the food may have been, what really impressed me was the service. Our dining room was populated by a handsome older American couple celebrating the gent's birthday over a dinner punctuated by several robin's egg blue Tiffany boxes, a very chic young Japanese couple, two Russian businessmen, and three assiduously elegant Argentinean women whose meringue-colored hair was elaborately coiffed in styles that reminded me of Goya's eighteenth-century portraits of the Spanish nobility, and I was awed by the way the wait staff made subtle calibrations to enhance the pleasure of each of these very different planets. The Japanese, both of whom had heroically embarked on the tasting menu, were served with deference and distance, the Russians with a homeopathic dose of complicit jocularity, the Americans with perfect English and a little flattery, and the Argentines with Gallic gallantry. Oh, and my trophy was being treated as the equal of the very knowledgeable Frenchman with whom I was dining, which I'll humbly admit is a prize indeed for any long-term American resident of Paris, since the limbo bar of Gallic knowingness has a clearance of about a half inch.

The wilder shores of gastronomic creativity to one side, this place falls all over itself to make sure you have a good time, with a steady rain of constant attentions and surprises that make an evening special. Some of them are superfluous—I don't need anyone to pose a napkin in my lap—but most are welcome, including the arrival of a miniature kebab of foie gras and toast to nibble over Champagne and a bread trolley that supplies you with a different bread for every course (curiously, the bread isn't baked on the premises but is bought in from Eric Kayser, one of Paris's best bakers, with headquarters in the 5th Arrondissement).

As is so often the case in haute cuisine restaurants, the starters were much more appealing than the main courses, so just as we were dithering over our choices, the maître d'hôtel arrived and suggested they'd happily serve tasting portions of several appetizers if we couldn't make up our minds. So I had the tuna and asparagus crus-cuits (raw and cooked) and a half portion of Savoy's signature artichoke and truffle soup. I found both the seared slices of raw tuna with shavings of raw asparagus and a node of tuna tartare and the soup underseasoned, but their presentation was lovely. Bruno's oysters with seawater gelée (aspic made from sea water), another Savoy specialty and a more interesting choice than either of mine, and his ladies-who-lunch classic of fresh baby peas with pea mousse and an egg coddled at a very low temperature so that the yolk was glossy alabaster, were similarly polite and pleasant.

Main courses reprised the themes of careful cooking and quality, tripped up by an overzealous culinary politeness. It's almost as though Savoy's modus operandi is to avoid offending any possible gastronomic sensibility, which means he low-balls his recipes, with often timid results. There was nothing I could reproach about my chop of turbot, which flaked easily but was still firm and had a vague nuance of white truffle, which rose from an artful but unfortunate dribble of white-truffle-flavored olive oil in the bouillon beneath a perforated plate posed on a shallow soup dish. Most of the egg yolk of an-other cooked-at-low-temperature egg dribbled into the bouil-lon as well, which meant that I was eating a correctly cooked but rather monastic piece of plain fish. Bruno's slices of meaty sole were cooked à la meunière (rolled in flour and sautéed in butter flavored with seaweed), and pleasant as this dish may have been, it would never have driven anyone into the ecstasy one hopes to experience at the summit of the French food chain.

We passed on the rather modest cheese trolley and instead split a "passion de légumes," carrot juice with finely chopped cit-rus peel, with a long-nosed carrot chip sticking out of a ball of root vegetable ice cream, a very adult dessert making a feint at the modern preoccupation with healthy eating. It was nice enough, especially when followed by the buckshot of luxury mignardises, or various sweet nibbles—marshmallow chunks (when and why did the French ever decide that marshallow was a desirable sweet for anyone over fifteen?), chocolates, caramels, and a delicious miniature strawberry-filled crêpe, but more of a child's sweet good-night peck on the cheek than the suggested lover's kiss. Overall, this meal was a charming but studiously po-lite performance without a single taste that would startle, tease, or puzzle, which is why I'd heartily recommend Guy Savoy to anyone who wants a perfect business meal or who is at the very beginning of their haute cuisine learning curve.

· ☙ ·

IN A WORD: Guy Savoy offers a well-mannered experience of luxurious contemporary French haute cuisine in a sleek modern dining room by the architect Jean-Michel Wilmotte. Soigné service delights the monied international crowd who've made this restaurant so enduringly popular.

DON'T MISS: Artichoke and black truffle soup; huîtres en nage glacée (oysters on a bed of cream in a gelée of their own juices); roasted duck foie gras with red cabbage nage; sea bass with spices; poached guinea hen and vegetables in a vinaigrette made with its liver; vanilla millefeuille.

· · ·

[**97**] **18 rue Troyon, 17th, 01.43.80.40.61.** MÉTRO: **Charles-de-Gaulle-Étoile.** OPEN **Tuesday to Friday for lunch and dinner. Saturday dinner only.** CLOSED **Sunday and Monday. www.guysavoy.com ▪ $$$$**

Hier et Aujourd'hui

BEFORE RAVING ABOUT HOW GOOD THE FOOD IS AT THIS storefront bistro—and it is—you should know that it has a rather challenging location near the Porte d'Asnières, which is not a part of Paris you've likely to have ever visited before. It's not dangerous, just remote, which is why my English friends Sue and Gary, who live in the rue de Varenne, were half an hour late for dinner before I saw their beautiful golden Labrador nose his way through the curtains at the door. By the time coffee was served, however, we all heartily agreed that this place is more than worth the schlep.

These days Parisians are used to traveling to unlikely parts of the city for good food, since few young chefs going out on their own can afford to set up shop in neighborhoods like Saint-Germain, and the curious advantage of these little journeys is that you not only end up eating really well for very reasonable prices but see another side of the city.

Hier et Aujourd'hui is a handsome place with ash gray walls, a beautiful old zinc bar, mahogany-stained tables set with Basque-style striped linens, and a winsome decor of fifties vintage bric-a-brac including a red-and-white clock advertising Quinquina and posters for Bhyrr, two bitter apéritifs that have fallen out of favor. This charming hybrid of Saint-Germain chic and vintage kitsch creates the kind of relaxed atmosphere you'd find in a small French town, and the service by Karin Ouet, the chef's wife, is warm, prompt, and cheerful.

I knew that Sue and Gary were wondering what we were doing here, so I explained that chef Franck Dervin is a promising young Turk who formerly worked with Alain Dutournier at the Bistrot de Niel and Bistrot de l'Étoile, two of Guy Savoy's baby bistros. I'd heard about this place from two different French food writers, both very discerning and demanding eaters, so I'd had it on my list for a while.

Things got off to an excellent start when a ceramic loaf pan of serve-yourself terrine de campagne was brought to the table with a big jar of cornichons and tiny onions, and wooden pincers to fish them out with. Obviously homemade, the terrine was dense and luscious with just a hint of garlic, and we came very close to embarrassing ourselves before it was removed and our first courses were served.

All of them were delicious. My foie-gras-stuffed ravioli with artichokes in a light cream sauce were tender and full of flavor, Sue loved her carpaccio of cod with artichoke puree and Parmesan shavings, and Gary immediately announced that he was going to copy his salad of baby spinach leaves with fine slices of viande des grisons (air-dried beef) in a creamy vinaigrette.

"This place is a real find," said Sue after tasting her parmentier d'agneau, a homey French take on shepherd's pie, with tender ground lamb and eggplant in a rich thyme-scented gravy under a crust of homemade mashed potatoes and bread crumbs. My daube de boeuf, tender chunks of braised beef in a winey sauce with carrots and ribbons of fresh asparagus, was exactly the sort of sincere, caring, homey cooking I constantly crave and which makes eating in Paris such a relentless pleasure. Gary's cod roasted with tomatoes and served with pommes boulangère (sliced potatoes baked with onions) was excellent, too. "If we ever move away from France, I know I'll miss food like this for the rest of my life," he said.

Dervin is as good with desserts as he is with main courses, including a chocolate mousse that sent Sue into ecstasies and a perfect vanilla millefeuille. When we enthusiastically complimented Karin Ouet on our meal, she grinned bashfully and said, "Mais, c'est normal. Nous sommes ici pour faire plaisir" ("But that's normal. We're here to give people pleasure"), which made me think of a favorite quote by Oliver Herford, the humorist, writer, and illustrator who has been called "America's Oscar Wilde," "Modesty: the gentle art of enhancing your charm by pretending to be unaware of it."

· ⟨image⟩ ·

IN A WORD: Getting here is an expedition, but this attractive bistro with friendly service and excellent food is well worth it, especially since the daily menu written on a chalkboard is one of the best buys in Paris.

DON'T MISS: Chef Franck Dervin changes his menu regularly, but dishes to look for include asparagus salad with mozzarella and tomatoes in pistou sauce; baby spinach salad with viande des grisons (air-dried beef); cod carpaccio with artichoke puree; foie gras ravioli with artichokes in cream sauce; hachis parmentier d'agneau (French shepherd's pie); daube de boeuf (beef braised in wine with carrots); roast cod with pommes boulangère (potatoes baked with onions); grilled salmon with lentille in a vanilla jus; vanilla millefeuille; chocolate mousse; mango soup; baba au rhum; Paris-Brest.

. . .

[**98**] **145 rue Saussure, 17th,** 01.42.72.35.55. MÉTRO: **Villiers.** OPEN Monday to Friday for lunch and dinner. CLOSED **Saturday and Sunday.** www.resto.hieraujoudhui.free.fr ▪ **$**

Le Petit Rétro

IT'S A PARISIAN PARADOX. THE WESTERN HALF OF THE CITY,
including the sprawling 16th Arrondissement, may be much
wealthier, but the center of gastronomic gravity has been steadily
shifting eastward for a decade. Lower rents in the 10th, 11th, and
12th Arrondissements are the main reason, since they make it possible for young chefs to spread their wings, but almost as important is the fact that the gentrification of these old working-class
neighborhoods has created a perfect audience, filling them with
people who seriously love unpretentious old buildings and good
food and who are eager for adventure when they go out.

In contrast, the Hermès-bedraped bourgeoisie is less avid gas-
tronomically, preferring vieille France menus like the chalkboard
lineup found at this long-running and very pretty bistro just off

the swanky place Victor Hugo. It's a lovely respite from modernity, though, since the landmarked Art Nouveau interior fancifully evokes the Belle Époque with glazed vanilla-colored tiles painted with a motif of poppies, and the kitchen ticks away like a good watch, sending out such impeccable bistro monuments as home-made duck foie gras studded with figs and creamy pumpkin soup. The entrecôte de Simmenthal (a steak of German Simmenthal beef) is tender but chewy and full of flavor, napped with a sauce of cream and pan juices, and coquettishly accompanied by a brown-edged fan of roasted potatoes. Similarly, the blanquette de veau (veal in lemony cream sauce) would warm the cockles of Charles de Gaulle's heart, and veal kidneys are perfectly rare and glossed with a nice sauce of grainy mustard. Though the older gentleman with a matching paisley tie and pocket square at the table next to me exclaimed "Quel horreur!" ("What a horror!") when he realized what made the steak tartare a l'andalouse, andalouse—some chopped chorizo had been mixed in with the beef—this mildly exotic riff on a much-loved French classic is actually very good. Crème brûlée and very good profiteroles are a fine way to end a meal here, an experience that's as interesting for revealing the bedrock of Gallic gastronomic chauvinism as it is for offering a textbook of traditional bistro dishes.

· ·

IN A WORD: The beautiful Art Nouveau tiled interior of this 1900-vintage bistro in a smart corner of the swanky 16th is a lovely setting for solidly good bistro dining.

DON'T MISS: Casserole of escargots and pleurottes (oyster mushrooms) en croûte; salmon-stuffed ravioli; oxtail terrine; blanquette de veau; veal kidneys in mustard sauce; entrecôte de Simmenthal;

côte du boeuf (rib steak); rack of lamb; apple tart with salted caramel ice cream; chocolate profiteroles; crème brulée.

. . .

[93] 5 rue Mesnil, 16th, 01.44.05.06.05. MÉTRO: Victor Hugo. OPEN Monday to Friday for lunch and dinner. Saturday dinner only. CLOSED Sunday. www.petitretro.fr • $$

Le Pré Catelan

TUCKED AWAY DEEP IN THE BOIS DE BOULOGNE, THE VAST park on the western edge of Paris that's one of the city's two green lungs (the other is the Bois de Vincennes on the southeastern edge), Le Pré Catalan is one of the most romantic restaurants in the world. Since the arrival of chef Frédéric Anton more than ten years ago, it has also become one of the city's best restaurants, since Anton is a boldly inventive cook who delights in creating dishes that are miniature studies in culinary theater—his cooking is carefully staged and decorated and has a lot of drama.

Though there's never a time of the year when I don't look forward to a meal in this sumptuous Belle Époque pavilion, it is especially wonderful during the summer, when it's a pleasure to escape the heat-stunned city. I've been here on many different occasions through the years, but for rather surprising reasons, my last meal was particularly memorable. Let me explain.

The approach of August, the de rigueur vacation month that's always been the anchor of family life, is a potentially perilous season in Paris. As soon as I heard Anna's voice on the phone, I knew what had happened. She and Gerard had been involved for two years but had been seeing less and less of each

other since Gérard got a new job that meant he went to New York regularly, and now, just before he'd left for Bali with his family for three weeks, plans he hadn't mentioned before, he'd told her that she deserved much more and he thought it would be better if they stopped seeing each other.

It was a hot, pretty summer day, and aching for Anna, a charming banker from Auckland who'd made the classic mistake of getting involved with a married man, I had an idea. "What are you doing for lunch today?" "I don't much feel like eating right now." "I understand, but a change of scene might do you some good."

I called a friend who's a concierge at one of the best hotels in Paris, asked if he could do me a favor, and two hours later we were sitting in the dappled shade of the chestnut trees at a table dressed in pretty pink linen next to a planter of scarlet geraniums. You might think this romantic bower was a curious place to bring someone with a broken heart, but wait.

Anna had never been here before, and as is true of anyone who comes for the first time, she was impressed and excited. "Isn't this lovely! I feel like we're a thousand miles from Paris," she said as we studied the menu while sipping flutes of chilled Champagne. Around us, besotted couples outnumbered business diners on this gorgeous afternoon when much of corporate Paris had already decamped to idle on Breton beaches or doze in the shade of Provence's olive trees to a scrim of cicadas after lunch. Across the way, however, a man with salt-and-pepper hair was dining with a pretty young woman in a fluttery polka-dot navy blue chiffon dress. Anna instantly seized on this tableau, which included a single wedding ring. "I feel like going over there and telling her to come to her senses before it's too late," she said, while I was mum. In a country with an institutionalized tolerance of adultery, it is easy for a culturally disoriented young foreigner to get caught up in these webs.

Our first courses came, and my grilled scallops in a lime-zest-spiked foam were light, succulent, and sexy. Anna loved her stuffed crab in an elegant gelée of its own coral. And she didn't mention Gérard again during our meal, although her eyes darted often to the table across the way. I had the sole in caramelized mango sauce with giant capers, and Anna, ready to buck herself up, devoured a brilliant composition of lamb that included grilled cutlets, a lamb sausage, a kidney, and a slice of filet in an intriguing licorice-flavored sauce with a side garnish of a large goat-cheese-filled raviolo. "This sauce is really interesting—I'd never have made the association between lamb and licorice, but it really flatters the meat," said Anna.

I couldn't wait for our desserts to come either, since Le Pré Catalan has one of the best pastry chefs in Paris. Young Christelle Brua didn't disappoint. Both of our desserts looked as though they'd been made in Fabergé's workshops. Decorated with quivering bits of gold leaf, my transparent green sugar sphere was filled with baked apple, crumbled shortbread, and whipped cream, while Anna's wild strawberries came under a meringue veil decorated with silver-colored candied almonds. "These are so pretty I could weep," said Anna. "But I've done enough of that for the time being." Over coffee, I gingerly raised the subject of summer vacations. "A friend of mine from London has invited me to a beach house he's rented in Puglia, but I'd been putting off making a decision until I knew what Gérard was doing," she sighed. "But maybe a long weekend down there would be nice. I don't know that part of Italy, but they say it's lovely." She sipped her coffee and glanced at the couple across the way. "I wonder if it looked that obvious when we were together. I hope not." I watched as a welcome breeze slightly ruffled the geraniums. "What a wonderful meal this has been," Anna said. "And I'm so glad I didn't come to such a special place as anyone's mistress."

· 🙊 ·

IN A WORD: Chef Frédéric Anton has made this famous sylvan getaway one of the best restaurants in Paris. Service in the elegant Belle Époque pavilion is courtly and soigné, and it also has one of the most impressive wine lists in Paris. Unfortunately, they no longer serve outside during the summer, a shame since they had one of the prettiest terraces in town, but this lavishly decorated dining room with refreshing views over the surrounding greenery is still one of the most romantic addresses in the city. This is just the place for some enchanted evening, although tables are usually easier to snag for lunch. Advance reservations are imperative.

DON'T MISS: Stuffed crab with a gelée of its own coral; grilled scallops in lime foam; l'os à moelle (beef bone marrow) in two preparations, grilled in the bone with black pepper and stuffed with baby peas and morel mushrooms; spit-roasted pigeon with a poivrade sauce and macaroni gratin with petits pois; lamb in réglisse (licorice) sauce with a goat-cheese-stuffed raviolo; sole with caramelized mango sauce; ris de veau (sweetbreads) with morel mushrooms and a Parmesan-glazed soubise (sauce of onions and cream); turbot in an almond crust with capers and baby onions in bitter almond jus; millefeuille; macaroon with bergamot ice cream and carmelized hazelnuts.

. . .

[94] Bois de Boulogne, 16th, 01.44.14.41.00. MÉTRO: Porte Maillot and then a taxi, since the restaurant is located deep inside the Bois de Boulogne, Paris's largest park. OPEN Tuesday to Saturday for lunch and dinner. CLOSED Sunday and Monday. www.lenotre.fr ▪ $$$$.

Le Stella

DEEP IN THE SILK-STOCKING PRECINCTS OF THE 16TH ARrondissement, Le Stella is a textbook example of a good brasserie. This is not a part of town where people cook much, so Le Stella babies its bourgeois clientele by shrewdly offering its

kitchen-averse regulars a different special dish every night of the week, including delicious hachis parmentier (the French version of shepherd's pie, but better) on Monday and a fine choucroute garnie (sauerkraut with pork and sausages) on Wednesday. Should you arrive by car, a parking jockey spirits away your car, and inside, in the wood-paneled dining rooms, the atmosphere is what the French call bon enfant, or polite and pleasant. The small glassed-in terrace contains the most sought-after tables, which are implicitly reserved for recognizable faces—regulars or politicians, businesspeople or the occasional showbiz personality—but the main dining room also offers some fascinating people watching.

Think *The Discreet Charm of the Bourgeoisie*. Or wealthy middle-aged couples composed of Madame with a helmet of expensively coiffed and colored hair and Monsieur in a blazer, fiddling with his BlackBerry as a way of forestalling some incipient bickering. With the exception of a few befuddled Japanese tourists, tables of bespectacled businessmen having conversations about "implementing" things, and dutiful adult grandchildren accompanying Grand-mère to a feed that will at the very least allow her to air out her fur coat, the fact is that a faint air of infidelity hangs over this dining room. While we gorged on meaty Gillardeau oysters and the better-than-average house-smoked salmon as first courses, the surgically impeccable brunette in a fringed tweed jacket next to us informed her husband that she was certain he hadn't been alone at their country house the weekend before (she'd been visiting her mother in Marseille). Gulp. Talk about a study in guilt, with a vague reference to "a friend" who'd stopped by and the furrowed brow that wondered, how did she find out? Fortunately, a big plateau of shellfish—oysters, clams, langoustines, sea snails, and shrimp—arrived in time to keep things on an even keel, momentarily at least, while we supped on a perfectly grilled sole and an excellent steak, accompanied by homemade frites and some rather pallid sauce béarnaise, the only off note in a very satisfying meal.

No one has dessert here, because everyone's counting calories, but it was fun to watch a beautiful young woman in a shaggy shearling coat tucking into a pyramid of ice-cream-stuffed profiteroles slathered with hot chocolate sauce, which are far and away the best choice here, while her companion, an older man, twirled his sour-smelling cigar and looked on with a hunger of his own. Since the restaurant doesn't take reservations, you may have to wait, but this democratic seating system leads to brisk service and means you can almost always get a table here. A perfect Parisian tableau, and a good meal to boot.

"I found a red sock," the aggrieved madame finally blurted out as we were putting on our coats. "And I don't wear socks." Maybe, but she sure knew how to put away the oysters.

IN A WORD: A well-mannered traditional French brasserie with better-than-average food and a diverting crowd.

DON'T MISS: Haricots verts with Parmesan shavings; smoked salmon; grilled sole; tarte fine aux tomates fraîches; tuna steak with pistou sauce; grilled cod with olive oil; beef brochette sauce diable; tête de veau; vacherin glacé sauce caramel.

. . .

[95] 133 avenue Victor-Hugo, 16th, 01.56.90.56.00. MÉTRO: Victor-Hugo. OPEN daily for lunch and dinner. ▪ $$

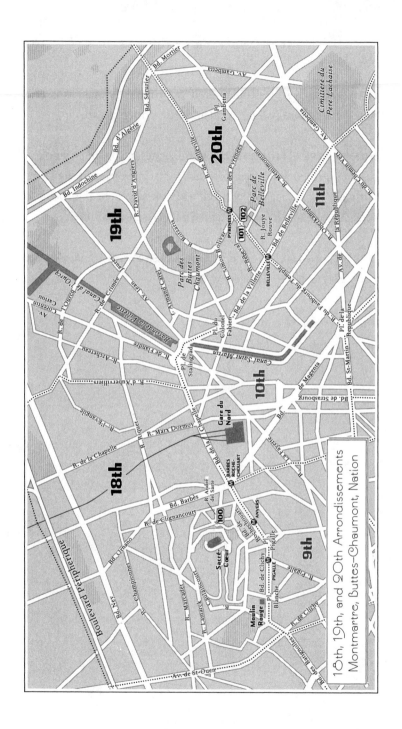

18th, 19th, and 20th Arrondissements
Montmartre, Buttes-Chaumont, Nation

Le Baratin

A CENTURY AGO, L'AMI LOUIS, THE EGREGIOUSLY OVER-priced Marais bistro that pulls an international crowd of high rollers more interested in a brand-name luxury experience than

good food, might have been something like this hole-in-the-wall in Belleville, the old working-class neighborhood in northeastern Paris where the singer Édith Piaf was born—a buzzy, unpretentious place with a smart, sexy, arty crowd, a fabulous chalkboard menu, and a slightly bluff style.

On a warm night in July, we settled at our bare wood table and started with glasses of a sublime and very unusual pétillant naturel Chasselas de Tavel, a naturally sparkling (no sugar added to promote fermentation) wine made from sweet Chasselas grapes. Le Baratin is a bistrot à vin par excellence, and justly proud of its nervy and very original wine list.

The restaurant, in a steep cobbled side street of crooked old houses and Arab groceries, is a simple pair of dining rooms with cracked tile floors, a service bar under three globe lights, and wonderful faces with stories you want to hear. One of them was that of the Uruguayan dancer and her French lover to our left. Even though she was in the corps of a top-tier company in a small French city, she still didn't have proper work or residency papers after ten years in France and so was on the verge of tears all night about whether or not to risk a trip home to visit her gravely ill mother (by the time coffee was served, she'd decided to go). To our right, a pair of scrubbed but funky Dutch architects discussed green buildings in Rotterdam with a New York–based French arts administrator who said he dreamed of working for the Brooklyn Academy of Music. No one in the room was talking about real estate, private schools, or hedge funds. As much as there's any real vie bohème left in Paris these days, you'll find it here. That being said, Parisian bohemians not only know and love their food and wine but have the scratch to pay for it. In rapidly gentrifying Paris, Belleville is the last and latest frontier, which is why dinner for two at this bistro in this remote and atmospherically run-down part of the city isn't the bargain you might be expecting in such an off-the-beaten-track neighborhood.

Still, the food is so good and generously served I'd go often if it were in my neighborhood. Raquel Carena, the chef, is Argentinean, which explains her brilliantly irreverent approach to bistro cooking. She has a style all her own that defies categories—if it's rooted in Argentinean home cooking, it's also surprisingly creative and international, lit up by her sincerity and desire to please. She often brings dishes to the table herself and beams every time she comes across an empty plate.

We were elated by first courses of hand-chopped red tuna tartare with pitted black cherries and grated cucumber with a scattering of fleur de sel and a little miso, a truly brilliant dish, and a chunky terrine of meaty monkfish livers, which the waiter accurately described as "foie gras of the sea." A soulful bottle of Saint-Joseph from the Rhône valley proved the perfect foil for delicious lemon-braised veal topped with chewy ribbons of grilled eggplant skin and garnished with baby vegetables and olive-oil-dressed rice pilaf. Another main course, a tender and perfectly seasoned souris d'agneau, was bright with Moroccan spices, and afterward, we had slices of the best Saint-Nectaire cheese I'd ever had—it smelled and tasted like the inside of a musty stone church in the country—and for dessert, a gratin of buttered apricots in almond meal.

We lingered over coffee—this a place where you want to spend an evening—and felt that all was solidly right with the world when we stepped out into the animated streets of Belleville a few hours later. This is a wonderful restaurant.

IN A WORD: A first-rate bistrot à vin in a far-from-the-madding-crowd location in Belleville. This is the type of place that Parisians guardedly share with friends, and it's a favorite of chefs on their night off.

DON'T MISS: The menu changes constantly here, but if the following are available, don't pass them by: bouillon de lotte au galanga (monkfish broth with galangal root, a gingerlike rhi-

zome); barbue poêlé aux asperges vertes (brill sautéed with green asparagus); pudding aux noisettes (hazelnut pudding).

. . .

[102] 3 rue Jouye-Rouve, 20th, 01.43.49.39.70. MÉTRO: Belleville or Pyrénées. OPEN Monday to Friday for lunch and dinner. Saturday dinner only. CLOSED Sunday. ▪ $$

Chapeau Melon

THE CHAPEAU MELON, ONE OF PARIS'S BEST WINE BARS, offers a perfect opportunity to discover Belleville, one of my favorite Paris neighborhoods. For people who really love Paris, and especially those who think they know it well, Belleville comes as a surprise, even a shock. While major cities like New York, Los Angeles, London, and Berlin are immediately and quite visibly international, the center of Paris remains primly French. On any given sunny afternoon in the Tuileries Gardens, for example, the only foreigners you'll see are students, domestics, and other tourists. Head up to Belleville, an old working-class neighborhood in the 19th Arrondissement, however, and you'll be surprised by what an almost antically international city Paris really is. Every fifth shopfront advertises the services that are the umbilical cord of any modern immigrant's life—prepaid calling cards, Internet access, fax transmissions, and money transfers—in Hindi, Chinese, Arabic, and a dozen other languages, and the streets are filled with people from every country in the world.

Recently, however, younger French-born professionals in search of affordable housing and a more richly textured urban

experience than that offered in most of the city's single-digit arrondissements have discovered the neighborhood, and their
presence is creating a demand for something other than the local
Chinese restaurants, gyro stands, and kosher couscous parlors.
The Chapeau Melon's chef-owner, Olivier Camus, understands
exactly what this crowd likes to eat, too, and crafts a single dinner menu daily that showcases French comfort food and dishes
that have a finely tuned international inspiration.

As we settled in for dinner on a Saturday night in this cozy
dining room with bare wood tables, celadon-painted walls, exposed beams, and wine displayed in open stock shelves, it was
easy to like this place even before the kitchen began performing.
Jazz played on the soundtrack, and Camus's wife poured us a
welcome glass of Bourgogne Aligoté before she recited the set
menu and asked if it suited. The whole atmosphere was decidedly chilled out and reminded me of my first exciting experiences of modern American-style bistros in Northampton and
Cambridge, Massachusetts, when I was a pennywise college student. What these New England tables had in common was a
guiding belief in the natural democracy of food, the idea that
good eating should be stripped of the trappings of power and
status that were built into the original French boilerplate for
restaurants. This idea of making good food available to as many
people as possible also thrived in other places, most importantly
San Francisco and to a lesser degree London and Berlin, before
finally taking root in Paris, initially in counterculture vegetarian
restaurants but more recently at higher levels of the local food
chain. Where it's most successful in Paris today is in the new
generation of bistrots à vin, wine-oriented bistros, which have
cropped up in some of the city's edgier and lesser-known neighborhoods, like Belleville.

Since I wholeheartedly agree that good, healthy, delicious food should be available to everyone, I had no trouble getting in the groove here, and what followed was an excellent meal. We began with artichauts barigoule, tender baby artichokes poached provençale style in a light vinaigrette and sprinkled with delicious piggy-tasting lardons. Next up was red tuna tartare, which had me scratching my head a bit, since I thought this dish was the creation of Raquel Carena at the nearby Le Baratin. Whatever its original authorship may have been, it was excellent, with fat cubes of fresh red Mediterranean tuna marinated in soy sauce, sesame oil, and ginger and garnished with black cherry halves. A delicate saffron-brightened fish bouillon garnished with steamed coques (baby clams) and crab-stuffed ravioli followed and was talented home-style cooking at its best—fresh, sincere, generous, and uncomplicated. My favorite dish on the menu was the paleron (shoulder) of beef, fork-tender but grilled so that it had a light crust of its own juices, and served with a jaunty green sauce of herbs and good olive oil, plus a side of vividly fresh steamed vegetables.

Since the human landscape was so appealing—a large table of diamond dealers and their wives from Antwerp visiting relatives who lived in the neighborhood, two male webmasters on what I'd guess was a third date, an older quartet of university types, and a motley crew at the table d'hôtes (a communal table where strangers sit together)—we decided to linger. I ordered the Pelardon, goat cheese from the Ardèche, with a drizzle of olive oil and a pinch of Espelette pepper, and Bruno had a slice of the rich brownie-like chocolate cake. While we were dawdling over coffee, the friendly, hardworking waitress paused by the table and asked, "Ca va?" ("Everything okay?"), and when I told her we'd had a wonderful meal, she grinned and said, "C'est la moindre des choses" ("That's the least we can do").

. ☙ .

IN A WORD: A pleasantly bohemian bistrot à vin with simple, delicious, homey cooking, this place is a good choice for dining as a group and also offers the opportunity to discover Belleville, one of Paris's shaggier and more colorful neighborhoods. This place is also one of the city's best buys.

DON'T MISS: The set menu—everyone eats the same meal— changes constantly here, but do order the Pelardon, a creamy goat cheese, if it's available.

. . .

[101] 92 rue Rébeval, 19th, 01.42.02.68.60. MÉTRO: Pyrénées. OPEN Tuesday to Saturday for lunch and dinner. Sunday lunch only. CLOSED Monday. • $

Chéri Bibi

TUCKED AWAY IN A PRETTY COBBLED STREET ON THE eastern slope of the Butte de Montmartre, the hill on which Montmartre is built, Chéri Bibi is a sure sign that the appealingly ramshackle and sociologically diverse Barbès-Rochechouart neighborhood is next up for gentrification. The mushroom-colored dining room with a façade of folding glass doors that open fully on warm nights and a hip decor of antique factory lamps, bare wood tables with kraft paper place mats, and found-at-the-flea-market Danish modern chairs has been packed with happy Bobos (bohemian bourgeois types) ever since it opened. Its immediate success is a reflection of the way it channels one of the most urgent culinary yearnings of hip Parisians, which is terroir, or a nostalgic desire to eat the way they did in the days when everyone in Paris still smoked Gauloises, drank wine at lunch, and blew off warnings about cholesterol in the unlikely event they even knew what it was.

Cheri Bibi is pure terroir, which means hearty, earthy, rustic French country cooking. The chalkboard menu leads off with starters like a superb homemade bacon-wrapped pork-and-prune terrine spiked with green peppercorns and served à volonté (help yourself) with a crock of puckery cornichons (miniature cucumber pickles), and there's also a soup of the day (maybe carrot and coriander), marinated herring, lentil salad and head cheese in anise-perfumed vinaigrette, oeufs mayonnaise, and bulots (sea snails) with aïoli (garlic mayonnaise). Mains include boudin noir (blood sausage), andouillette (a sausage made from the pig's colon and intestines), beef braised with red peppers and cocoa beans, sausage, and bavette (skirt steak) with sautéed shallots, and all of them come with a choice of sides—homemade frites, mashed potatoes, sautéed vegetables, or salad. Follow with a serving of Laguiole cheese from the huge wheel in the middle of the dining room, or go for strawberries sprinkled with fresh basil, fresh fruit salad, or the heavenly chocolate mousse. The service by two blowsy waitresses is friendly and fun but professional, and the whole place has a sweet, funky vibe that's très Parisien.

· ·

IN A WORD: Fun and frisky, this lively bistro in an authentically bohemian part of Paris is a great choice for anyone who wants a great feed for moderate prices and a buzzy scene that's a living snapshot of the city today. It's also an excellent address for fans of real old-fashioned terroir-style cooking, which runs to hearty, traditional country-style French food.

DON'T MISS: The chalkboard menu changes often, but dishes to look for include terrine de campagne aux pruneaux; marinated herring; lentil salad; head cheese in anise-perfumed vinaigrette; oeufs mayonnaise; bulots (sea snails) with aïoli (garlic mayonnaise); andouillette; skirt steak with sautéed shallots; boudin noir; blanquette de veau (veal in a lemony cream sauce); roasted shoulder of lamb for two; grilled sausage with potato puree; rice pudding; chocolate mousse.

. . .

[100] 15 rue André-del-Sarte, 18th, 01.42.54.88.96. MÉTRO: Anvers or Château Rouge. OPEN Tuesday to Saturday for lunch and dinner. CLOSED Sunday and Monday. ▪ $

BUT WHAT ABOUT? OR WHY CERTAIN FAMOUS RESTAURANTS AREN'T INCLUDED IN THIS BOOK

· · ·

YOU MAY BE WONDERING WHY SOME VERY WELL KNOWN Paris restaurants are not profiled in this book, so let me briefly address some of the more obvious omissions.

ALLARD. The food's still good at this old-time bistro in Saint-Germain, but the incidence of Coke bottles on the tables in the two small dining rooms and the vertiginous prices on the menu reveal that a tipping point has been reached. To wit, don't be at all surprised to run into someone you know here—this is now an American bistro in Paris.

L'AMBROISIE. Chef Bernard Pacaud is a brilliant cook, and this intimate dining room on the lovely place des Vosges is quite beautiful, but the joyless atmosphere and sanctimonious service have unfailingly dampened my spirits during every meal I've ever had here. When you're spending this much money, I insist it should bring on rhapsody.

L'AMI LOUIS. The prewar atmosphere of this power broker's bistro is indisputably delicious, but even though the food is decent enough, the real thrill comes more from getting a reservation—tables are highly sought after—than anything you'll eat there. The lofty prices make it a pretty egregious example of conspicuous consumption, too, especially when you can find better roast chicken and foie gras elsewhere.

APICIUS. Since chef Jean-Pierre Vigato's handsomely decorated town house restaurant serves as a sort of de facto clubhouse for Parisian power brokers, unknown diners often get lost in the shuffle.

BENOÎT. The food's still pretty good at this luxury bistro, which is not far from the Hôtel de Ville, Paris's city hall, and is now part of chef Alain Ducasse's restaurant empire, but the atmosphere was badly wounded when it added a new dining room. I also regret that its uniqueness has been spoiled by branches in Tokyo and New York.

BOFINGER. The beautiful decor at this historic brasserie on the edge of the Marais can't compensate for the kitchen's mediocrity and the offhanded service.

CARRÉ DES FEUILLANTS. Chef Alain Dutournier is a really nice guy, and some of his dishes are excellent (I loved the Jerusalem artichoke and foie gras cake with truffles and veal sweetbreads with oyster sauce). Unfortunately, I can't imagine why anyone would come here unless they were invited, since it's just not a good time.

LA COUPOLE. I love the history of this famous Montparnasse brasserie, but I've never warmed to the heavy-handed renovation of the dining room ten years back, and it has been ages since I've had more than a half-decent meal here. Service is often glacially slow, and it is overpriced relative to the quality of the cooking. If you are a Hemingway fan or just fascinated by Paris during the twenties, stop by for a drink at the bar or maybe just a plate of oysters.

LA GRAND VEFOUR. Yes, the eighteenth-century decor is exquisite, including painted glass ceilings and brass plaques with the names of famous patrons like Colette and Cocteau, and there are few lovelier places in Paris than the Palais Royal. The food is good, too, but nowhere near as memorable as the setting, because chef Guy Martin's cooking suffers from a politesse that negates the primal pleasure that is always at the heart of great haute cuisine.

HÉLÈNE DARROZE. Because Hélène Darroze is a charming woman, I really wish I could like this one-star on the Left Bank. Unfortunately, I've never had a more than better-than-average meal here. The cooking's uneven and imprecise, the dining room's dull, and the bill lands on the table with a disheartening thud.

LE DIVELLEC. Popular with politicians, but it's a total mystery why this stuffy, mediocre, and exorbitantly expensive fish house on the Esplanade des Invalides retains its reputation.

LASSERRE. Jean-Louis Nomicos is a wonderful chef, but the prices here are blood-curdling, and the experience of a meal is much too grandmotherly to be as much fun as his food.

MAXIM'S. Just say no. The Belle Époque decor is the only appetizing thing left about this world-famous tourist trap.

MICHEL ROSTANG. This two-star in the 17th Arrondissement has drifted off into an irrelevant senescence.

PRUNIER. It's been low tide at this handsome Art Deco restaurant, once one of the city's most prestigious seafood tables, for a long time.

LA TABLE DE JOËL ROBUCHON. Though the food here is superb, Robuchon's Left Bank counter-service-only restaurant is a lot more fun than this oddly decorated and rather stuffy dining room in the 16th.

RELAIS LOUIS XIII. One can only assume that the Michelin inspectors have forgotten that this dusty old dowager still lurks in their guide. Why it still has two stars is a total mystery.

AU TROU GASCON. Once Paris's temple of southwestern French gastronomy, this well-known place is but a shadow of its former self, with distracted service and a seriously disappointing cassoulet.

ACKNOWLEDGMENTS

I would like to thank the many people who taught me how to eat and also the friends with whom I've shared many happy meals in Paris: Bamma, Emma, my mother and father, Laurie Eastman, Tom Crane, Marc Parisot, David Bruel, Judy Fayard, Michele Loyer, Anne Bogart, Sue and Gary Young, Albert Sonnenfeld, Noël Riley Fitch, Nadine Frey, Steven Rothfeld, Bob and Lynn Peterson, Barbara Nagelsmith, Suzy Gershman, Dorie Greenspan, Jean-Marie and Marie-Therese Midavaine, William Sertl, Ruth Reichl, Jocelyn Zuckerman, Nanette Maxim, Charlotte Shagolsky, John Van Ness Philip III, Kato Wittich, and Charles Carroll, among many others. I'd also like to thank Susanna Porter, my editor; Jillian Quint, her talented assistant; and Deborah Ritchken, my remarkable agent, without whom this book would never exist.

RESTAURANTS BY TYPE

RESTAURANTS
BY PRICE RANGE

EXPENSIVE ($$$)

VERY EXPENSIVE ($$$$)

OPEN ALL OR PART OF WEEKEND

...

NOTE: Weekend hours vary. Restaurants marked with an asterisk (*) are closed on Sunday.

INDEX

Restaurant names in **boldface** are the
102 restaurants profiled in the book.

ABOUT THE AUTHOR

· ·

ALEXANDER LOBRANO grew up in Connecticut
and lived in Boston, New York, and London before
moving to Paris, his home today, in 1986. He was
the European correspondent for *Gourmet* magazine
from 2000 until it closed in 2009, and now writes
regularly on food and travel for *The New York Times*
and many other publications in the United States
and the United Kingdom.